THELYPHTHORA
or
A Treatise on Female Ruin

VOLUME III

TAKEN FROM MY LIBRARY SHELF
AND REPRINTED IN LIKE FORM
Original Fonts Version
Don Milton

Born Again Publishing, Inc.

All Text, Images, and Text Images
Copyright 2009 Don Milton
All Rights Reserved

Dedicated to the men who lost their lives, their livelihood, and their place in history because they chose the Bible, not custom.

> Trust in the LORD with all thine heart;
> and *lean not unto thine own understanding*.
> In all thy ways *acknowledge Him, and He shall direct thy paths*.
> Proverbs 3:5-6

ABOUT THE EDITOR/PUBLISHER

For the last ten years, Don Milton has pastored ChristianMarriage.com, an online ministry dedicated to providing theological answers to questions about marriage. Pastor Don has published numerous books on the topics of Courtship and Christian Marriage as well as Law & Justice. He recently published his own novel, The Prince of Sumba, Husband to Many Wives, and is currently working on a historical novel. He received his Bachelor of Arts in Linguistics from the University of Washington in 1987.

Don has a wonderful wife and three children. He would like to have more.

Other Books Published by Don Milton

Title	Author	Availability
Prince of Sumba Husband to Many Wives	Don Milton	Now
Exhortatory Address to the Brethren in the Faith of Christ	Martin Madan	Now
A Dialog on Polygamy	Bernardino Ochino Don Milton	Now
Letters to Joseph Priestley	Martin Madan	May 2009
Thelyphthora Volume II A Treatise on Female Ruin	Martin Madan	May 2009
Thelyphthora Volume III A Treatise on Female Ruin	Martin Madan	May 2009
Juvenal and Persius Volume I	Martin Madan	May 2009
Juvenal and Persius Volume II	Martin Madan	May 2009
John Milton on Polygamy	John Milton	May 2009
Many More Titles	Don Milton & Others	Fall 2009

To Purchase Books or to Contact Don Milton
Visit - DonMilton.com or write:

Don Milton
PO Box 10162
Scottsdale, AZ 85271-0162

ABOUT MARTIN MADAN

In 1746, thirty-five years before the Reverend Martin Madan wrote this book, he founded the London Lock Hospital. London Lock was the first voluntary hospital that treated venereal disease.[1] Shortly after Madan founded the Lock Hospital, the institution opened a new building and it became known as *The Female Hospital*. He then began to hold worship services in areas of the hospital *that afforded him the ability to preach as well as to lead a congregation in the singing of hymns* but soon it became crowded, so he set out to build a chapel. With donations from wealthy patrons he was able to build a chapel that seated up to eight hundred people.[2] This may not seem large compared with today's mega-churches but it's still a very large fellowship and it was one of the largest of his day. The wonderful thing about Madan's chapel was that it received enough in tithes to become a strong source of support for the hospital.[3] It was there that the singing of hymns first took hold as part of Christian worship.[4] The members of Lock Chapel sang from a hymnal that Madan, himself, had published. He published the hymnal as a benefit to future generations as well as to raise money for the hospital.[5] From the Chapel at the Lock, hymn singing spread quickly throughout the English speaking world with Madan's hymnal the standard. His mastery of musical worship brought thousands to the Chapel at the Lock and his hymns have brought many more thousands to a saving knowledge of our Lord.[6] In less than thirty short years from the first printing of Madan's hymnal, fully two thirds of the hymns sung, even in the parishes of the Church of England, had been lifted; *word for word, note for note, from Madan's own hymnal.* Madan's hymnal had in fact become the core of the Church of England's hymnal.[7] The Baptists' hymnal came out twenty five years after Madan's.[8] The hymnal that he published was called A Collection of Psalm and Hymn Tunes Never Published Before, the proceeds from which were for the benefit of the Lock Hospital.

Madan held the position of Chaplain at the Lock till the day he

About the Author - Martin Madan

died. This was partly due to the fact that he eclipsed all of his contemporaries in promoting, as well as defending, the faith. It was Madan who defended Whitefield and the Methodists against the vicious satire of playwright, Samuel Foote, in 1760, (See his Exhortatory Address to the Brethren in the Faith of Christ at the back of this book) so it was not surprising that he continued to defend the faith and biblical morality till the day he went to be with the Lord."[9]

Four years after the publication of this book, Madan excoriated another group of rascals, the judges of England, for their inconsistency in rendering justice. In his seminal work, *Thoughts on Executive Justice*, he outlined the need for sure and swift punishment of criminals. After his death he was falsely accused of having favored hanging for theft, but he stated in the very book that they quoted out of context against him, that he agreed with the maxim that '*a less punishment, which is certain, will do more good than a greater [punishment], which is uncertain.*'[10] After another two years Madan defended the faith against Unitarian, Joseph Priestly in his *Letters to Joseph Priestley*. Another two years and Madan published his translation of Juvenal and Persius from Latin to English with copious explanatory notes. Today it remains unmatched in thoroughness.[11] On occasion Madan still preached at the Lock Chapel and yet he still found time to write dozens of letters excoriating those who would gamble on the horse races.[12]

Despite all these accomplishments, not to mention his many published sermons, Christian historians have failed to chronicle his ministry in their accounts of the great evangelists of the Eighteenth Century, not to mention the great legal minds of the Eighteenth Century. This and other books in this series, will attempt to correct that deficiency, a deficiency which has left an important part of Church history unrecorded; the transition from singing Psalms to singing hymns. And it was that transition that the Lord used to spark the great revivals of the hundred years that followed Madan's ministry. Prior to Martin Madan's successful promotion of hymn singing, there were only random cases of hymn singing. A church here, or a church there would allow hymn singing, and Christians at non-church venues as well as at dissenting churches sang hymns. However, it took the success of the Reverend Martin

About the Author - Martin Madan

Madan's chapel and its music to make it acceptable. The new hymn singing combined biblical concepts with calls to repentance into a moving form of worship. The hymn provides a way for biblical concepts to be presented in poetry set to music. Many lost souls have been deaf to all other forms of preaching, but have been converted by the hearing of a single hymn.

As you read this book, may you be blessed in knowing that its author was the man who polished some of the most famous words in today's hymnals, the man who composed and arranged the music behind many of those hymns, and the man who cared for and counseled the cast aside women of his time; Martin Madan, the Father of the Evangelical Hymnal.

The preceding *About Martin Madan* section as well as the following footnotes are used with permission, having been gleaned from Prince of Sumba, Husband to Many Wives, Chapter 12 - Martin Madan, A Memory of Love by Don Milton - Copyright 2009

1. "The first special hospital was the Lock Hospital near Hyde Park Corner, founded in 1746 by Martin Madan, who became its first chaplain."
A History of English Philanthropy
by Benjamin Kirkman Gray
London - P.S. King & Son, Orchard House, Westminster - 1905

The following is an account of some of the types of patients that could be found at the Lock Hospital.

"There are merit-mongers, among the most abandoned sinners. Two women were, some time since, admitted into the Lock Hospital, in order to be cured of a very criminal disease. Mr. Madan, who visited them during their confinement, laboured to convince them of their sin and spiritual danger, 'Truly,' said one of them, 'I am by no means so bad as some of my profession are : for I never picked any man's pocket, in my life.' The other said, 'I cannot affirm that I never picked a man's pocket; but I have this in my favour, that I never admitted any man in my company, on a Sunday, until after nine at night.'
The Works of Augustus M. Toplady page 168.
You will remember Toplady as the writer of that famous hymn,

About the Author - Martin Madan

Rock of Ages. He was a very close friend and admirer of the Reverend Martin Madan, having also preached at the Lock Chapel.

Good News from Heaven; or, the Gospel a Joyful Sound. At the Lock Chapel, near Hyde Park Corner, June 19, 1774. By the Reverend Augustus Toplady.

Recorded on page 375 of The Monthly Review Volume 52 1775

Madan wrote a tract concerning the sequence of events that led to the conversion of one such prostitute. Despite her conversion and new way of living, she soon died of the illnesses she acquired as a prostitute. This is chronicled in: *A Remarkable and surprising account of the abandoned life, happy conversion, and comfortable death of Fanny Sidney, a young gentlewoman, who died in London in April, 1763, aged 26 years.* By the Reverend Martin Madan

2. "The Lock Chapel was (officially) opened March 28, 1762" but the Reverend Martin Madan conducted services prior to that in other areas of the institution that afforded him the ability to preach as well as to lead the congregation in the singing of hymns.

Dictionary of National Biography - Edited by Sidney Lee - McMillan and Co.1893 - Page 288

Through Martin's exertions a new chapel, capable of seating 800 persons, was erected in the garden of the hospital, he himself contributing 100 pounds.[100 pounds converts to $20,000 in today's U.S. dollars. University of Michigan conversion table.] It was opened on March 28, 1762 and by 1765 was entirely free of debt.

The Madan Family and Maddens in Ireland and England By Falconer Madan 1933 - Page 112

3. "In the case of the Lock Hospital, the musical movement coincided with the Evangelical. Its chapel was used not only by its inmates, but by a strongly contrasting *West End Evangelical congregation who rented sittings.*"

These rented pews helped pay for the expenses of the hospital.

The Princeton Theological Review - Volume XII - 1914
The Princeton University Press - Princeton, N.J. - Page 87

4. "He (William Romaine) held the extreme Calvinistic position as to the exclusive use of inspired words in Praise, and was able to impose his views upon his own congregation. But he could not

stay the rising tide of Hymn singing or make a breach between the Gospel and the Hymns of the Revival. *In Martin Madan the new Hymn singing found an effective sponsor.* The humorous and sturdy John Berridge was as early on the field as Madan, but less effective."
The Princeton Theological Review - Volume XII - 1914
The Princeton University Press - Princeton, N.J. - Page 73,74
5. In the preface to the Hymnal that the Reverend Martin Madan published, "The Collection of Psalm and Hymn Tunes sung at the Chapel of the Lock Hospital" Mr. Madan writes:
"I have at last, with no small care and trouble, completed this Book of Tunes for the use of the Chapel; and as the publication of them may be of service to the Charity, I must desire your acceptance of the Entire Copy, hoping that, by the sale of this Music, some addition may be made to your fund for maintaining and promoting the charitable work which you have undertaken."
6. The Church of England's hymnal began with Martin Madan's Collection of Psalms and Hymns (1760).
The New Schaff-Herzog Encyclopedia of Religious Knowledge by Johann Jakob Herzog, Philip Schaff, and others. Copyright 1909
7. In 1788, the publisher of the fifth edition of the Church of England hymnal, "appropriated fully two thirds of the contents of Madan's Collection."
The Princeton Theological Review - Volume XII - 1914
The Princeton University Press - Princeton, N.J. - Page 76
8. The first Baptist hymn-book was Rippon's (1787).
The New Schaff-Herzog Encyclopedia of Religious Knowledge by Johann Jakob Herzog, Philip Schaff, and others. Copyright 1909
9. It was Martin Madan who defended Whitefield and the Methodists against the vicious satire of playwright, Samuel Foote in his Exhortatory address to the brethren in the faith of Christ published in 1760
10. Thoughts on Executive Justice with respect to our Criminal Laws Published in 1785 - Page 63
11. A New and Literal Translation of Juvenal and Persius; with Copious Explanatory Notes, by which these difficult satirists are rendered easy and familiar to the reader. In Two Volumes.

About the Author - Martin Madan

By the Rev. M. Madan -Printed for the Editor, at Mr. Lewis's, No 157, Swallow-Street, Near Piccadilly MDCCLXXXIX (1789)
12. "It was formerly the abode of the celebrated [famous] Dr. Madan [Martin Madan], of whom we have given an account. During his residence here, [Birmingham, England] he interposed his authority as a magistrate, to prevent the introduction of illegal games into the town during the race week; he gave notice to those persons, who were in the habit of letting [renting] their houses for this purpose, that it was contrary to the laws of their country, and if they persisted in doing it, they must take consequences. Several tradespeople, who disregarded this notice, were sent to prison, which so exasperated the inhabitants, that they burnt his effigy, near the spot where the pump now stands."
Some Particulars Relating to the History of Epsom by Henry Pownall 1825
"I possess twenty-three letters from him to George Hardinge, Esq., M.P., July 9, 1789-March 14, 1790, [Against illegal gaming] written in good spirits and with some wit."
The Madan Family by Falconer Madan 1933
"Mr. Madan, however, the most respectable clergyman in the town, [Birmingham] preaching [1787-1789] and publishing... [against Priestley's Unitarianism] ...I addressed a number of "Familiar Letters to the Inhabitants of Birmingham," in our defence."
An Appeal to the Serious and Candid Professors of Christianity By Joseph Priestley - Page 105

Thelyphthora III

A BRIEF NOTE ABOUT 18TH CENTURY FONTS

Every day you distinguish between a **hard c** and a **soft c** as well as a **hard g** and a **soft g**. You do it by context and because you understand that written English is not absolutely phonetic. In other words, you naturally understand the difference between written English and spoken English. Would you ever think that the word CIRCUS meant calling names?

cir - (kir)   cus - (sus)   kirsus - curses

The example seems ridiculous because you are able to tell the difference between a **hard c** and a **soft c** by context. Therefore, I will trust you, the reader, to be able to tell the difference between a **hard f** (represented in modern English as **f**) and a **soft f** (represented in modern English as **s**). Just 225 years ago, all readers of English were capable of telling this difference. If you cannot, then I recommend keeping it a secret, for none will believe that you are capable of understanding the arguments presented in this book if you can't read.

Thelyphthora III

THELYPHTHORA;

OR,

A TREATISE ON

FEMALE RUIN,

IN ITS
CAUSES, EFFECTS, CONSEQUENCES,
PREVENTION, AND REMEDY;

CONSIDERED ON THE BASIS OF THE

DIVINE LAW:

Under the following HEADS, viz.

MARRIAGE,   ADULTERY,
WHOREDOM, and   POLYGAMY,
FORNICATION,   DIVORCE;

With many other INCIDENTAL MATTERS;

PARTICULARLY INCLUDING

An Examination of the Principles and Tendency of
Stat. 26 GEO. II. c. 33.

COMMONLY CALLED

THE MARRIAGE ACT.

VOLUME III.

ΔΙΑ ΔΥΣΦΗΜΙΑΣ ΚΑΙ ΕΥΦΗΜΙΑΣ.

2 COR, vi. 8.

" Whosoever attempteth any thing for the PUBLIC (especially if it per-
" tain to RELIGION, and to the opening and clearing of the WORD OF
" GOD) the same setteth himself upon a *stage*, to be glouted upon by
" every evil eye; yea, he casteth himself headlong upon *pikes*, to be *gored* by
" every *sharp tongue*. For he that meddleth with men's *religion*, in *any* part,
" meddleth with their *custom*, nay, with their *freehold*; and though they find
" no content in *that* which they *have*, yet they cannot abide to hear of
" altering."

Translators of the BIBLE. *Preface to the* READER.

LONDON:
Printed for J. DODSLEY.

M.DCC.LXXXI.

MEMORANDUM.

"The grand queſtion to be tried is ——
"Whether a SYSTEM filled with *obligation* and
"*reſponſibility*, of MEN to WOMEN, and of
"WOMEN to MEN, even unto *death* itſelf,
"and this eſtabliſhed by INFINITE WISDOM,
"is not better calculated to prevent the *ruin*
"of the *female ſex*, with all its horrid conſe-
"quences, both to the public and indivi-
"duals, than a SYSTEM of *human contrivance*,
"where neither *obligation* nor *reſponſibility*
"are to be found, either of MEN to WOMEN,
"or of WOMEN to MEN, in inſtances of the
"moſt *important* concern to BOTH, but eſpe-
"cially to the *weaker ſex?*"

See Vol. i. Pref. xxiii, xxiv.

CONTENTS of VOL. III.

PREFACE
INTRODUCTION — — Page 1

CHAP. XII.

Shewing by what Means, *and by what Degrees, the Laws of* JEHOVAH, *concerning* Marriage, *were opposed and abrogated, and a* NEW SYSTEM *invented and established, by* CHRISTIAN CHURCHMEN — — 4

CHAP. XIII.

Observations on the foregoing — applied to the Subjects of this Treatise — — 254

CHAP. XIV.

Of the true ORIGIN *and* NECESSITY *of* MARRIAGE-CEREMONIES — 309

CONCLUSION — — 352

ADDENDA — — — 358

LETTER *to* R. HILL, *Esq;* — — 366

ERRATA.

Omitted Vol. I.

Page 33. l. 22. *for* antinuptial—*read* antenuptial.
 34. l. 28. 2d edition, ditto.
 97. 1st edit. p. 95. 2d edit. *for* uxores duas—*read* duas uxores——wives two—*read* two wives.
 371. n. l. 13. 2d. edit. *for* filio—read Silio.

Vol. III.

Page 20. l. 27. *for* fons—*read* fores.
 128. l. 23. *after*—in an old book—*add*—of *Camden's*.
 129. l. 23. for *ibi*—read *tibi*.
 184. l. 19. *after* granted—*add*—where grantable.
 213. n. l. 1. *for* that escaped—*read* which escaped.
 293. l. 17. after *marriage*—add—as in God's fight.
 294. l. 4 & 6. ditto.
 335. l. 18. *for* wife—*read* wife,

PREFACE

TO THE

THIRD VOLUME.

THE AUTHOR was in great hopes, that, when he had finished the *Second Volume* of this *work*, his labours were at an end; nor had he any intention of carrying the *treatise* to any greater length. But, notwithstanding the clear and plain manner in which he thought he had laid the several matters therein contained before the *Reader*, and on a weight of *evidence*, which seemed to carry its own conviction with it—he was sorry to find himself not sufficiently *understood*, and that what was charged as *error*, and mere *human invention*, was still to be regarded in a much more respectable light.

The great and interesting *question* which was laid before the public for *examination* and *trial*, appeared at the end of the *Preface* to vol. I. It was repeated in the same words, by way of *memorandum*, facing the *first page*, vol. II. The reason of this was, that the *Reader* might be the more easily induced to carry in his mind the *question* which he was to *try*, while he was attending to the *evidence* on which it was to be determined.

Instead of taking the *whole* of the *evidence* together, as applying to the *whole* of the *question*, partial quotations of the *work* have been made and censured, and the *question* itself kept entirely out of sight. This, as far as the *Author* has yet seen, has been the method of opposition; therefore he saves himself the trouble of any farther remarks on his opponents, than to recommend to them a more serious and attentive perusal of the *work*, than they seem to have hitherto given it, and to connect the importance of the *question* with the *authority* of the *evidence* on which it is supported.

The *Author* has most evidently taken the *affirmative* side of the *question*, and flatters himself that he has uniformly pursued it throughout the *whole work*; nor has he the least notion of changing his opinion, till it can be proved, that *punishment* is an incentive to the commission of *crimes*—and that a most severe *responsibility* for our *actions*, tends to promote a *licentiousness* in our *determinations*.

Being conscious that nothing but the LOVE OF TRUTH, and a strong desire to make it known, as involving the *preservation* of his *fellow-creatures*, could have ever led him to the publication of a performance which carries with it so much opposition to our whole *system* respecting the *commerce of the sexes*—and thinking the affair of too much importance to be left in *doubt* as to its *original*—he not only has been at the pains to shew its unconformity to the *Divine system*, in the former parts of this work, but, as a farther proof of that point, now undertakes to manifest its derivation from, and almost entire and total conformity with, the *church* of *Rome*.

He could wish particularly, that those *pious* * ministers of the *gospel*, who have done

---

* One of these has lately published *two volumes of letters*, in which I find the following excellent advice.

His *correspondent*, it seems, was under some perplexity, from objections which had been made to the *writer's Calvinian* principles, and which had induced *somebody* to draw *consequences* of no very *favourable* kind to the *writer's plan*, set forth in his *printed sermons*—the *writer* being willing to satisfy his *correspondent*, and to settle his mind on the subject, sends him the letter in question, and, by way of introduction to what he says, begins thus—viz.

"In the first place, I beg you to be upon your guard
"against a *reasoning* spirit. *Search the scriptures*; and
"where you can find a plain *rule* or *warrant* for *any*
"*practice*, go *boldly* on, and be not discouraged because
"you may not be clearly able to answer or reconcile
"every *difficulty* that may either occur to your *own*
"mind, or be put in your way by *others*. Our hearts
"are very *dark* and *narrow*, and the very root of all
"*apostacy* is a proud disposition to question the *necessity*
"or *propriety* of *divine appointments*. But the child-like
"simplicity of faith is to follow God without *reasoning*;
"taking it for granted, a thing must be *right* if *He* di-
"rects it, and charging all seeming inconsistencies to
"the account of our *own ignorance*."

The part which this *worthy* and *valuable* man (for *such* I have long known him to be) has taken with respect to *Thelyphthora*, constrains the *Author* to remind him of his own *salutary advice*, as well as to recommend an observance of it to every *Reader*. It must be confessed, that it is much easier to *give* advice than to *take* it.—See *Cardiphonia*, vol. ii. p. 68.

PREFACE TO

Thelyphthora the *honour* of publicly *preaching* against it, as well those who *have red* it, as those who have *not* (for this, it seems, has made *no* † difference) would give this *third volume* a very diligent perusal, as it may save them the trouble of inventing arguments to

---

† In a pamphlet which I have seen, published by way of *dialogue* between *Philalethes* and *Monogamus* — whom the writer introduces (as Mr. BAYES in roduces the *Two Kings of Brentford* smelling to the same nosegay) in the most perfect harmony and agreement throughout—there is an anecdote of "a *certain minister*, who being asked if
" he had red *Thelyphthora*, or intended to read it, replied
" in the *negative*: and being asked what objection he
" had to giving it a reading, he answered—He did not
" chuse to try how much *arsenic* his constitution would
" bear."—" PHIL. This answer expressed a most *judi-*
" *cious* sentiment, indeed," &c.

Hamlet says, that " *a knavish speech sleeps in a foolish*
" *ear*"—and it may be thought, that, if this had been the case with this " *judicious answer*," it would have been rather more for the credit of this " *certain mi-*
" *nister*," than to represent him as condemning a *work*, not only *never having red it*, but under a fixed determination *never to read it at all*. It must be not a little *edifying*, to hear so *scrupulous*, so *conscientious* a *divine*, preach on Exod. xxiii. 1.—or on Matt. vii. 1, 2.—or on that question of *Nicodemus*, John vii. 51.

As for those who *have red* the *work*, the *Public*, as well as the *Author*, is obliged to them for openly declaring their sentiments upon it, and for giving their *reasons* on which those *sentiments* are grounded—no *cause* can ever be *fairly tried*, but by an *impartial* examination of *witnesses* on *both sides*. How far it may be thought by *others*, that *Thelyphthora*, or any part of it, has met with an answer, I cannot say; but as for the *Author* himself, he remains—*qualis ab incepto*—and can only adopt the words of a learned and reverend *correspondent*, who writes him thus—" All *letter-writers* and *publishers* which I
" have hitherto red, only, in effect, tell me that your
" *book* is *right*."

elude

elude the force of *scripture-testimony*, and qualify them, if they chuse to *migrate*, for becoming Doctors of the Sorbonne—with a—

    Dignus, dignus est intrare
    In nostro docto corpore.
                    Moliere.

One thing, however, may be worth observing in this place, which is, that some of the most violent against *Thelyphthora*, have *themselves* laid down, in their own comments on the *Bible*, the very *principle* on which the grand argument, which runs throughout the book, is founded—*viz.* that of the "obligation which men are under to *marry* the women they *seduce*."—One says—on Deut. xxii. 29—"Seduction of an unmarried woman was punished with a fine to the father, and with an obligation to marry the woman, without power to divorce her." His observation on this is, that—"he who robs a woman of her honour, can never make her reparation but by taking her for his wife."—

Another thus comments on the same passage—"Happy will it be for that country, in which this *divine statute* is carried into execution—it will save many from ruin, both of *body and soul*."

The Author of *Thelyphthora* very explicitly declares, that this "DIVINE STATUTE" includes *all men* without exception, as to their being *married* or *not*, for which he appeals to * the words of the

* See vol. i. p. 254—9. 2d edit.

statute,

statute itself, compared with those of ver. 22. and ver. 25; and asserts, that it was never *repealed.* (See vol. i. Introd. p. 10.) And, furthermore, he would hereby be understood to *challenge* his adversaries to prove the contrary.—One thing is clear, that God *has not* repealed it; and it is equally clear, that man *cannot.*—The *Author* is entirely of opinion with the last-mentioned *commentator*, that, " if this DIVINE STATUTE was car-
" ried into * execution, it would save many
" from ruin, both of *body* and soul;" and on *this position* has he ventured his work into the *world.*

It must be confessed, that the above *comments* are so *cautiously* worded, as to leave a *niche*, as it were, in which may be placed the word *unmarried*—"*If any* unmarried *man*," &c.—This has actually been done by some—(see before vol. i. 258. 2d edit.)—but as it has not been done by the LAWGIVER HIMSELF—and I am for giving HIM credit for knowing *best* how to express HIS OWN MEANING—I doubt not, that, if HE had had any *other* than what appears from the *passage itself* as it stands, and indeed from the whole texture of the *Jewish law*, He would not have left it, either to the JEWISH *rabbies* or CHRISTIAN *expositors*, to have made it out —but have been as *particular* with regard to the description of the *man*, as HE is with respect to that of the *woman.*——I own my-

* How the *spirit* and *intention* of it might, in some measure, be complied with, even in a *monogamous* country—see vol. i. p. 290, and n. 2d edit.

self

self to be one of those people who *despair* of ever seeing an *edition* of the DIVINE LAW *auctior & emendatior*—or any other *plan* whatsoever proposed, equal in *wisdom, purity,* and *holiness,* or so nicely and exactly calculated to preserve the *chastity* of women from the violation to which it is now subjected, by an almost total *irresponsibility* of the men towards them.—For this, we little think ourselves *chiefly,* if not *wholly,* indebted to the *Pope* and his *clergy*—but so it is, as from the authentic testimonies, recorded in the following extracts from their proceedings, will be made manifest.

The daring insolence of *mortals,* in laying aside the *oracles of* GOD, and, in defiance of the fixed and determinate *laws of Heaven,* taking upon themselves to frame such *plans,* and to devise such *schemes,* as seemed to them good—*making* or *unmaking marriage,* as in GOD's sight, just as they saw most conducive to their own *interest* or *ambition*—raising *impediments* which are unwarranted by the scriptures, and inventing *obstacles* which oppose the mind of GOD as revealed in those scriptures — *vacating obligation* which GOD hath *made,* and *continuing obligation* which GOD hath *vacated*—*putting those asunder whom* He *hath joined together*—and *joining together* those whom He hath *put asunder*—forbidding to *marry* where He has *allowed* it, and even *commanded* it, and *allowing* to *marry* where He has *forbidden* it—this, by *dispensing* with *His laws*

laws in some *instances*, and *rejecting* them in *others*—making *no sin* where GOD hath *made it*, and making it where GOD hath *not made it*—assuming *powers* and *offices* in GOD's name, which He hath no where warranted—obscuring by human *rites* and *ceremonies* the simple and clear nature of *divine institutions*—putting *human laws* in the place of GOD's *commandments*—dealing distress, destruction, and ruin among their fellow-creatures, under colour of GOD's authority—and, to this end, *misconstruing* and *misinterpreting* the very scriptures which were revealed for their preservation—thus *seething the kid in its mother's milk :*— all this, and much more, will be opened to demonstration, in the following extracts from the *annals of the church of Rome.*

It then will evidently appear, by what *means*, and by what *degrees*, *marriage*, and every thing belonging to it, has been taken out of GOD's hands into the hands of *men*, and on what authority that *system* is built, which we are accustomed to think so *highly* of, and, consequently, from whence is derived that source of *female misery*, which so loudly calls for *redress*, and of that *power* to *destroy* without limitation or restraint, now indulged to mankind.

———*Longa est* injuria, *longæ*
Ambages, *sed summa sequar* fastigia *rerum.*
VIRG.

THELYPH-

THELYPHTHORA.

INTRODUCTION.

THE Apoſtle Paul, 1 Tim. chap. iv. 1—3. foretells many of thoſe errors which afterwards aroſe in the *Chriſtian* Church, through the *ſeduction* of thoſe evil *ſpirits*, which would poſſeſs the minds of men, and lead ſome to teach, and others to follow their pernicious ways.—THE SPIRIT (ſaith he) *ſpeaketh expreſsly*, that, *ſome ſhall depart from the faith*, (i. e. *the faith once delivered to the ſaints*. JUDE 3.) And he inſtances one particular among others to be—FORBIDDING TO MARRY, ver. 3.— thus diſannulling the order of GOD and *Nature*, and expoſing mankind to all the temptations and miſchiefs of *unchaſtity*.

Theſe *ſeducing ſpirits transformed themſelves into angels of light*, (See 2 Cor. xi. 14.) and taught the *Chriſtians* to oppoſe and reject the plain and poſitive *command* of GOD, and, under the deceitful guiſe of higher degrees of *piety, purity*, and *holineſs*, to prefer *celibacy* and *virginity,* which GOD has *not commanded,* before *marriage,* which He has *ordained* and *commanded,* for the *propagation, continuance,* and *preservation* of the HUMAN SPECIES.

The *precepts* and *examples* of the *Hebrew* scriptures, in which the *mind* and *will* of the CREATOR were fully *revealed,* availed nothing — these were thrown aside from bearing *their testimony* in the matter.—The writings of the New Testament afforded certain passages, which were wrested from their *meanings,* and distorted and pressed into the service of *error* and *delusion.*

This *mystery of iniquity* (See 2 Thess. ii. 7.) began to work very early; and in some of the earliest *apologies* of the *Christian Fathers,* a *single* life is spoken of in terms, which clearly prove the preference which was given to it in their esteem.

All this was greatly increased — εν υπο-κρισει ψευδολογων — *through the hypocrisy of men speaking lyes,* [Castal. in loc.] and laid the foundation of what happened, when, in after times, *Churchmen* found it very highly to their advantage, to make the world believe, that the *antient laws* of GOD, relative to the *commerce of the sexes,* were all *antiquated* and *abolished* — that JESUS CHRIST had introduced an entire *new system*—and the *Pope,* as CHRIST's *Vicar,* was to *model* that *system,* as *He* and the *Church* should think proper.

In order to elucidate and evince this, it shall

shall now be my business to lay before the *Reader*, in a regular series, the defections of *men* from the *laws* and *ordinances* of the MOST HIGH, with regard to the *above* subjects—by which it will appear, how evidently we stand indebted to *Romish* priestcraft and superstition, for almost every idea which the *system* of the *Protestants* exhibits to us respecting *matrimony*, and all that concerns it.

I have only to observe, that the writer, whom I chiefly follow in the ensuing collections, is *Du Pin*, who, though a *Romanist*, and a doctor of the *Sorbonne*, was a very honest writer, too much so for the *Church* he lived in; and therefore he was censured, and bitterly persecuted, at the instigation of the *Bishop* of *Meaux*, for speaking his mind so liberally. The free censures which he passed on the writings of the ancient fathers of the Church—and his asserting the privileges of the *national* churches against the pretensions of the *court* of *Rome* —were sufficient to awaken the thunder of the *church artillery*—and to bring on him a charge of *heresy*—which ended in a decree of the parliament of *Paris*, for the suppression of his book.

This is a *mode* of *argumentation* which *Churchmen* have often had recourse to, when the *craft has been endangered*, and when writings which have threatened the *maladie du metier*, have appeared before the eyes of the world.

CHAP. XII.

Shewing by what Means, *and by what* Degrees, *the Laws of* JEHOVAH, *concerning* Marriage, *were opposed and abrogated, and a* NEW SYSTEM *invented and established, by* CHRISTIAN CHURCHMEN.

CENTURY I. and II.

<small>CENT. I. and II.</small>

IT is no easy matter to lay before the *Reader*, a detail of historical facts, relative to the transactions of the *latter* part of the *first Century*, and the beginning of the *second*, from any of the *Ecclesiastical Histories*; I know of none which were written at that time; for the *works*, which bear the name of *Dionysius* the *Areopagite*, were forged in the 5th *Century*, and illustrated with annotations by *John* of *Scythopolis* in the 6th. See *Mosheim*, vol. i. p. 298, 408. note u. Macl. edit.

The first testimony, therefore, with which I shall begin, is of the *epistolary* kind, and this, under the hand of *Clemens* Bishop of *Rome*. At the end of *Wetstein*'s New Testament, vol. ii. are to be found two *epistles* of " St. *Clement* the *Roman*, disciple of " St. *Peter*, taken from the book of the *Sy-* " *riac* MS. of the New Testament." *Wetstein*, in order to prove they are genuine, cites two testimonies, one of St. *Jerome*, the other of *Epiphanius:* the first of which,
c. *Jovinian,*

c. *Jovinian*, lib. i. writes thus — " Hi
" sunt eunuchi, quos castravit, non neces-
" sitas, sed voluntas propter regnum cæ-
" lorum. Ad hos & *Clemens* successor *Apos-*
" *toli Petri,* cujus *Paulus Apostolus memi-*
" *nit* (Phil. iv. 3.) scribit *epistolas,* om-
" nemque penè sermonem suum de virgini-
" tatis puritate contexuit, & deinceps mul-
" ti *Apostolici* & *Martyres,* & illustres tam
" sanctitate quam eloquentia, quos ex pro-
" priis scriptis nosse perfacile est."

" These are *eunuchs*, which, not neces-
" sity, but their own will, hath *castrated*
" for the kingdom of heaven. To these
" *Clement,* the successor of the apostle
" *Peter,* (of whom the apostle *Paul* makes
" mention Phil. iv. 3.) writes epistles, and
" almost his whole discourse relates to the
" purity of *virginity.* After that, many
" *apostolical* men and *martyrs,* and illustrious
" as well for sanctity as eloquence, whom
" it is very easy to know from their own
" writings, did the same."

Epiphanius, (Hæres. 30. of the *Ebionites,*
n. 15.) says, " That *Clement* taught *virgi-*
" *nity,* in all the circular epistles which he
" wrote, and which were red in the
" Churches."

The *epistles* themselves appear in *Syriac*, with a *Latin* translation; by which it seems evident, that this *saint* was as great an advocate for *virginity* as *Jerome* was himself.

Clement says, — " Whosoever professeth
" before

"before the Lord, that he will preserve his *chastity*, ought to be girt with every holy virtue; and if indeed he hath *crucified his body* for the sake of piety, he prays against the Word, which saith— INCREASE AND MULTIPLY, and the whole mind, and cogitation, and concupiscence of this world," &c.—and afterwards—"For he who desires for himself these great and excellent things, on that account is discharged, and separates himself, from the whole world, that he may go away, and live a divine and heavenly life, like the *holy angels*," &c. "On this account he separates himself from all the desires of the body, and not only prays against that —" BE FRUITFUL AND MULTIPLY"— but desires that hope, promised, prepared, and placed in heaven with God, who promised with his mouth and lyeth not, who is greater than *sons* and *daughters*, and will give to *virgins* a famous place in the house of God, more *excellent than sons and daughters*, and more excellent than to those who were yoked together in holiness, and who are not polluted by their *matrimonial intercourse*."

A deal more of such *impious piety* is to be found in other parts of these *epistles*; but these quotations may serve to shew, how very early it became a fashion, in the *Christian church*, to put imagination in the place of scripture, and to invent schemes
of

of *sanctity*, which directly militated against the *will* and *word* of GOD, as revealed in the *holy* scripture.

What GOD had *honoured* with His *primary* blessing (Gen. i. 28.) they were to *deprecate*—what he *commanded* they were to *avoid*—and, in short, it seems as if the way to be thoroughly *holy*, was to counteract all that GOD had *done* and *said* upon the subject of marriage, by every method they possibly could, even to the " avoiding the speech and society of the " *other sex*, as the *contagion of a plague*." How this foundation was built upon in later times, the sequel will very sufficiently shew.

If the *reader* will turn to Is. lvi. 4, 5. which is the scripture alluded to in the latter part of the above quotation, he will see how the word of GOD could be perverted and abused, to answer the purposes of these delusions.

As for the *genuineness* of these two *epistles*, the reader may find what is said on that subject by *Wetstein*, vol. ii. N. T. Proleg. at the end of the *volume*; who seems to entertain little doubt of the matter.

EUSEBIUS PAMPHILUS, Bishop of *Cæsarea* in Palestine, a writer of the *fourth century*, whom *Mosheim* speaks of, as " a " man justly famous for his profound " knowledge of ecclesiastical history," (Mosh. vol. i. p. 186.) has left us an *history of the church*; and in that part of it which

Cent. I. and II. which relates to the above period, he tells us (B. 3. c. 29.) that—" at this
" time the *herefy* called the herefy of the
" *Nicholaites*, continued a very fhort time;
" of which alfo the *Revelation* of *John*
" makes mention. Thefe boafted of *Ni-*
" *cholas* (one of the *deacons*, who, toge-
" ther with *Stephen*, were ordained by the
" apoftles to minifter to the poor) as the
" author of their fect." *Eufebius* then cites *Clemens Alexandrinus*, who flourifhed about the year 192, as a voucher for the following ftory, which he profeffes to tranfcribe from *Clemens*, word for word.—He (i. e.
" *Nicholas* the *deacon*) they fay, having a
" beautiful *wife*, being, after our Sa-
" viour's afcenfion, blamed for his jea-
" loufy by the *apoftles*, brought his wife
" forth, and permitted her to marry
" whom fhe had a mind to, faying—δει
" παραχρασθαι τη σαρκι—that *we ought to*
" *abufe the flefh*. Thofe therefore who
" follow his *herefy*, fimply and rafhly
" affenting to this faying, and imitating
" this deed, do moft impudently give
" themfelves over to *fornication*. But I am
" given to underftand that *Nicholas* made
" ufe of no other woman, befides her he
" married; and that thofe of his children
" which were daughters, remained *virgins*
" when they were old; and his *fon* con-
" tinued *undefiled* by *women*. Which
" things being thus, his bringing his
" *wife* (over whom he is faid to be *jealous*)
" to

"to the *apostles*, was a sign of his reject-
"ing and bridling his passion; and by
"those words of his, that *we ought to
"abuse the flesh*, he taught *continence*, and
"an abstaining from those pleasures,
"which are with so much earnestness
"desired by men. For, I suppose, he
"would not, according to our Saviour's
"commandment, *serve two masters*—Plea-
"sure and the Lord.

"Moreover they say, that *Matthias*
"taught the same doctrine, that we should
"war against the flesh, and *abuse it*, al-
"lowing it nothing of pleasure; but that
"we should enrich the soul with faith
"and knowledge.

"But *Clemens*, whose words we have
"even now cited, after that passage of his
"before quoted (faith *Eusebius*) does
"reckon up those *apostles* that are found
"to have been *married*, upon account of
"such as despise *marriage*, saying, what
"will they reprehend even the *apostles*
"also?"

Now though there are historical facts recorded by this *Clemens*, as well as by *Eusebius* himself, which deserve about as much credit as *Mother Goose's Tales* *, yet it

Cent.
I. and II.

---

* Among others, that foolish story of a *devil*, that had taken up his residence at *Rome*, to whom *Simon Magus* went when *Peter* had preached him out of *Judea*, and by the assistance of this *devil*, *Simon* pre- vailed

CENT. I. and II. it is easy to perceive, that *marriage* itself fell into great disrepute among the very early *Christians*:—and *Dr. Cave*, as has been already noticed, (see *Thelyph.* vol. ii. p. 120. 1st edit. p. 112. 2d edit.) has collected evidence enough of this fact, to leave it without a doubt.

This *Clemens* of *Alexandria*, whatever he might write on behalf of *marriage* itself, did not approve of *second marriages*. *Du Pin*, who reckons *Clemens* among the writers of the *third century*, says, that though he does not entirely *condemn second marriages*, yet he *blames* them; that he held the *dæmons* to have sinned through *incontinence*; that it is not *lawful* to *marry*, but with a design of begetting children.

The learned Bishop NEWTON, in his ingenious and edifying " Dissertations on " the Prophecies," (vol. ii. p. 443.) observes from *Theodoret*, who was a writer of the *fifth century* (see *Mosheim*, vol. i. 246. Edit. Macl.) that " *Saturninus* or *Satur-* " *nilus*, who flourished (early) in the se- " cond century, was the first *Christian* " who declared matrimony to be the *doc-*

---

vailed on the inhabitants of *Rome* to set up an image to him, and worship him as GOD. But on *Peter's* following *Simon* to *Rome*, and preaching there, *Simon* and his *familiar* were silenced, his power extinct, and the man himself destroyed.

Another foolish story *Eusebius* cites out of *Clemens Alexandrinus*, of *Peter's* wife suffering martyrdom, and of the conversation between *Peter* and her on the occasion.

" *trine*

" trine of *the Devil*. But according to
" *Irenæus* and *Eusebius*, *Tatian*, who had
" been a disciple of *Justin Martyr*, was
" the first author of this *heresy*; at least
" he concurred in opinion with *Satur-*
" *ninus* and *Marcion*, and their followers
" were called *Encratites — Continents —*
" from their *continence* with regard to *mar-*
" *riage* and *meats*.

" The *Gnostics* likewise, as *Irenæus*
" and *Clemens Alexandrinus* inform us, as-
" serted, that to marry and beget children
" proceeded from the *devil*; and, under
" pretence of *continence*, were impious
" both against the *Creature* and the Cre-
" ator, teaching that men ought not
" to bring into the world others, who
" would be unhappy, nor supply *food* for
" *Death*."

Tertullian

Absolutely condemns *second* marriages, as being *adultery*—as did the whole sect of the *Montanists*. This father apologizes for the contempt of marriage among the early *Christians*, from their apprehension that the end of the world was near, and that this circumstance vacated the necessity of begetting children. See before, *Thelyph.* vol. i. p. 170. 2d edit. n.

Athenagoras

Commends *virginity*—condemns *second* marriages, calling them *honest adultery*.

CENTURY III.

Minutius Felix

Says—The *Christians* commonly *marry* but *once*, and that they have no other defign in their marriage, but the having of children.

Origen.

The violence which this father did on himfelf is well known;—he was much blamed for it in general—but, Demetrius, bifhop of *Alexandria*, commended his zeal, and the fervency of his faith, and bid him not be difcouraged on that account. In his time they did not admit perfons that were *twice* married into *holy orders*.

He fays, we ought not to *make ufe* of *marriage*, but * only for the fake of having children. He at laft fell into many errors and ftrange opinions—and there were difputes in the *church* whether he was *faved* or *damned*:—much it fignifies to him, which way the difputants determined the queftion.

Cyprian,

Who, when he was a *Catechumen*, refolved on *continency*, fays much of the

---

* Compare 1 Cor. vii. 4, 5.

great

great advantages of *virginity*; that it was the nearest state to that of *martyrdom*; that *virginity* is not of absolute necessity, but a great deal more *excellent* than *marriage*—and desires the *virgins* to remember him when they receive the recompence of their *virginity*—"Words," says *Du Pin*, "which
"make it appear, that, in *St. Cyprian's*
"time, they believed that the saints in-
"terceded for us before God."

The book of the *celibacy of the clergy* is extremely useful (says *Du Pin.)* In it he *proves*, that *churchmen* ought not to live with *women*.

Methodius,

Bishop of Olympus, and afterwards of Tyre, who, in a book intituled the *Banquet of Virgins*, has given as much *pious* nonsense on the subject of virginity, and its preference to marriage, as almost all the preceding fathers put together.

In Du Pin's summary of the discipline of the *3d century*, he says, that it was lawful for *priests* to keep the wives they married before they were ordained, but marriage was never permitted after ordination; but both the one and the other was allowed to *deacons*. *Monks* were not as yet instituted; but there were abundance of persons of both sexes among the *Christians*, that lived in a state of *celibacy*, and chearfully submitted to the austerities of an ascetic life. There were likewise some women,

CENT. III. women, in the *third age* of the church, that folemnly obliged themfelves to keep their virginity all their life-time.

CENT. IV.

CENTURY IV.

For an account of the Emperor Constantine's encouragement of *celibacy*, fee before, *Thelyph.* vol. ii. 281. n. 1ft edit. 252. n. 2d edit.

Eusebius of *Cæfarea*,

Praifes the ftate of virginity as more perfect, and the celibacy of priefts, without *blaming* marriage.

Athanasius,

In a letter to *Ammon* the monk, refutes the error of fome, who condemned the ufe of marriage, and fhews, from fcripture, that it is *permitted*, and that it is impiety to condemn it, though virginity is a *more perfect* ftate, and *deferves greater rewards*.

Hilary,

In his commentary on Pfalm cxix. obferves, that *celibacy* is more *perfect* than a ftate of *marriage*.

He approves of *vows*, and *invocation of faints*, and praifes *celibacy*.

Didymus of *Alexandria*,

Of whom *St. Jerome* was a difciple—
teaches,

teaches, that the use of marriage, though it is permitted, is called *sin* in comparison of *virginity*, which is a much more excellent state.

Cyril of *Jerusalem*,

Takes notice that *virginity* is the more perfect state, but that married persons *may* hope for salvation, provided they use marriage aright. That their intention should not be to satisfy a brutal passion, but to have children. That we ought not to condemn *even* those who proceed to *second* marriages; and that this *weakness* should be pardoned in those who stand in need of this remedy to avoid fornication.

St. Ephraim of *Syria*,

Answered one of his *monks*, who asked him, who they were that might use that liberty which *St. Paul* gives to marry, *rather than to burn?* that it concerns only those who are not bound, and who live in the world, but not those who have renounced the world, and embraced a religious life.

He has a treatise, to shew the excellencies of a monastic life above the secular.

St. Basil of *Cæsarea*,

Was the first founder of a monastic life in *Pontus* and *Cappadocia*. He taught, that there are many things *forbidden* in the *Gospel* which the *Law permitted*; that the passage

CENT. IV.

sage of *Genesis,* " *Increase and multiply,*" does *not* respect the * *New Testament.* He observes, that *second* marriages are a remedy against fornication, and not an inlet to immoderate lust; but he condemns *third* marriages as a kind of *fornication,* and says that the custom of the church was to *excommunicate* those who married a *third* time, for *five* years—that, in other places, they were only put under *penance* for two or three years. He enjoins the same thing to *bigamists,* for one or two years: though he would have neither the one nor the other reduced to the lowest penance—that they should be in the first years in the rank of *hearers*—the last years they should partake of the *prayers*—though they were still excluded from the participation of the *eucharist* 'till their penance was finished, and they had given signs of their conversion.

Can. 12. He declares, that the *canons* wholly exclude all *bigamists* from ecclesiastical functions.

---

* The reader may have observed before, p. 6. how early the *Christian* fathers began to *break ground* for a siege against the Old Testament, with respect to marriage. Here the *trenches* are fairly opened;—as we proceed, we shall find the *besiegers* very active—and that when the *Pope* and his *clergy* could bring the heavy artillery of their *canons* and *decrees* to bear, they played upon it 'till they left little else standing, beside its *impregnable testimony* against their wicked contempt of the *divine law.*

Can.

Can. 18. *St. Basil* observes, that the antients did not treat the *virgins* consecrated to GOD, who abandoned their profession, more rigorously than *bigamists*; they imposed only a penance of *one* year: but he adds, that the church, and the number of *virgins*, increasing every day, they should be treated as *adulterers*.

Can. 19. He observes, that men make no vow nor profession of virginity, as *virgins* do; that those who enter into a monastical state seem tacitly to embrace *celibacy*; but, to oblige them to it, it was necessary they should be asked, and that they should make profession, and then if they should pass to a voluptuous life, they should be punished as *fornicators*.

Can. 24. Is against *widows*, who, being *deaconesses*, married afterwards. He would have them more severely punished than *bigamists*, if they be above 60 years old. He excuses them if they be younger, because it was the bishop's fault to receive them too young.

By Can. 25. It is provided, that he who shall *marry* a woman after he hath *abused* her, shall be put under penance, but he shall have *leave* to keep her for his wife. *N. B.* The law of GOD positively says, *she shall be his wife*. See Exod. xxii. 16. Deut. xxii. 28, 29.

In Can. 26. He declares that *fornication* is never *marriage*, and that it cannot lawfully be the beginning of marriage; and therefore

CENT. IV.

therefore it would be better to part thofe who have committed this fin, than to marry them together; but yet, if they have a mind to marry, they fhould not be hindered, left fome greater mifchief fhould follow.

Qu? If by *fornication* this *father* means, the coming together without the rites of the church—how doth this *canon* agree with the fcriptures above referred to?

Can. 40. A flave, who marries without confent of his mafter, has committed *fornication*, his marriage being void.

Can. 50. The laws do not forbid nor punifh *third* marriages, and yet the church looks upon them as *fhameful* actions.

The treatife of true virginity, contains many precepts for preferving *virginity*. In it he extols very much the ftate of *virgins*, &c. There are in this treatife fome paffages which may offend nice ears; but it is to be confidered (fays Du Pin) it is addreffed to a bifhop, and not to the *virgins* themfelves. But qu.? If the *virgins* did not read or hear it, how were they to be the better for it?

This *father* fays much of *a law* of JESUS CHRIST—and of *the morality* of JESUS CHRIST—and feems to be one of thofe, who laid a foundation for feparating the Old Teftament from the *New*, by making CHRIST a new *lawgiver*, and a teacher of a new fyftem of *morality*, independently of the law of *Mofes*.

ST.

St. Gregory Nazianzen

Says, that marriage is commendable, where the parties are contracted with a defign of having children; but he prefers virginity to marriage.

In his poem in praife of virginity, he handles, with much wit and eloquence, the queftion about the pre-eminence of celibacy above marriage—he then brings in *married perfons*, and thofe who obferve *celibacy*, fpeaking for both their opinions; each of them fays all that can be faid in favour of their ftate, but the *latter* have the *better*.

St. Gregory Nyssen

Wrote a treatife on virginity, wherein he defcribes the advantages of *virginity*, and the inconveniences of *marriage*.

This father fpeaks out about a *new law* and an *old law*, and feems to leave the *latter* out of the queftion. "*Sacrilege*," fays he, "was punifhed under the *old law*, by "ftoning to death—yet this punifhment "was mitigated under the *new law*, and "now facrilegious perfons are treated lefs "harfhly than *adulterers*."

There is a paffage in this *father*'s writings, which fhews how little regard they paid to the *moral* law of the Old Teftament.—" Though the fcripture " (faith he) " reproves all fins feverely, yet the "*fathers*"

"*fathers*" (*i. e.* of the *Christian* church) "have made *no laws* but against *murder.*" He imposes twenty-seven years penance for *wilful murder,* and for involuntary murders the same space of time as for *fornication,* yet he allows "this penance to be diminished according to the fervor of the penitent."

So that God's law, Gen. ix. 6. was quite laid aside. A strong instance this, of the small attention they paid to the *Old Testament* in forming their systems.

Timothy of Alexandria

Would have persons that are married, abstain from the use of marriage *Saturday* and *Sunday,* that they may be capable of receiving the holy communion.

Siricius, *Pope of* Rome, *anno* 385,

Can. 7th. He declares, that every *clergyman* who shall marry a *second wife,* or a *widow,* shall be turned out of holy orders, and reduced to lay communion. And he declares, that if for the future any *bishop, priest,* or *deacon,* shall not continue *unmarried,* he is to hope for no more pardon; because it was necessary to cut off, with the knife, those sons which could not be cured by other remedies.

The 8th Can. is against those who get themselves *ordained* after they have had *several wives.*

Can. 9.

Can. 9. Says, that a man may be an *acolyth* or *subdeacon*, provided that he marries but once, and then does not marry a *widow*. That, after, he should be ordained *deacon*, if he obliges himself to live *unmarried*.

St. Ambrose, Bishop of Milan,

Wrote *three books* in praise of *virginity*. In which he treats at large on the excellency of *virginity*. He shews that this virtue came from heaven, that God is the author of it, that the Heathens neither knew it, nor practised it as they ought; that the *Jews* themselves did not esteem it, and that it was not common among men 'till Jesus Christ came into the world. Afterwards he gives a catalogue of the advantages which virginity has above the marriage-state. " I do not condemn " marriage," (says he) " but I will prove " that *virginity* is more excellent;"—and then says all he can to frighten women from marrying.—He reproves mothers who hindered their daughters from coming to hear him, lest they should embrace virginity, and commends those *virgins* who devoted themselves to God without their parents leave.

He wrote also a treatise of *widows*, wherein he exalts the state of *widows*, who do not marry again, as approaching near to the perfection of *virgins*. He does not absolutely

CENT. IV. lutely condemn either *first* or *second* marriages, but he prefers the state of *virgins* and *widows* before that of *married women*.

He complains that there were few at *Milan*, who *profited* by his instructions; whilst a great many virgins, not only from *Bologna* and *Placentia*, but from *Mauritania*, came to receive the veil at *Milan*.

St. Epiphanius

Praises *virginity*, but does not condemn marriage, nor yet *second* marriages; but declares plainly, that the church does not admit any to holy orders, but such as observe *celibacy*, and that she excludes *bigamists*. He confesses, that there are still some places where the *deacons* and *sub-deacons* do not observe *celibacy*, but adds,—" This is " done upon sufferance, because of the " weakness of men, or the multitude of " people." Lastly, he says, " It is a great " sin to violate the *vow* of *virginity*."

Having briefly extracted some *opinions* of the *Fathers*, I will now lay before the reader, the *wisdom* of some of the *Councils*.

Council of Eliberis, *anno* 305.

Can. 7th. Those that relapse into *adultery*, after they have undergone *penance*, shall not be received even at *death*.

Can. 8th. Subjects a woman to the same

same penalty, who has forsaken her husband, without cause, to marry another.

Can. 14. Treats *virgins* with much moderation, who have lost their *virginity:* if they *marry* those who have abused them, they are restored to communion at the end of one year, without being obliged to do penance; but imposes *five* years penance if they had to do with other men.

Can. 19. Ordains, that communion shall be refused, even at the point of death, to *bishops, priests,* and *deacons,* who have committed *adultery.*

Can. 61. Imposes penance of five years upon him that marries his *wife's sister,* unless the extremity of sickness oblige us to give him the peace of the church sooner.

Can. 65. If a clergyman knows that his wife commits *adultery,* and sends her not away, he is unworthy of the communion of the church, even at the point of death. *N. B.* This *canon* is an authentic evidence of the marriage of the clergy in the church of *Spain* at this time.

Can. 69. Imposes but five years penance on those who have fallen but *once* into the sin of *adultery.*

Can. 70. If a woman commit adultery with the consent of her husband, he is unworthy of the communion at the point of death; but if he divorces her, he may be received after ten years penance.

Can. 78.

Can. 78. Imposes on him who commits *adultery* with a *Pagan* or *Jewish* woman, a penance of *three* years, if he confesses his crime, but of *five* years if detected by the testimony of others.

Council of ARLES, *anno* 314.

Can. 10. Those who find their wives in the act of *adultery*, must be counselled not to marry others, though the law permits them to do it.—BRAVO!

Council of ANCYRA and NEO-CÆSAREA, *anno* 314.

There are twenty-five canons of the Council of ANCYRA.—The 10th concerns the celibacy of *deacons*. If they declared, at the time of their ordination, that they would marry, they shall not be deprived of their function if they did marry; but if ordained without making this declaration, and afterwards married, they should be obliged to quit their employment.

Can. 16 and 17. Imposes long penances on those who have committed crimes contrary to nature. See Lev. xx. 13.

Can. 20. Imposes *seven* years penance for *adultery*. See Lev. xx. 10.

Can. 21. The synod observes, that the antient *canons* delayed the absolution of those women, who, having committed the sin of *adultery*, *murdered* their *infants*, 'till death;

death; but, to mitigate this punishment, it imposes upon them only *ten* years penance. Note, For *adultery* and *child-murder!*

N.B. The canons of this council are signed by eighteen bishops. BRAVI TUTTI.

NEO-CÆSAREA.

Can. 1. If a *priest* marries after he has been ordained, he ought to be *degraded.*— If he commit *fornication* or *adultery*, he ought to be punished more rigorously, and put under *penance*.

Can. 3. The time of *penance* of those who marry *often*, is regulated by the *canons*, but it may be shortened proportionably to the conversion of the *penitent*, and the fervour of his *penance*.

Can. 7. Forbids *priests* to be present at the marriage of *bigamists*.

Can. 8. He cannot be admitted into holy orders, whose wife has been convicted of *adultery*.

Can. 9. If a *priest* who has committed the *sin of the flesh* before ordination, confess his crime, he ought no more to offer, but he shall enjoy all his other rights: for as to *other sins*, 'tis thought, that they are pardoned by the imposition of hands. But if he does not confess his crime, and cannot be convicted of it, he shall be left to his own conscience.

Can. 10. A *deacon* committing the same crime before his ordination, shall be placed in the rank of the other ministers.

Council of NICE, anno 325.

This was called an *Oecumenical*—*i. e.*—a council of the *whole world*, becaufe it was called together by the emperor *Conftantine* from all parts of the *Roman* empire, and was compofed of the *eaftern* and *weftern* bifhops.

Can. 3. Forbids *bifhops*, *priefts*, and *deacons*, and other *clergymen*, to keep women in the houfe with them; yet it excepts mothers, fifters, and other perfons of whom there could be no bad fufpicion. *N. B.* Nothing is faid of *wives*.

In this *council* a canon was propofed for obliging *bifhops*, *priefts*, and *deacons*, who were married before ordination, to obferve *celibacy*; but *Paphnutius*, a venerable confeffor and prelate, withftood this, and brought the council to confent, that every one fhould be left to their liberty, and need not abftain from their wives unlefs they were willing fo to do. See *Jortin Rem*. vol. ii. p. 249.

Council of LAODICEA, between 360, 370.

Can. 44. *Women* ought not to come near the *altar*.

Can. 52. That *marriages* fhould not be celebrated in *Lent*.

Council of VALENCE, anno 374.

Can. 1. Thofe are not to be ordained who have been *twice* married, or thofe who have

have espoused a *widow*, whether they did it before or since their *baptism*: but they do not intermeddle with the ordinations of *bigamists* made before their decision, lest they should disturb the *church*.

Can. 2. *Penance* shall not be allowed immediately to those *virgins* who *married* after they had made a vow of *virginity*, and they shall not be received until they have made *full satisfaction*.

Council of SARAGOSA, *anno* 381.

Can. 8. Forbids *virgins*, that are devoted to JESUS CHRIST, to be *veil'd*, except they be forty years of age.

Councils of ROME and of MILAN against JOVINIAN, *anno* 390.

Though we ought not to despise marriage, yet *virgins* are more to be honoured. Their second letter contains *proofs* of these truths; and it is shewn, that the Blessed Virgin lost not her *virginity* by bringing forth JESUS CHRIST into the world.

First Council of CARTHAGE, *anno* 348.

Can. 2. Forbids those persons who profess *virginity*, to cohabit or to have familiarity with any persons of the other *sex*, under pain of *excommunication* for the *laity*, and of *deposition* for the *clergy*.

Can. 4. Contains the same prohibition to *widows*.

CENT. IV.

Councils of CARTHAGE, *anno* 397.

Can. 4. Forbids the confecration of *virgins* before the age of twenty-five years.

Can. 17. Forbids *clergymen* to cohabit with ftrange women, and permits them only to live with their mothers, grandmothers, aunts, fifters, nieces, and thofe of their *domeftics* who dwelt in the houfe with them before their *ordination*.

Can. 19. Readers are to be obliged, when they come to age, to *marry*, or to make the *vow* of *chaftity*†.

Can. 33. When *virgins* lofe their relations who took care of them, the *bifhop*, or, in his abfence, the *prieft*, ought to place them in a *nunnery*, or commit them to the care of women of known probity.

Can. 36. *Priefts* fhall not confecrate *virgins* without the *bifhop*'s permiffion— they are abfolutely forbidden to make the holy *chryfm*.

Council of CARTHAGE, *anno* 398, called the *fourth*.

There are 104 canons relative to the ordination of *bifhops*, &c.; and it is ordained, that every *bifhop* fhall be interrogated about the errors *common* in *Africa*, and among others—" Whether he does not condemn " *marriage*, and *fecond marriages*? Whe- " ther he believes it is the fame GOD who

† This is fomething like " a *wife*, or a *mittimus*."

" is

" is the author of the *Old* and *New Testa-*
" *ment*, the *Law* and the *Gospel?*"

Can. 10. *Virgins* who would be consecrated by the *bishop*, should present themselves in habits agreeable to their profession and vocation, like to those which they are to use for the future.

Can. 11. Those who are *contracted*, and would receive the *benediction* of *marriage*, ought to be accompanied by their kindred, and to abstain from the use of marriage the night after the *benediction*.

Can. 104. Excommunicates *widows* who marry again, after they have made profession of *celibacy*.

D°, *anno* 401, called the *fifth*.

Can. 70. Ordains *bishops, priests,* and *deacons,* to have no more to do with their *wives*, under pain of degradation; for the *lesser orders*, it does not oblige them to *celibacy*.

Council of Toledo, *anno* 400.

Can. 1. They permit the order of *deacon* to be given to *married* persons, provided they be *chaste*, and observe *continence*; but they impose no other penalty upon a *priest* or *deacon*, that has not lived in *continence*, and who had children before the law which the bishops of *Lusitania* made upon this subject: they impose upon them no other penalty but that they shall not be capable of rising to a higher dignity.

Can. 3.

CENT. IV.

Can. 3. If a *reader* marry a *widow*, he cannot be advanced to higher orders, at most he shall be only *sub-deacon*.

Can. 4. A *sub-deacon*, who marries again, shall be put into the rank of *porters* or *readers*, without being capable of reading the *epistles* or *gospels*. He who marries a *third* time, shall be *separated* from the church for the space of *two years*, and after he is reconciled, he shall never rise higher than the rank of *lay-men*.

Can. 16. Imposes *ten years* penance for *adultery*.

Can. 17. He who has a *concubine* and *wife* both together, ought to be *excommunicated*, but he ought not to be *excommunicated* who has † only a *concubine*; so that it is necessary for every one, that is a member of the church, to satisfy himself either with one *wife* or one *concubine*. This canon (says *Du Pin*) may give some trouble to those, who know not that the word *concubine*, which is at present *odious* ‡, was formerly taken for a woman, to whom the marriage promise was given, though she was not *married* with all the solemnities which the laws required in marriage, as St. *Austin*

---

† This *Canon*, as *Dr. Jortin*, Rem. vol. ii. 294, observes, proves the *allowance* of *concubinage* in the *Christian* church, so late as anno 400; therefore this will hardly be pretended to be *altered* by the New Testament.

‡ It never became so, 'till the *Pope* and *his clergy* insulted the GOD of the Old Testament, by setting His *dispensations* at nought.

has explained it, chap. 5. of the book about the *advantages of marriage.*

Can. 18. We ought not to communicate with the *widow* of a *bishop*, a *priest*, or a *deacon*, if she marries again; she ought not to be reconciled until the point of death.

Can. 19. Inflicts the same penalty on the daughters of *bishops*, &c. who marry after they have been consecrated to God.

N. B. This council was composed of *nineteen* Spanish bishops.

In the abridgement of the *doctrine* of the *fourth* age of the church, it is said—
" They approved of marriage, and would
" have the persons to be married, con-
" tracted in the *face of the church*, and in
" the presence of a *priest*, who gave a
" *blessing.* They honoured *virginity*, and
" commended those who professed it, and
" looked upon those as *sacrilegious* persons
" who violated that profession. They had
" much reverence and veneration for the
" *blessed virgin* and the *saints*, they prayed to
" them, and also honoured their *reliques.*
" They prayed for the dead. We have of-
" ten (says *Du Pin*) taken notice of their
" opinion concerning the authority of *holy*
" *scripture* and *tradition.* They taught
" that there was but one *Catholic church*,
" out of which there was no *salvation*, and
" to *whose authority* all men ought to *sub-*
" *mit*, because it can neither cease to be,
" nor *err* in matters of faith.
" Whereof

CENT. IV.

"Whereof one may say in general (adds "*Du Pin*) that the doctrine of the *fourth* "age was the belief of the *church* of that "age, and so, the *church* not being capa- "ble of changing her belief, it necessarily "follows, that the doctrine of that time "is not at all different from that which "the *church* teaches still at this day."

In the abridgement of the *discipline* of the *fourth* age, we are told—"*Prayer* for "the *dead* was a common practice in the "*church*, they were commemorated at the "celebration of the *eucharist*; the *invoca*- "*tion* of *saints* and *martyrs*, and the cele- "bration of their *festivals*, were common "in all the churches; the use of *crosses* "was frequent; the sign of the *cross* was "made very often; there were images in "many churches.

"A *blessing* was given for *marriage*; but "the church never gave it for † *second* mar- "riages, and they even put *bigamists* under "*penance* for some time. Marriages con- "tracted between persons who could not "lawfully marry, according to the *civil* "*laws*, were looked upon as *null* §. *Di*- "*vorce* for *adultery* was *permitted* in *some* "churches. The *monastic* state was esta- "blished in *this age*, and became very "common in a little time."

† Still they were *good and valid marriages*.
§ Qu? Were these *marriages null* in GOD's sight.

CEN-

CENTURY V.

St. John Chrysostom,

In his 19th and 20th sermons, which are on 1 Cor. 7. takes occasion to speak against *dancing*, and other profane pomps at *weddings*—" To what purpose (faith he) " do ye bring in a *priest* to crave a blessing, " and the next day yourselves commit base " actions?"

From this, and other passages in the *fathers*, it does manifestly appear, that the marriage-contract, though sometimes made, according to some *canons*, in the *face* of the *church*, was of a *civil* nature, and that the only thing the *priest* did, was to pronounce a *blessing*; unless indeed he partook of the diversions of the *wedding-feast*, which also seems to have been the custom, and that pretty heartily too; for the council of *Laodicea*, Canon 14, says, " that *clergymen* ought not to be present at *shews* or *balls*, that are made during *marriage-feasts*, but arise and be gone before the *mask* begins."— So that we may conclude, there were many abuses of this kind, which gave rise to this canon.

In *Chrysostom*'s 24th sermon on 2 Cor. 4. he gives great praises to *virginity*, and to a *monastic* life; which he thus describes:— " Do you take notice of those *monks* who " live

"live privately, and dwell upon the tops of mountains? What austerities and mortifications do they not practise? They are covered with ashes, cloathed with sackcloth, loaden with chains and irons, shut up in little cells; struggling continually with hunger, they spend their time in watchings, TO BLOT OUT PART OF THEIR SINS." He observes also, that, though *virginity* is a supernatural gift, yet it is unprofitable, if it be not accompanied with *charity* and *meekness*.

He proves that *second* marriages are not forbidden, though it is *better* to *forbear*.

In his book *of Virginity*, he says, "*marriage* is *good*, that's my opinion, but virginity is *better*. This I own, and if you will have my sense, it is as much above matrimony as *heaven* is above the *earth*, and makes *men* like to *angels*."

Afterwards he makes an objection—"If it be *better* to live *unmarried*, why did GOD institute *marriage?* Why did he make *women?* And, should all men embrace *virginity*, how should mankind be propagated?"—To answer these objections, *St. Chrysostom* goes back as far as the *creation* of man, and takes notice, that "while he was in the earthly *paradise* with *Eve*, he was taken up with a conversation with GOD, and he was then freed from *lust* and the *desires* of the *flesh*, and lived in perfect *virginity*, and "the

"the whole world was at that time a vast
"solitude. But man, having disobeyed
"God's commands, and becoming mortal
"and corruptible, with that happy life
"which he enjoyed, he lost also the *glory
"of virginity:* so that *sin* being the cause
"of *death*, became at the same time the
"cause of *marriage*. It is probable that
"though there had been no marriage, yet
"the world ‡ might have been peopled,
"and God have created *other men* as he
"had done the *first*." Adding, that "it
"is not the frequent use of *marriage* that
"multiplieth mankind, but God's bles-
"sing:" and he believes that "marriage
"is more necessary to the world at present,
"for a remedy against incontinency, *than
"for the preservation of mankind;* he grants
"that it is necessary for the *weak*, but that
"*virginity* is far more honourable and pro-

‡ This passage puts one in mind of *Leslie's* observation on the famous *mystic*, *Madame Bourignon*—who said—"there was no need for Christ to suffer
"in order to the redemption of mankind, God might
"have effected it some other way."—"This *devil* of
"a *saint*," says *Leslie*, "gives a direct lye to the scrip-
"ture, Luke xxiv. 46. which saith—*Thus* (εδει)
"*it* BEHOVED CHRIST *to suffer*, &c."—How far short this *angel* of a *Father* is from giving the *lye* to the book of *Genesis*, wherein we find *marriage* instituted in the days of perfect *innocency*, must be left to the judgment of the *reader*, on the perusal of what is said in the above paragraph. However severe *Leslie's* animadversion on *Madame Bourignon* may appear, it is fully warranted by what Christ said to Peter on a similar occasion. See Mat. xvi. 22, 23.

"fitable

Cent. V.

"fitable too: he pretendeth, that what-
"foever *St. Paul* faid of *marriage,* ought to
"induce men to embrace *virginity.*"

He wrote two treatifes, "*Againſt the co-*
"*habitation of clerks with women*"—and
"*A diſcourſe to a widow;*"—he exhorts
her to continue in her *widowhood*. He
made another little book on purpoſe to
ſhew, that *ſhe ought not to marry again;*
where he *proves,* that though *ſecond* marriages be not abſolutely *forbidden,* yet it is
much better to continue in *widowhood*.

This *eminent father,* in his diſcourſes on
the *euchariſt,* affirmed, that the *bread* and
wine become the *body and blood* of Christ;
that we ought not to doubt of it, ſeeing
Christ himſelf affirmeth it — that fire
from heaven conſumeth the things offered, and changeth them into the *body*
and *blood* of Jesus Christ.

In the *Chriſtian* maxims, which are ſe-
lected from his ſermons, he lays it down,
that, "*ſolitarineſs,* and a *monaſtic* life,
"are more to be deſired than the greateſt
"kingdoms."

Pope Innocent I.

Can. 4. Forbids *orders* to a perſon who
has married a *widow*.

Can. 5. Extends this prohibition even
to thoſe who have *married* ſuch a woman
before *baptiſm*.

Can. 6.

Can. 6. The same with regard to those who have been *twice married*.

Can. 12. Prohibits the admitting *virgins*—that, being consecrated to GOD, *married*, or were *corrupted*—to *penance*, before the death of the person with whom they have committed the *crime*.

Can. 13. Enjoins *penance* to virgins that *marry*, after promising *virginity*, though they had not been solemnly *veiled* by the *bishop*.

Can. 1. Epist. 3. He confirms *Siricius* his law, concerning the *celibacy* of *priests* and *deacons*. Yet he forgiveth those, who through ignorance observed it not, on condition that they should continue in that order, and rise no higher. But he ordains that those should be *degraded* who *violated* it *knowingly*.

In Letter 5. To two bishops of *Abruzzo*, he bids them *depose* the *priests* that were accused of having had children since their *ordination*, if they be convicted of *that crime*.

Letter 9. Declareth, that a man who *married* another woman, while his wife was in captivity, ought to return to the former; because a *second* marriage *cannot* be *lawful*, except the former wife be dead or separated by divorce.

Letter 22. To *Rufus*, and other bishops of *Macedonia*, dated anno 414, he tells them, that " he was much surprized " by "by a letter directed to the see of *Rome*, as the *chiefest* of all *churches*, because they consulted him about things that had *no difficulty*, and concerning which he had plainly declared his opinion. One is, the ordination of such as had married *widows*." Pope *Innocent* saith, "That there is no dispute that they should not be ordained;" and affirms, "that it was the practice of *all*, both *eastern* and *western* churches; nay, he would have those to be *degraded* who are found to be in orders."

The *second* is concerning those, who having lost a former wife, being yet *unbaptized*, had married a *second* after *baptism*. Some were of opinion, that this kind of *bigamy* did not hinder them from *ordination*. Pope *Innocent* alledgeth several reasons, to prove that such a practice is not to be followed.

St. Jerom

Was born about the year 345. In his treatise of *Virginity*, to *Eustochium*, he highly extols it. In his directions to her for the maintenance of it, he advises her to shun reading *profane* books; and, to inforce what he says, tells her, that "he, "being once too earnest in reading *Cicero*, "*Plautus*, and other profane authors, he "fell into a violent fever, and, by it, "into a kind of agony, and then was
"caught

"caught up in the spirit *to the tribunal of* "Jesus Christ; where, having been "soundly *whipt* for reading profane au"thors too much, he was forbidden to "read them any more." He assures *Eustochium* that " this story *is not a dream,* "and calls the *tribunal where he appeared,* "and the *judgment that was given against* "*him,* to attest the truth of what he "says." Yet, when *Rufinus* upbraided him afterwards, that, for all that, he had not given over reading profane books, he laughs at his simplicity, and jests upon him for taking a *dream* for *truth*. So much for this *saint*'s ‖ sincerity!

In his polemical treatises, his bitterness against his opponents is excessive. When he disputeth with *Helvidius*, he commendeth *virginity* to that excess, that it was thought he designed to condemn *matrimony*;—and he discourseth after such a manner of *virginity,* as would almost persuade men, that it was necessary to lead that sort of life, in order to be *saved*. Labour, fastings, austerities, and various mortifications, together with solitude and pilgrimages, make up the subject of almost all his advices and exhortations. His de-

‖ *Le Clerc,* Quæst. Hieron. iii. p. 62. says—" *Ingenium* Hieronymi *totum fuit ad jactationem, & dissimulationem compositum."* The genius of Jerome, *was wholly turned to bragging and dissimulation*. See *Confessional,* 3d edit. p. 406—408.

Cent. V.

light was to hear of the lives of monks and hermits, and he easily believed whatsoever was told him upon that subject, though never so extraordinary.

In short, from the account which *Du Pin* gives of this *Saint Jerom*, his composition seems to have been a mixture, like that of the *Cynic Diogenes*, in point of temper and disposition, and like that of the visionary of *La Mancha* in point of *judgment*. See before *Thelyph*. vol. ii. 123—128. 1st edit.——p. 116—121. 2d. edit.

St. Austin.

It being said, by some enemies to the *Christian* faith, that God had abolished the *old law*, either out of *inconstancy*, or because He was *weary* of it, *St. Austin* answered—that "God is *unchangeable* in "all that concerns *Himself*; and that, as "He hath given precepts and ordinances "for the good of man, so it is for the "*same* end that He sometimes *changeth* "them, as He judgeth it may be more "*convenient* for them."

N. B. The *Creator*'s changing His laws, in order to suit the *creature's convenience*, is a curious idea!

He adds, that, "we should not believe, "that, since the coming of Jesus Christ, "those things can be observed, which were "either *permitted*, or *prescribed*, only for "the time of the *old law*; though at that "time

" time they were to be taken in their pro-
" per fenfe." He inftanceth in the *polygamy* of the *patriarchs*, becaufe they lived
† *holily* in marriage, with a profpect of having children; and he confidently preferreth
that ftate, before that of fuch men, who,
having but *one wife*, abufe matrimony to
fatisfy their § brutifh luft.

He taught, that of all that is done for
the *dead*, nothing availeth them where
they are, but the offering of the *Eu-
charift, prayers,* and alms-deeds: that
thefe things are not ufeful to *all*, but only
to fuch as *deferved*, in their *life-time*, to reap
benefit by them after their *death*.

He wrote againft *Jovinian*, who was
called an *heretic*, and an enemy to *virginity*, for perfuading fome *Roman* virgins to
marry, and for maintaining that " mar-
" ried perfons might be as *holy*, as perfons
" in a ftate of *celibacy*." *Jovinian*'s opinion was rejected at *Rome*; and *Saint Auftin*
wrote a book, to fhew, that *Jovinian*'s
opinions might be refuted without condemning *marriage*; in which he examines
how men could have had children had they
perfifted in a ftate of *innocence*.

† Qu? How could the *patriarchs* be faid to " *live*
" *holily* in marriage," if they lived in a *ftate* forbidden
by the *primary inftitution?*

§ From this paffage, and many more, it is very
clear, that this *father*, as well as others, differed very
widely from *St. Paul*, in their notions relative to the
ufe and *ends* of *marriage*. See poft, p. 42. N. B.

He

CENT. V.

He declares that man guilty of *adultery*, who should abuse a *virgin*, when he has a design to marry another. As for the young woman, she is guilty of *sin*, but not of *adultery*, if she is true to that man, and designs not to *marry* when he leaveth her. He doth not excuse from *venial* sin, either the man or the woman, who have another prospect in marriage than the begetting of children. *N. B.*

He determines, that, though human laws permit a man to *marry again*, when he is divorced from a *former wife*, yet it is not *lawful* for *Christians*.—He concludes, that *marriage* is of itself a *good* thing, but one of those *good* things which we should not look after, but in order to a greater *good*, or to avoid a *great evil*. That, before CHRIST, the most *continent* might *marry*, to multiply that people from whom the *Messiah* was to be born; but *now*, as many as are able to contain, do *well* not to *marry*. That, for *this* † reason, men were permitted formerly to have *several wives*, but *now* no man is to have more *than one wife*. That the *gospel purity* is so great in this point, that a *deacon* was not to be ordained, who

† What an entire confidence had these *fathers* in the *credulity* of mankind, to venture forth their *reveries*, on *reasons* so absurd and foolish, as to be against all *reason*? As if the command to *increase* and *multiply* the human species, Gen. i. 28. was not as necessary for one period of the world, as for another. See post, p. 47.

had

had ever had more than *one wife*. He approves their opinion who underſtand this maxim in its *whole extent*, and without reſtriction, as did *Jerom*, by excepting thoſe who contracted a *former* marriage before *baptiſm*. And, as a young woman who had been defiled when ſhe was a *catechumen*, cannot be conſecrated as a *virgin* after *baptiſm*, even ſo it hath been thought reaſonable, that the man, who hath had more than *one wife*, whether before or after baptiſm, ſhould be looked upon as wanting one *neceſſary* qualification for *orders*.

His book *Of Holy Virginity*, ſays, that " *virginity* is one of the moſt excellent " gifts of GOD."—He exalteth the excellency of *virgins* conſecrated to GOD, by the example of the virginity of the *mother of* GOD, who, according to him, had made a vow of *continency* before the *angel* appeared to her.—He ſays, that *virginity* ſhould not be choſen as a thing *neceſſary* to *ſalvation*, but as a ſtate of greater *perfection*; and aſſerts, that *virgins* ſhall have a particular REWARD in *heaven*.

He exhorts huſbands that have left their wives to live in *continency*, alledging the example of *churchmen*, who abſtain ſo religiouſly, though they often were forced to take that profeſſion upon them againſt their wills.

He believes, that, by the inſpiration of GOD,

CENT. V.

GOD, the *martyrs* know the necessities of the faithful, and *hear* their *prayers*. He does not question but *martyrs* help the living; but he knows not whether they do it by themselves, or whether GOD doeth it by *angels* at their request. He confesseth, that we cannot know by which of these means, or whether by *both*, the *martyrs* work *miracles*.

St. *Austin*'s answer to the following question is very curious, *viz.*—" If con-
" cupiscence is evil, and an effect of sin,
" if all children are born in sin, how
" comes *matrimony* to be approved, which
" is the *effect* and *spring* of this *sin*?"
Answer. " Though *lust* be a *defect*, and
" a consequence of the first man's *sin*,
" which remaineth even in the baptized,
" yet conjugal chastity is to be approved,
" which makes a good use of an *evil*
" thing."

Here St. *Austin*, as well as St. *Chrysostom*, (see before p. 35.) evidently makes the natural desire of the sexes to each other, *evil in itself*—an horrible blasphemy against GOD, who implanted it in man's nature for the wisest purposes, in the days of man's *innocence!* otherwise how could the command—" *increase and multiply*"—have been *then* given, Gen. i. 28?—and the way in which this was to be done, expressly *commanded*, Gen. ii. 24.? With as much reason these *fathers* might have said, that

the

the appetite of *hunger* is evil, and the effect of *sin*, though GOD provided food for man. Gen. i. 29.

St. Austin has been styled the father of the *Latin church.*

The *Rhemists* quote this *father's* authority for thus commenting on 1 Cor. vii. 29.—" He exhorts that *those who have*
" *wives*, should not wholly bestow them-
" selves in the vain transitory pleasure and
" voluptuousness of their flesh, but live
" in such moderation, that *marriage* hin-
" der them, as little as may be, from spiri-
" tual cogitations: which is best fulfilled of
" them, who, by *mutual consent*, do *wholly*
" contain, whether they have had children
" or none, contemning *carnal issue* for the
" joys of heaven—and *these* marriages be
" more blessed than any *other*, saith *St.*
" *Aug.* de *Serm. Dom. in Monte*, L. i.
" c. 14."

Council supposed to be held at ROME under Pope INNOCENT I.

Can. 1. and 2. Speak of those *virgins* penance, who having solemnly put on the *veil*, and received the *priest's* benediction, commit incest, or contract prohibited marriages. Penance is likewise imposed upon those that made a single vow of *virginity*—though they made no solemn profession, nor received the *veil*—when they happen

to

Cent. V. to marry, or suffer themselves to be taken away.

Can. 3. Concerns the *sanctity* of *bishops, priests,* and *deacons:* they are told, that they ought to give example to the people; that they are obliged to remain *unmarried,* and several reasons are alledged for it. *Priests* and *bishops,* say they, are to preach *continence* to the people: with what confidence shall they do this, if they keep it not themselves? They are obliged to offer frequently the *holy sacrifice,* to *baptize, consecrate,* and *administer:* to do it with the greater reverence, they must be *chaste* both in body and spirit.

Can. 11. Speaks very ambiguously concerning a man's marrying his uncle's wife, or an aunt's marrying with the son of her husband's brother.

Council of CARTHAGE. Anno 407.

Can. 8. Forbids *divorced* persons to be married to others. This regulation is there judged to be conformable to the *law of the gospel,* and the decision of the apostle *St. Paul.* (Quere, where?)

Ditto. Anno 418 and 419.

Can. 3. Confirms the rule of the council of *Carthage,* anno 401, concerning the celibacy of *bishops, priests,* and *deacons:* it

is

is said that their ministry obligeth them to it.

Faustinus confirms this order in the 4th canon.

Can. 16. Readers are obliged to *marry* when they come to the age of *puberty*, or to make a *vow* of *continency*.

Can. 18. Forbids giving the *eucharist* to the *dead*.

St. ISIDORE PELUSIOTA

Prefers a single life before marriage.— He observes, that the *polygamy* of the antient *patriarchs* was *then* very excusable, because it was necessary that they should have a numerous posterity; but it may not be *now* used as a pretence to ‡ cover our incontinence.

He taught, that the veil, that covers the

‡ This "most lame and impotent conclusion" from the premises, which speak of quite another matter, would almost tempt one to say of these *fathers*, as Lord Chief Justice *Holt* said of one of the *heralds*, who appeared as a witness in a *cause*, wherein the determination of some question depended on a distinction in *heraldry*. The *herald* giving but a *blind* account of the matter, and tiring the patience of the court with many absurd answers —" Well," said the Chief Justice, " I perceive, that this *silly* fellow " don't understand his own *silly* trade." The *reader* will find many instances of this, in the perusal of these extracts from the *fathers*, whose *trade* and *occupation* seem to have been *system-making*: in which they were as great proficients, with respect to *divinity*, particularly as relating to *marriage*, as the projectors at *Laputa* were in *experimental philosophy* and *mathematics*. See GULLIVER.

CENT. V.

sacramental elements, doth *undoubtedly* overspread the *body* of JESUS CHRIST, and the *Holy Spirit* turns the wine into the *blood* of JESUS CHRIST. He approves of the honour given to *martyrs*, and the respect which is bestowed on their *reliques*; and disallows the presenting of offerings at their altars in honour of them.

He relates a story of a young woman, who coming into the sight of a young man, who was in love with her, cured him of that fond passion, by presenting herself with her hair *crop'd*, and her head covered with *ashes*.

As *St. Isidore* professed a *monastic* life, he extols a *monastic* state, and recommends the cloathing of *monks* to be of hair, and their food to be nothing but *herbs*.

ST. CÆLESTINE,

Chosen *Bishop* of *Rome* anno 423. He decreed — that none be ordained *bishop*, who hath been *married twice*, or hath married a *widow*: which he ordains as a rule, not only for the future, but he requires, that the ordinations already made in prejudice of this law, be looked upon as *unlawful*, which may not be allowed in force.

ST. LEO,

Chosen *Pope* anno 440, deservedly reckoned (says *Du Pin*) among the *fathers* of
the

the *church*. He lays it down, as a condition neceſſary for holy orders, not to have married above *one wife*, and ſhe not to have been a *widow*. He commands the *biſhops*, to whom he wrote, to deprive them of their *biſhoprics* who were found to had *two wives*, or had married a *widow*.

He orders, that the miniſters of the altar, that is to ſay, the *deacons* and *ſub-deacons*, ſhould be ſubject to the law of *continence*, as well as the *biſhops and prieſts*. He adds, that being *laics* or *readers*, they may be *married* and *have children*; but being arrived to the ſacred miniſtry of the altars, it is not to be permitted to them. That their *marriage* ought to be changed from *carnal* to *ſpiritual*, that ſo they may neither forſake their wives, nor have any carnal knowledge of them. *St. Leo* is the firſt that extended the law of *celibacy* to *ſub-deacons*.

He declares, that a *clergyman* who gives his daughter in marriage to one that hath a *concubine*, ought not to be treated as if he had given her to a perſon already married, becauſe *concubines* cannot be * counted *lawful wives*, nor the familiar commerce with them *marriage*, unleſs they be free, endowed, and joined together by *public marriage*.

That, young women, whoſe relations

---

* See before, p. 30. and vol. i. Append. to chap. 2.

have married them to persons that have *concubines*, do not sin in dwelling with those to whom they are married.

That it is not the sin of *adultery*, but a virtuous action, for a man to *cast off* his *concubine*, that he may live only with his wife. The *concubines*, spoken of in this place, are slaves, with whom men lived as with their wives, without having any commerce with others, though they were not solemnly married to them.

He could *wish* that those who have done *penance* when they were *boys*, would not *marry*; yet he *excuses* young men who do it to avoid incontinency. See 1 Cor. vii. 9.

He orders that the *monks* who have *married* should be made to do *penance*, because they cannot leave that profession without *sin*, when they have once embraced it, but are obliged to perform their *vows*.

He condemns *virgins*, who married after they had voluntarily put on the habit, though they were not yet consecrated.

Can. 4. He commands *bishops*, *priests*, and *deacons* to live unmarried; and observes, that the use of marriage was not allowed to *sub-deacons*. *St. Gregory* says, that " it was hard to refuse it to the *lat-* " *ter*."—But quere,—Why more so than to the *former* ?

The *Gallican* bishops wrote to *St. Leo* a letter full of high commendations and compliments, and they call the church of
Rome

Rome—"*Apostolica sedes, unde religionis nostræ fons & origo manavit."*—" The apostolic church, from whence comes the origin and source of our religion."

In one of his sermons, on *St. Peter*'s day, he says, that, that *apostle* never forsakes his church, but continues to be the *foundation* of it—that *St. Peter* is not only *bishop* of the *Roman* church, but the *head* of all the churches in the world.

St. Hilary, Bishop of Arles,

A man of remarkable eloquence, and of great zeal.—He did much good in his visitations to the *Gallican* churches. He often went to see *St. Germanus*, with whom he made an enquiry into the life and manners of the clergy. While he was with him, a certain *bishop*, named *Celidonius*, was accused before him, because he had *married* a *widow* before he was ordained, which is forbidden by the *canons*, and the *authority of the Holy See.* The case being discussed, with all fairness imaginable, and the witnesses heard, he pronounced, that he whom the *holy canons* deprived of his *priesthood*, ought to forsake it of himself: the poor bishop resolved with himself to go to *Rome*; he complains that he had been used with too much severity.

St. Hilary, understanding this, puts himself immediately upon his journey to go to *Rome*. The coldness of the season, the height

CENT. V.

height of the *Alps*, and other troubles in the journey, could not take off the edge of his zeal; he conquered them all, and went to *Rome* on foot: after having paid his *devotion* to the tombs of the *apostles* and *martyrs*, he went to *St. Leo*, gave him all due respect and veneration, and humbly besought him, that he would make *no alteration in the ordinary discipline of the church*.

HILARY, Bishop of ROME,

Was of opinion that *bishops* who had been *twice married*, or had married a *widow*, ought to be deprived.

GELASIUS I. Bishop of ROME,

Repeats the antient *canons* concerning the qualifications of such as they ought to ordain—that they ought to be but *once married*.

Council of CHALCEDON.

Can. 15. Forbids the ordination of a *deaconess* before ‡ forty years of age, and without strict examination; and declares, that if she shall *marry* after she has been some time in the service of the church, she shall be *excommunicated* with her *husband*.

Can. 16. It is not permitted to *virgins*, devoted to GOD, to *marry*. They who

‡ 1 Tim. v. 9.

have

have done so shall be excommunicated—yet the *bishop* of the place may treat them with such lenity and mildness as he thinks fit.

I. *Council* of ORANGE, *anno* 441.

Can. 22. For the future no married persons shall be ordained *deacons*, unless they make a profession of living in *chastity*.

Can. 23. If it be found out that one of those *deacons* do not abstain from his wife, he shall be *deprived*.

Can. 24. Excepts from this law, those who have been ordained heretofore. The only *penalty* it inflicts on them is, that they cannot obtain any higher orders.

Can. 25. Those who have been *twice married*, though *never so worthy*, shall be admitted to no other orders than that of *sub-deacon*.

Can. 27. Of *widows* professing *chastity*—orders, that it shall be done before the *bishop*, and that it be discovered by their widows garments, or by a kind of veil put upon them, as it is the *Roman* custom, and is decreed by the council of *Toledo*, can. 4. and of *Carthage*, can. 104.

Can. 28. Such as break their vow of *virginity*, whether *men* or *women*, shall be made to do *penance*.

CENT. V.

II. *Council* of ARLES, about *anno* 442.

Can. 2. No man may be made a *priest*, who is *married*, unless he will renounce the *use of marriage*—which they call by the name of *conversion*.

Can. 21. A *penitent* may not *marry*.

Can. 52. Is against those who marry after they have vowed *virginity*.

Council of ANJOU, *anno* 433.

Can. 4. The *clergy* shall not dwell with *women*.

Can. 5. They shall be treated very severely, who forsake their state of penance or *virginity*.

Can. 11. No person shall be ordained *deacon* or *priest*, who hath had more than one *wife*.

Letter of LUPUS Bishop of TROYES, and EUPHRONIUS Bishop of AUGUSTODUNUM, to THALASSIUS Bishop of ANJOU.

This letter contains, 1. Rules concerning the different ways of celebrating the *vigils* of the *festivals*.

2. About the *clergy* that had been *twice married*. They say that it may be *tolerated* in the lesser orders, as high as a *porter*: but *exorcists* and *sub-deacons* ought not to have been *twice married*. 3. They say, that

that it were better for the clergy to abstain from marriage, but in this they must follow the *custom of the churches*. As to the *exorcists* and *sub-deacons*, they must not be suffered to marry a *second* time; that, in the church of *Augustodunum*, none of the *clergy*, not the *porters* themselves, are allowed it.

Council of Tours, 461.

Can. 1. and 2. Recommend a single life to *bishops, priests,* and *deacons*.

Can. 3. Forbids them to dwell with *women*.

Can. 4. Prohibits the *clergy*, who might marry, to marry *widows*.

CENTURY VI.

Pope Symmachus.

He condemns those who marry *widows*, or *virgins* consecrated to God, although they who are married mean well. He ordains that such shall be cast out of the communion of the church: and he forbids *widows* who have lived a long while unmarried, and *virgins* who have been a considerable time in monasteries, to *marry*.

Ennodius, Bishop of Pavia,

Took *orders* by consent of his wife, who, for her part, embraced a chaste and religious

religious life. He wrote a *poem* in praise of *virginity*.

St. Fulgentius.

His letter concerning the *conjugal duty* and the *vow*, is upon a particular case. Some had asked *Fulgentius*—" Whether a " married person was obliged to keep a vow " of continence?" St. *Fulgentius* makes many observations concerning the use of marriage, and the obligation of vows. He remarks upon the first head, " that the " use of marriage is *allowed*, when it is " intended for the procreation of chil- " dren; but when it has no end but plea- " sure, although it is not a crime like " *adultery*, yet it is always a *small sin*, " which is *blotted out by prayer and good* " *works*."

As to the vow, he says, that, " there is " no doubt, but, by it, an obligation is " contracted to do the thing which was " vowed." But he maintains, that " the " vow of *continence* made by one of the " married persons, cannot oblige the other, " nor dispense with that person who made " the vow from paying the conjugal duty " to the other, at least unless both parties " had concurred in making the vow." Having laid down these principles, he concludes—" that if the persons who wrote " to him, had *both* made a vow of *conti-* " *nence*, then they were obliged to keep " it;

"it; and that if they found themselves
"tempted by carnal desires, they should
"humbly pray to GOD to give them grace
"† to resist them; but if only *one* of the
"*two* had made a vow of continence, that
"party was obliged to pay the conjugal
"duty to the other who had not made it."

The EMPEROR JUSTINIAN,

Began his reign in 527, and died in 565.

He added many laws to those made by the princes his predecessors; *viz.*

If a *monk* enter into orders, he is forbidden to *marry.*

He who would be made a *bishop,* must be one who was never *married* but *once,* and also one who was not espoused to a *widow.*

The same precautions shall be observed in the ordination of inferior *clergymen.*

The *deaconesses* shall be ordained only of *virgins,* or of *widows* who were never *married* but *once,* and who have passed the *fiftieth* year of their age. If any younger are ordained, they shall enter into a *monastery.*

In treating of *marriages,* he first men-

---

† Here is a fair *preceptive* precedent, as before, p. 6. for praying to GOD, to invert the *order* of *nature*—to annihilate his own *command*—and to *defeat* his own *purpose* in the creation of the *male* and *female,* and in ordaining *marriage!* See 1 Cor. vii. 5, 9.

tions the causes of the dissolution of marriage. He distinguishes them into two sorts: the *first*, are those, which he calls *ex bona gratia*, because it is to be presumed that both parties are willing. 1. When one of the two who are joined together makes a *vow* of *chastity*. 2. When the husband is impotent for the space of *three* years. 3. When he is a captive, or absent for the space of *five* years, without hearing of him: but not when he is a slave, or condemned to the mines, or exiled and banished for ever. 4. That if a woman be espoused who is found to be a slave, the marriage shall be *null* for the future, unless he was her master, who married her as a free woman, in which case she shall continue free. 5. *Constantine* had permitted a woman, whose husband had been *four* years in the wars, without writing to her, or giving her any marks of his affection, to marry another.

Justinian repeals this law, and ordains that a woman cannot marry again until the end of *ten* years; and also till she has solicited her husband to return, and presented her petition to his captain or his colonel, whereby it may be evident that he has no mind to return to his wife.

These are the causes of dissolution of marriages which *Justinian* calls *ex bona gratia*.

The other causes are those which are *rigorous:*

rigorous: as, if a *man* or a *woman* be convicted of *adultery, murder, poisoning, theft, treason, robbery*, or any other crime: and if it happen that the *woman* be guilty of these crimes, she shall continue *five* years without being capable of marrying again; and also if it be she who convicts her husband of them, she shall at least continue *one* year before her *second* marriage.

Justinian adds also three causes for which women may be divorced. If they make themselves *miscarry*. If they *bathe* with other men. If they speak of *marriage* to *others* while their husband liveth.

Justinian repealed what he had before ordained concerning persons who were in the army, and ordains, that it shall never be lawful for a woman to marry again, unless she has sufficient proof or witnesses that her husband is dead.

Another law contains reasons for which a *divorce* may be granted. A man may *divorce* his wife—if she has conspired against the state—if she be convicted of *adultery*—if she has attempted her husband's life—if she has dwelt or washed with strangers against her husband's will—if she be present at public sports in spite of him. The woman may also be parted from her husband—if he be a criminal to the state—if he has attempted her life—if he would have prostituted her—if he cohabits with other women, after his wife

has

Cent. VI.

has admonished him to forsake their company.

As to what concerns the clergy—they must have no *concubine,* nor natural children; but they must be *virgins,* or such as are married only *once* to one woman.

If he who is to be ordained, has not a wife, then, before he is ordained, he must engage to live in *celibacy*; but he who ordains a *deacon,* or *sub-deacon,* may permit him to marry after his ordination.

That if a *priest,* or *deacon,* or *sub-deacon,* espouse a woman after his ordination, he is to be turned out from the *clergy.*

That a *reader* may marry—but if he contract a *second* marriage, or espouse a *widow,* he cannot ascend to higher dignity among the clergy.

That if any marry after they have been among the *clergy,* they shall return to their first condition.

He restores the *antient custom,* whereby married persons were allowed to separate, with the consent of one another, without any other formality.

St. Benedict.

This gloomy mortal, famous among the monks, shut himself up in a frightful cave.—He declares that his *rule* contains only the *first elements* of a religious and spiritual life, and that the *books of the fathers* contain it in *perfection.*

N. B. One

N. B. One should think that the scriptures bore a *price* something under *par*, in the eyes of these *enthusiasts*.

Pope PELAGIUS II.

In one of his decrees, he allows that a man may be ordained *deacon*, who, having left his wife, had children by a *maid-servant* without espousing her, although it be against the *laws* and the *canons*, merely on account of the want of those who are disposed to be *clergymen*.

He ordains also, that this *maid-servant* shall be put into a monastery, to make there profession of *continence*.

St. JOHN, surnamed CLIMACUS.

This *saint* was called *Climacus*, from his work intitled Κλιμαξ, *i. e.* a *scale* or ladder.

This *scale* contains thirty *degrees*, which are so many *Christian* and *religious* virtues. The 15th contains the praises of *chastity*. There he shews the consequences of this virtue, and the enormity of the crime which is opposite to it; he condemns it, even to the motions of *lust*, which happen in the time of *sleep*. He prescribes for a remedy, that they should clothe themselves with sackcloth, and cover themselves with *ashes*; that they should pass the night standing; that they should suffer hunger and thirst; and that they should lodge in the

the tombs, and be humble and charitable.
—See 1 Cor. vii. 9.

St. Gregory, Pope 590,
Surnamed THE GREAT.

St. Gregory *proves (epist.* 39. lib. ix.) that *marriages* are not *dissolved* by the entrance of one of the married persons into a religious house, although human laws permit the man to part from his wife, or the woman from her husband, that they may go into a monastery.

He adds, in *epist.* 44. of the *same* book, where he handles the *same* question, that the law of God does not allow a man to forsake his wife for any cause but *adultery*; nevertheless, he permits *married* persons to part from one another, that they may enter into a religious house, when this is done with the consent of both parties.

St. Gregory took it ill, that the *subdeacons* of *Sicily* were obliged to *abstain* from their *wives*, according to the custom of the church of *Rome*. This law appeared to him harsh and unreasonable, because they found not *continence* established by any law for them, and they were not obliged to keep it before they were ordained. He feared lest *something worse* should happen if this *yoke* were imposed upon them.

He orders, that none shall be *ordained* for the

the future, who do not promise to live in *continence*.

He declares, that he will put in execution the order of the *Pope*, his predecessor, about the *continence* of *sub-deacons*, and that those who are married shall be obliged to abstain from the *use* of *marriage*, or else to forsake the service of the altar.

He would not have the *wives* punished, of those who desired rather to quit the service than renounce them, nor the women hindered from marrying again after their death. He orders, that, for the future, no *sub-deacon* shall be made, who is not obliged beforehand to observe *celibacy*.

He forbids to ordain a *deacon bishop*, who had a very young *daughter*, by whose age it manifestly appeared that he had not long observed *continence*.

He promised the Empress *Constantina*, some of the *filings* of St. *Peter*'s chain, if the *priest* who was appointed for filing them could have any; for the *file* would not take hold, when those who desired to receive them do not deserve to receive them.

He sent every where some of these *filings*, enchased in *keys*.

This *St. Gregory* sent *Austin* a *monk*, of the order of *St. Benedict*, with forty *missionaries, French priests* and *Italian* monks, to establish *Popery* in *England*, under the notion of preaching the *Christian religion*. *Austin* was the first *archbishop* of *Canterbury*;

CENT. VI.

bury; he was nominated to that high office anno 597, by *Pope Gregory*, with the confent of *Ethelbert*, King of *Kent*. "The *Chriftianity* which this pretended *apoftle* and fanctified *ruffian* taught us, feemed to confift principally in two things; in keeping *Eafter* upon a proper day, and in being *flaves* to our fovereign Lord God the *Pope*, and to *Auftin* his deputy and vicegerent. Such were the boafted bleffings and benefits which we received from the miffion and miniftry of this moft audacious and infolent *monk*. He is ftrongly fufpected, as *Du Pin* acknowledges, of having excited the *Saxons* to fall upon the *Britons*, and to cut the throats of twelve hundred *monks* of *Bangor*." See *Jortin*, Rem. vol. iv. p. 417. Alfo *Fox*, vol. i. p. 132.

The faid *St. Auftin* fent to *St. Gregory*, for a refolution of fundry queftions. Among others—

Q. Whether *ecclefiaftics*, who have not the gift of *continence*, may *marry*; and if they do, whether they may return to fecular affairs?

A. They may *marry*, if they be not engaged in *holy orders*, and fuch ought not to want fubfiftence; but they fhall be obliged to lead a life agreeable to the ecclefiaftical ftate, and to fing the *pfalms*.

Q. To what *degree* may the *faithful* marry together?

A. A Roman

A. A *Roman* law, of *Arcadius* and *Honorius*, permitted marriages between *cousin-germans:* But *St. Gregory* did not think these marriages lawful, for *two* reasons.

1. Because *experience shews that no children are born of them.*
2. Because the *divine law* forbids them.

Q. Where?

This St. *Austin* sent also to *St. Gregory* for a resolution of sundry very *filthy* questions; which, with the answers to them, may be found in *Du Pin*, vol. v. p. 93. *Eng. Transf.* Likewise an account of the monstrous *lyes* which *St. Gregory* published in *four books*, p. 98, 99. See also p. 92.

Lucius Charinus

Says, that the God of the *Jews* was a God of *wickedness*—that, on the contrary, Christ is a God of *goodness*—He condemns marriage, and looks upon *generation* as the work of the *devil.*

N. B. Let those think on this, who talk of a *new law* of Christ, more *pure* and *holy* than the *law* of the Old Testament, and who represent the God of the *Jews* as allowing *polygamy*, and Christ as calling it *adultery.*— Let them consider, that, frequently, there may be a *verbal*, where there is little *real*, difference.

CENT. VI.

Council of AGATHA, *anno* 506.

Can. 1. Renews the prohibitions of the *antient canons* about the ordinations of *bigamists*, and of those who had married *widows*. It permits those who are already ordained *priests* and *deacons*, though they be *bigamists*, or married to *widows*, to retain the *name* of their order, but deprives them of the exercise of their *function*.

Can. 9. The laws of the Popes *Innocentius* and *Siricius*, about the *celibacy* of *priests* and *deacons*, shall be observed.

Council of ORLEANS, *anno* 511.

Can. 21. A *monk* who quits the monastery and *marries*, can never enter into holy orders.

Council of GERUNDA, *anno* 517.

Can. 6. All the orders of clergymen, from *bishops* down to *sub-deacons*, are forbidden to *cohabit* with their *wives*, or if they will dwell with them, they are commanded to have with them one of their *brethren*, who can give testimony of their *continence*.

Can. 8. None shall be admitted into the *clergy*, who have had carnal dealings with a woman, after the *death* of their *wife*.

Council of EPAONE, *anno* 517.

Can. 2 and 3. Renew the *canons* against the ordination of *bigamists*, and those who have done *penance*.

Can. 21. Forbids to consecrate ‡ *widows* for *deaconesses*; insomuch that if widows are willing to be converted, i. e. to lead a religious life, the benediction of *penance* shall only be given to them.

Can. 25. Forbids to place the *reliques* of saints in country chapels, unless there be clergy in the neighbouring parish, who can *honour* them, by singing in these chapels from time to time.

Can. 30. None shall marry a *cousin-german* or the *issue* of a *cousin-german*.

Can. 32. Separates from the church the wife of a *priest* or *deacon* who marries, and him that espouses her, until they be parted.

Can. 34. Imposes *two* years penance on him who puts his *slave* to *death* by his own authority.

Can. 40. The *bishops* who will not observe these canons, shall be guilty both before GOD and their brethren.

‡ *St. Paul* and this *council* are at irreconcileable variance. See 1 Tim. v. 9.

Cent. VI. Council of LERIDA or ILERDA, *anno* 524.

Can. 1. Forbids *clergymen* to shed *human blood*, under penalty of being deprived of the communion for *two* years.

Can. 2. Imposes *seven* years penance upon those men or women that *murder* infants conceived and born in *adultery*. If they be *clergymen*, they also shall be put under penance, and not be restored again to their order: they shall only be permitted, after *seven* years, to sing in the quire. But as to those who give *drugs* for committing these * detestable *crimes*, 'tis said they shall not receive the *communion* till *death*.

Can.

---

* The *system* which the *church* was erecting on the demolition of the *divine law*, was attended with the most fatal and dreadful consequences, such as will never be got rid of, 'till the *laws of the Creator* shall be once more fully restored among us.

Horace's fable of *Prometheus*, bears no little resemblance to the case before us, and may easily be paraphrased to our purpose.

> *Audax* JAPETI *genus*
> *Ignem fraude mala gentibus intulit.*
> *Post ignem ætheriâ domo*
> *Subductum, macies, & nova febrium*
>   *Terris incubuit cohors:*
> *Semotique prius tarda necessitas*
>   *Lethi corripuit gradum.*

When men of *Japhet*'s daring race
The laws of Heaven could efface,
  And substitute their *own*;
Of murders dire a ghastly brood,
And crimes, the impious fraud pursu'd,
  'Till then almost unknown.

Oppress'd

Can. 6. He who has defiled a *widow*, or a *nun*, shall be *excommunicated*, the *nun* shall also be *excommunicated*, unless she part from him, in which case she shall be put under public penance.

Fourth Council of ARLES, *anno* 524.

Can. 3. Renews again the prohibition so often repeated, not to ordain a *penitent* or a *bigamist*.

Second Council of TOLEDO, *anno* 531.

Can. 1. Concerns *infants* which the parents offer to be *clergymen*. It ordains, that, at the age of *eighteen*, they shall be asked, in the presence of the clergy and people, what is their design; and if they promise to observe *chastity*, they shall be made *sub-deacons* at the age of twenty. If they discharge this ministry well, they shall be *deacons* at twenty-five; but good heed shall be taken that they do not MARRY, or that they keep not company with *women*, and if they be convicted of doing it, they shall be looked upon as *sacrilegious* persons, and turned out of the *church*.

> Oppress'd with shame, o'erwhelm'd with fear,
> The teeming *mother* will not dare
> Her *infant*'s life to save;
> The dagger's point its blood shall stain,
> Or the slow poison's deadly bane
> Shall make her womb its grave.

CENT. VI.

As to those who will not oblige themselves to observe *celibacy*, they shall be left to their liberty; but they shall not be promoted to holy orders, until such time as they shall *renounce* the *use of marriage*, after they are arrived to the age of maturity.

Second Council of ORLEANS, *anno* 533.

Can. 8. A *deacon* who is *married*, being in captivity, cannot be restored to his ministry.

Can. 17. Women who have received the *benediction* given to *deacons*, *contrary* to the *canons*, shall be turned out of *communion*, if it be proved that they *marry:* yet if, upon admonition of the *bishop*, they cease to *cohabit* with their husbands, they shall be received into communion, after they have done *penance*.

Can. 18. The *deacon*'s blessing shall no more be given to women.

Council of CLERMONT in ARVERNIA, *anno* 535.

Can. 13. *Priests* and *deacons* shall live in *celibacy*, and if they be found to keep company with their wives, after they are promoted to these dignities, they shall be deprived of them.

A man must not marry his *wife's sister's cousin-german*, or the *issue* of her *cousin-german*.

Third Council of ORLEANS, *anno* 538.

Can. 6. Forbids ordaining those who have *twice married*.

Can. 7. If *clergymen* who have been ordained with their own consent, being *unmarried*, do afterwards *marry*, they shall be excommunicated. If they were ordained against their will, they shall only be *deposed*, and the *bishop* who ordained them be suspended for one year.

Clergymen who commit *adultery*, shall be shut up in a monastery all their life-time, yet without being deprived of *communion*.

Can. 10. A man must not marry his *cousin-german* or *her issue*.

Can. 33. An *imprecation* against those who observe not *these canons*.

Fourth D°, *anno* 541.

Can. 10. Suspends a *bishop* from the sacerdotal function, who had ordained a *bigamist*, or him that married a *widow*.

Can. 17. Priests and deacons shall not have a *bed* and *chamber* common with their *wives*.

Fifth D°, *anno* 549.

Can. 4. *Clergymen* who are obliged to *celibacy*, and do not observe it, shall be *deposed*.

Can. 19. If women who come to a monastery and take the habit, do afterwards marry,

marry, they shall be *excommunicated*, together with those that marry them: but if they *part*, and do penance, they shall be restored to communion.

Second Council of Tours, *anno 567*.

Can. 12. The *bishop* shall live with his *wife* as with his *sister*, without giving any cause of *suspicion*.

Can. 14. Forbids *priests* and *monks* to take any person to *bed* with them. It orders that monks should not lie, *two* or *three* in several cells, but in one *common hall*, where some shall watch while others *take their rest*.

N. B. This *canon* was, for *certain reasons*, a very necessary one.

Can. 15. Monks who go out of their monastery to marry, shall be parted and put under penance.

Can. 19. Hinders the *clergy* who are obliged to *celibacy*, from lying with their *wives*.

Can. 20. Renews the penalties on those who marry *virgins consecrated* to God, or who *consent* to these *marriages*.

Synod of Antisiodorum.

Can. 12. The *eucharist* shall not be given to the *dead*, nor the *kiss of peace*.

Can. 20. *Priests, deacons*, and *sub-deacons*, who shall have *children*, shall be deposed.

Can.

Can. 24. It is not lawful for an *abbot* or *monk* to *marry*.

Can. 36, 37. Women not to receive the *eucharist* with the naked hand, or to touch the linen cloth which covers the body of *our Lord*.

Can 42. Women to have the *dominical* for receiving the communion. Some think this is the linen upon which they receive the *body* of JESUS CHRIST, being forbidden to receive it with their naked hand. Others think it a kind of veil which covers the head. Whatever it be, this *synod* declares, that, if they have it not, they shall wait 'till another *Sunday* to receive the *communion*.

Council of MASCON, *anno* 581.

Can. 3. No women shall enter the chamber of a *bishop*, but in the presence of two *priests* or two *deacons*.

Can. 11. *Clergymen*, obliged to *celibacy*, shall be deposed if they violate the obligation.

Can. 12. *Virgins* consecrated to GOD, who *marry*, shall be *excommunicated*, both they and their husbands, till *death*. If they *part*, they shall continue under *penance*, during the pleasure of the *bishop*.

Council of LYONS, *anno* 583.

Can. 1. *Clergymen* forbidden to have *any familiarity* with their *wives*.

Second

CENT. VI.

Second Council of Mascon, *anno* 585.

Can. 16. Forbids the *widows* of *subdeacons, exorcists,* and *acolythists,* to marry again.

This council, which was very numerous, consisting of 6 archbishops, 37 bishops, 20 deputies from other bishops, and 3 bishops who had no see, ordained—in

Can. 15. That *laymen* should shew *respect* to *clergymen,* and to salute them if they meet them on horseback in the way; to *light off* their horse and salute them, if they meet them on foot.

Third Council of Toledo, *anno* 589.

Can. 5. Renews the laws of *celibacy* for *priests* and *deacons.*

Can. 9. Leaves *widows* and *maids* at liberty to *marry* or keep *celibacy,* and *excommunicates* those who hinder them from observing their vow of *chastity.*

Can. 17. Against those *fathers* and *mothers* who put their children to death.

Council of Barcelona, *anno* 599.

Can. 4. If a virgin who has renounced the customs of the world, and promised to observe *continence,* or any other person who has desired of the *priest benedictionem pœnitentiæ*—i. e. the blessing for leading a religious life, for this is often called *pœnitentia*

tentia and *conversio*—do *marry*, or, being taken away by force, will not part from their ravishers, they shall continue excluded from the communion of the *faithful*, and shall not have so much as the comfort of *conversation*.—This canon may also be understood literally of penance, because it was not lawful for *penitents* to *make use* of marriage (if married) or to marry (if single).

CENTURY VII.

St. Isidore

Succeeded to the bishopric of *Sevil* about the year 595. He is likewise for the *celibacy* of the *clergy*. He says, that a *bishop* ought always to have lived single, or to have had but *one* wife — that *priests, deacons,* and *sub-deacons* should be bound to *continency*. Among other works of discipline, he wrote *the rules of the monks,* accommodated to the use of his country.

St. Columbanus,

An Irish *monk*. He contended, that the *celibacy* of superior clerks was commanded —that married persons should abstain from the *use of marriage* for *three* days before the *communion*—that men were to be put to penance for *bigamy* and *usury*—that *women*

men might receive the sacrament with a black veil on — that, in case of *necessity, confession might be made to* God.

St. Eligius,

A great lover of ecclesiastical discipline, and follower of the traditions of the fathers, *Cyprian, Austin, Gregory,* &c.—however, he exceeded them all; for, in one of his homilies, he lays it down, that "it is as great a crime for a man to lie with his wife, as to eat flesh in *Lent.*" This may easily be believed to be very true; but, as *St. Eligius* meant it, who believed that eating flesh in *Lent* was a very horrible sin, it certainly exceeds, if possible, the *folly* of all the preceding *saints* and *fathers* put together.

Theodorus of Canterbury,

Ordained bishop by Pope *Vitalian,* and sent into *England* in 668, to govern the church of *Canterbury.* He laboured much in the establishing of the *faith* and church-discipline in *England.*

In the *eleventh* chapter of the *ritual* attributed to him, there are many questions about *married* persons. It is said there, they ought to abstain from the *use* of matrimony *three* days before the communion—*forty* days before *Easter*—*forty* days *before* and *after* childbearing. That a lawful marriage cannot be dissolved, but with the consent

consent of both parties; but either of them may give his consent, that the other may withdraw into a monastery, and then, that the other may marry again, as if he had not been married before. If the husband be made a slave, the wife may marry at the year's end. That a man may marry again within *one month* after his wife's death, and a woman within *one year* after her husband's decease. That a woman, who hath vowed widowhood, cannot marry again; if she should, it shall be free for the husband to let her fulfil her vow or not. That the *bishop* may dispense with *vows*. It is free for one baptized to *keep* or *put away* his wife being a *Pagan*. If a woman forsake her husband, within *five* years after he may take another wife. If she be carried away captive, he may marry another *one* year after—but if she cometh again, he shall leave this *last*. It is lawful, among the *Greeks*, to marry in the *third* degree, and among the *Romans* in the *fifth* only.

Children are in the power of their father 'till sixteen years old, but, that time being past, they may enter into a *religious order*.

Council of EGARA, *anno* 614.

Confirmed the decree made in that of HUESCA, concerning the *celibacy* of the *clergy*.

Fifth

Fifth Council of PARIS.

Can. 1. The antient *canons* shall be kept.

Can. 14. Prohibits marriage with a maiden that has taken a religious habit. It excommunicates those that contract such marriages, 'till they separate themselves.

Council held in FRANCE, about *anno* 614, the *place* uncertain.

Can. 12. Forbids *presbyters* and *deacons* to *marry*, upon pain of being turned out of the *church*.

Second Council of SEVIL, *anno* 619.

Can. 4. Is against the unlawful ordinations made at *Astigi*, where persons that had married *widows* had been ordained *clerks*. The *ordinations* are declared *null*, and they are forbidden to be raised to the order of *deacons*.

Council of RHEIMS under SONNATIUS.

Can. 7. Threatens to excommunicate those who shall violently take away from the *church* the *criminals* fled into it.

The original of this privilege, allowed by the *Heathens*, and afterward by the *Christians*, to their *temples* or *churches*, was certainly taken from the divine constitution given to *Moses*, respecting the *six cities of refuge* in the *Jewish* nation (Numb. xxxv. 6.)

though

though not altogether conformable to it: for *Moses* made the cities only a *refuge*, and that only for such manslayers as had *killed their neighbours unawares*; but the *Heathens* made their temples an *asylum* for all manner of wickednesses. So *Livy* says of the *asylum* erected by *Romulus* at *Rome*: *Asylum aperuit, quo quisquis perfugerit,* ab omni noxa *liberatus esset.* " He opened an *asy-*
" *lum,* where, whosoever fled to it, should
" be freed from every crime." So *Herodotus* speaks of *Hercules*'s *asylum* at *Athens*. These *refuge-temples* were afterwards much increased among the *Heathen,* and at length, about the year 300, came to be in use among the *Christians;* for they thought it a shame, that the temples of the *Heathen* gods should enjoy so great a privilege, as to be refuges for the oppressed, and the *Christian* temples should be destitute of it: whereupon they were made such by the edict of *Theodosius* and *Valentinian,* and also by the *canons* of the *councils.* But although such grants might be of very good advantage among *Christians,* being kept within due bounds of the first institution, to be a protection for the *innocent* and *oppressed;* yet, as they have been, and still are, abused in the *Roman* and other *churches,* being made a refuge for *murderers (assassins) rebels,* and other *enormous criminals,* they are grievous both to the church and all civil societies. See Editor's

CENT. VII. Editor's note on *Du Pin*, Eng. edit. vol. vi. p. 57.

Can. 23. Forbids ravishing *widows* or *virgins* consecrated to GOD.

N. B. The word *ravishing* means *taking them away*.

Fourth Council of TOLEDO.

Can. 19. Forbids advancing those to the *priesthood* who have made themselves *eunuchs*—those that have had *many wives*, or have married *widows*—as also those that have had *concubines*.

Can. 44. Clerks marrying *widows*, shall be separated from them by the *bishop*.

Can. 56. Distinguisheth two sorts of *widows*—some *secular*, who do not leave the *secular* habit, and other *religious*, which take a religious habit—and declares, it is not *lawful* for these to *marry*.

Sixth Council of TOLEDO, *anno* 638.

Can. 8. Explains a constitution of *St. Gregory*'s, whereby they suppose he gave leave to a young man, who underwent penance under fear of death, to *cohabit* with his *wife*, till he was come to an age in which it were *easier* to live *chastly*. They say, that if he, or she, that was not put to penance, survive, he may marry again.

Ninth Council of TOLEDO, 655.

Can. 10. They declare the sons of clergymen, who were obliged to *celibacy*, incapable of inheriting.

Tenth Council of TOLEDO, 656.

Can. 5. Decrees that those who leave the habit of *widowhood*, after they have worn it, shall be *excommunicated*, and shut up in monasteries.

Fourth Council of BRAGA, 675.

Can. 4. Ecclesiastical persons are forbidden to dwell with a *woman*, excepting their *mother only*, but not their *very sisters*, or any other *near relations*.

Council held at CONSTANTINOPLE, anno 692.

Can. 3. Those of the *clergy*, *presbyters*, or *deacons*, that had married *two wives*, if they will not leave that custom, shall be deposed. As to those whose *second* wives are dead, or who have left them, they shall keep the honour and place of their dignity, being forbidden only to perform the functions of it, it being not fitting, that he, who ought to heal his own wounds, should *bless* others. As for them who had married *widows*, or had married, being *priests*, *deacons*,

CENT. VII.

deacons, or *sub-deacons*, they shall for a time be suspended from their function, but they grant them the power of being *restored* when they *leave* their *wives*, on condition, that they shall not be raised to a superior order. Lastly—they ordain, that all those who have been married *twice* after baptism, or have had *concubines*, shall not be made *clergymen*.

Can. 4. Such *ecclesiastical* persons as shall company with a *virgin* consecrated to GOD, shall be *deposed*. Laymen *excommunicated*.

Can. 5. Forbids *clerks* to have with them *women*, not related to them, except those which the *canons* allow them to dwell withal. It extends this prohibition to *eunuchs*.

Can. 6. Forbids those that are in orders, including the *sub-deacons*, to marry after their ordination.

Can. 12. Ties the bishops of *Afric* and *Lybia* to the law of the *celibacy*.

Can. 44. Against *monks* guilty of *fornication* or *married*.

Can. 48. The wife of him who is to be made a *bishop*, shall be put away from him, and shall withdraw into a *monastery*, at a distance from the *bishop*'s residence.

Can. 83. Forbids giving the *eucharist* to the *dead*.

Can. 93. Condemns the marriages of those

those *men* and *women*, who are not sure of the death of their *wives* or *husbands*. But after those marriages have been contracted, and when the first husband comes again, he is *ordered* to *take his wife again*.

CENTURY VIII.

St. Boniface, Archbishop of Mentz, about *anno* 719.

In letter 11, he consults the bishop *Pethelmus* about the customs of *France* and *Italy*, by which it was forbidden to marry her to whose child he had been * *godfather*. Whereupon he says, that, till then, he thought there was no *harm* in it, having never found that it was forbidden by the *canons* or *decrees of the holy bishops*. He desires him to inform him, whether he has

---

* When it is considered, that *godfathers* and *godmothers* are to be reckoned among *animalia non descripta*—there being no trace of them in the ordinance of *baptism* as revealed in the *Bible*—the *impediment* of *marriage*, which arose from a supposed *spiritual cognation* between each other and the *baptized*, &c. must appear the more unwarrantable and absurd—But when men once depart from the scriptures, where will they stop?

CENT. VIII. met with any thing about it in the *ecclesiastical* writings.

Near the end of a letter to *St. Cuthbert*, he tells him—" that it were convenient to
" restrain the women and virgins of *Eng-*
" *land*, from going in such numbers to
" *Rome*, because the greatest part of them
" were *debauched*, and caused great scandal
" in the whole church; for there is scarce
" a city, saith he, in *Lombardy* or *France*,
" where there are not some *English* women
" of a wicked life."

Pope GREGORY II, *anno* 714.

He prohibits marriages between persons related in the *fourth* degree. He enjoins the *bishops* not to ordain such as have been *twice married*—not to suffer any man to have *more wives* than *one*—to esteem *virginity* more highly than marriage.

Pope GREGORY III, *anno* 731,

Forbids marriage to the *seventh* generation.

Prohibits a *widower* to marry above twice.

Pope ZACHARY, *anno* 741.

Boniface, a *German* bishop, writes to *Zachary* on many subjects: among the rest, he he desires to know what he should do with those *bishops, priests,* and *deacons,* who lived in many *disorders* and *debaucheries?* *Zachary* answers him, that he ought not to suffer them to perform the functions and offices that belong to their orders and degrees.

N. B. St. Paul would have answered— *If they cannot contain, let them marry.*

Boniface also enquires, whether it be true, that one of his country had obtained a *dispensation* from *Gregory* III. *(Zachary's predecessor)* to marry his *uncle's widow,* which had been his *cousin-german's* wife, and had received the *veil?* The *Pope* answers—That his *predecessor* did not grant such a licence, because the *holy see* allows nothing contrary to the constitutions of the *councils,* and the *holy fathers.*

He prohibited a man from marrying his *father's god-daughter,* because of the *spiritual consanguinity.*

St. John Damascene

Highly extols the state of *virginity*.

St. Chrodegand, Bishop of Mentz.

Can. 15. *Clerks* guilty of *heinous crimes,* such as *murders, adultery, robbery,* or the like, shall be chastised on their body; shall be exiled, or cast into prison, as *long as the bishop pleases*; and shall moreover do *public penance.*

Pope STEPHEN II. *anno* 752.

Can. 2. Excuses a priest who had baptised with wine instead of water; and he intimates *that baptism* to be valid, in these words: *Infantes sic permaneant in ipso baptismo*—" The infants shall so abide in that baptism."

CHARLEMAGNE.

This *Emperor* may be reckoned among the Latin ecclesiastical authors, as well as *Constantine* among the *Greeks*, for he not only laboured in the establishment of church discipline, but moreover he made several laws, wrote letters, and caused some treatises of ecclesiastical matters to be composed: these are called *Capitularies*.

He empowers *bishops* to order the life of *widows*.

That they shall observe the *canons* concerning the *manner* of veiling *virgins*. The prohibition of contracting marriages, was extended to the fourth degree of consanguinity.

Women were forbidden to come near the *altars*.

They forbad to receive children into monasteries without the parents consent, and to veil *virgins* before *thirty* years of age, and *widows* before the *thirtieth* day after their husband's decease.

Prayers for the dead much practised.

Council

Council of BARKHAMSTEAD, *anno* 697.

Can 3. *Adulterers*, if *laymen*, put to *penance*—if *clergymen*, to be *depofed*.

Can. 4. *Foreigners*, guilty of that *crime*, fhall be expelled the realm.

Can. 5. and 6. Thofe of the nobility, overtaken in that *fin*, fhall be fined in an *hundred pence*, and the peafant in *fifty*.

Can. 7. An ecclefiaftical perfon guilty of *adultery*, if he break off that habit, fhall continue in the *priefthood*, provided that he hath not malicioufly refufed to adminifter *baptifm*, or that he be not a *drunkard*.

Council of ROME, under GREGORY II. *anno* 721.

Can. 1—11. Againft them that marry their *kindred*, perfons *confecrated* to GOD, or the *wives* of *priefts* and *deacons*, or who fteal away *widows* or *maidens*.

Can. 14—16. Againft a private man who had *married* a *deaconefs*.

Council of GERMANY under CARLOMAN.

Can. 6. He or fhe, that hath committed *fornication*, fhall be imprifoned, and fhall do *penance* there with *bread* and *water*; and if he be a *prieft*, he fhall be *fhut up* for *two years*, having been *whipt* till the blood comes; and then the *bifhop* fhall lay on him what *penance* he *pleafes*.

CENT. VIII.

If it be a simple *clerk* or *monk*, he shall be whipt *three times*, and then shut up for *one year*. The *nuns*, which have received the veil, shall be used after the same manner, and shaved.

N. B. What an instance of tyranny over their fellow-creatures, were these people to exhibit! they prevent them from using the means, and remedy, which GOD hath commanded *in his word*, and then punish them most severely, for the natural consequences of their own prohibition! This observation will still hold good to this hour, as will be observed in its proper place.

Can. 7. Enjoins *monks* and *nuns* exactly to follow *St. Benedict*'s rule.

Council of ROME under Pope ZACHARY, *anno* 743.

Can. 1. *Bishops* shall not dwell with *women*.

Can. 5. Anathematizeth those who marry a *priest*'s or a *deacon's wife*, a *nun*, or a *religious woman*, or their *godmother*.

Can. 6. Forbids marriage with a *cousin-german*.

Can. 7. Anathematizeth those who steal *maidens* and *widows*, to marry them.

Can. 8. Against those *clerks* or *monks* that let their hair grow.

Council of SOISSONS, *anno* 744.

Can. 8. *Clerks* shall have no women in their houses, except their *mother*, *sister*, or *niece*.

Council of VERBERIE, *anno* 752.

Can. 1. Those that marry in the *third* degree of consanguinity, shall be *put asunder*, and, after having done penance, they may *marry others*. Those in the *fourth degree* only shall not be separated, but only be put to penance if they be married; or otherwise not suffered to marry.

Can. 2. If any man hath had commerce with his *daughter-in-law*, he shall dwell no longer, neither with the mother nor with the daughter; and neither the *daughter*, nor he, shall *marry others*, but the mother may marry another.

Can. 3. If a *presbyter* marry his *niece*, he shall be obliged to leave her, and lose his degree. If any body else marry her, he shall be obliged to leave her, but shall have liberty to marry another.

Can. 5. If a wife conspire the husband's death, he may leave her, and marry another.

Can. 7. Slaves, who have a *concubine*, may leave her to marry their master's maid-servant, though they *do better* if they keep the first.

Can. 8. Permits the *master* to oblige his

CENT. VIII. his *slave* to marry his *maid-servant*, if he hath had any carnal knowledge of her.

Can. 9. Imports, that, if men be forced to go away from the place of their habitation, and their *wives* refuse to follow them, without any other reason but their love to their own country, it shall be free for those men, whose *wives* have thus left them, to marry others; but not for the wives to *marry* again.

Can. 10. Forbids him to marry who hath lain with his *mother-in-law*, and the *mother-in-law* likewise, and permits the *father-in-law* to marry again.

Can. 11. Inflicts the same punishment on defilers of their *daughter-in-law*, or *sister-in-law*.

Can. 12. He that lies with *two sisters*, shall have neither, though one of them were his *wife*.

Can. 17. Permits a woman, who complains that her husband never did cohabit with her, to try the *proof of the cross*; and if it appears, by *this trial*, that the thing is so, then she may do *what she pleaseth*.

Can. 19. The slave who is set at liberty may *put away his wife*, being a bond-woman, and *marry another*.

Council of VERNEVILLE, *anno* 755.

Can. 15. Enjoins both *nobles* and the *common people* to be *married publicly*.

Council

Council of METZ, *anno* 756.

Can. 1. Againſt *inceſts* committed either with a *perſon conſecrated* to GOD, a *ſhe-goſſip*, a *god-mother*, whether at *baptiſm* or *confirmation*, or with a *couſin-german*.

Can. 2. Appoints the *depoſition* of the *ſuperior clergy*, convicted of theſe *crimes*, and the *inferior* are to be *whipped* or *impriſoned*.

Second Council of NICE, *anno* 754.

Can. 22. Forbids *monks* to eat with *women*, unleſs it be needful for their *ſpiritual* good, or upon a *journey*, yea though they be their *relations*.

Council of AQUILEIA, *anno* 791.

Can. 4. Againſt *women's* cohabiting with *clergymen*.

Can. 8. Prohibits unlawful marriages between *kindred*, and *clandeſtine* marriages. It ordains that no marriages ſhall be contracted, but between parties which ſhall be known not to be a-kin; that there ſhall be an *interval* between *betrothing* and *marriage*; that the preſence of the *prieſt* ſhall be requiſite; that kindred, which ſhall be found to have married within the degrees prohibited [by the *canons*] ſhall be ſeparated, and put to penance—that, if it be poſſible, they ſhall remain *unmarried*; but yet, if they will have children, or if they cannot

CENT. VIII.

cannot keep their virginity, they shall be permitted to marry others, and their *children* deemed *legitimate*.

N. B. In this *Popish* law we may trace one *source* of the delay of *marriage* by asking *banns*—the vacating *clandestine marriages*—the presence of a *priest* made necessary—all which, however improved in later times, owed their existence to *Popish* contrivance, and all for the advancement of *priestly* emolument and authority.

Can. 10. Forbids a man or woman, which have been divorced for *adultery*, to marry again. It affirms, that JESUS CHRIST in this case only permitted a man to *put away his wife*, but * *not* to *marry another*, and confirms this opinion by the *authority* of *St. Jerom!* The common practice was then contrary to this law.

Can. 11. *Virgins* or *widows*, which have promised to live *single*, and have taken the habit, though they have not received the *consecration* from the *bishop*, if they do secretly *marry*, or suffer themselves to be *defiled*, they shall be punished according to the rigour of the *civil laws:* and besides this, they shall be *put asunder*, and do penance all their life-time, unless the *bishop*, considering the greatness of their *repent-*

---

* Doubtless Matt. v. 32. and xix. 9. are alluded to.—Here is one proof, among many others, of the perversion and abuse of those texts.

ance, shew them some *favour*; but at the *point* of *death* they shall not be deprived of the *viaticum*.

CENTURY IX.

Council of METZ, anno 813.

Can. 55. Forbids *parents* presenting their *own children* at the *font*; or marrying one's *god-daughter*, or one's partner in the *suretyship* at a child's *baptism*, or even the person, whose *son* or *daughter* one has brought to be *confirmed*.

Council of MENTZ, anno 847.

Forbids all marriages, whether *incestuous*, or within the degrees of consanguinity *prohibited by the laws*.

Council of PAVIA, anno 850.

Can. 9. Forbids the benediction to be given to those *women*, who marry after they have been deflowered.

Marriage is forbidden to those who are under *penance*.

Can. 10. Declares that men cannot lawfully *marry* the persons they have *forced*; and allows such persons no *absolution*, but just at the point of *death*. See Deut. xxii. 28, 29.

CENT. IX.

Council of ROME under LEO IV. *anno* 853.

Can. 29. Commands, that *women*, who professed a *religious life*, should not *marry*.

Can. 36. Prohibits men's putting away their wives, and marrying others, unless in case of *adultery*, and *orders*. If a man and his wife are willing to part, to embrace a *religious life*, they must do it with consent of the *bishop*.

Can. 37. Forbids * *polygamy*.

Can. 38. Against *marriage* within the *degrees forbidden*.

Second Council of TULLIUM or TOUL, *anno* 860.

Can. 2. *Widows* or *virgins* devoted to the service of GOD, who *marry*, shall be *imprisoned*, and put to *penance* 'till their death.

Council of WORMS, *anno* 868.

Can. 9. Contains a law of *celibacy* for all in sacred orders.

Can. 21. *Widows* who have taken the *veil*, prayed in the church among the professed *nuns*, offered oblations with them, and promised to continue in that state, shall never leave it.

---

* The authority on which this *practice* is forbidden, being the same on which *marriage itself* is prohibited, in so many instances unknown to the *scriptures*, must, to be sure, be truly respectable!

Can. 34. Prohibits to marry a *god-mother* or *god-daughter*.

Can. 35. Condemns to the penance of *murderers*, those *women* who cause *abortions* in themselves.

Can. 36. Subjects to *penance*, and separates him from his *wife*, who hath lain with his *wife's daughter* by another husband.

Can. 44. Condemns *adulterers* to *seven* years penance.

Second Council of Douzy, *anno* 868.

Duda, a *nun*, being with child by *Huntburtus*, a *priest*, an assembly of *bishops* met, and ordered *Duda* that she should be put to *penance*, and scourged by the *abbess*, in the presence of her *sister nuns*, and not be received into communion 'till after *seven* years penance. They condemned *two nuns* who knew of it, but did not discover it, to *three* years penance, after being moderately chastised with the *rod*. It is not said what became of *Huntburtus*.

Qu? How many *child-murders* must such proceedings be the occasion of? The *canons* which we find against *these*, and causing *abortion*, are sad proofs of their frequency.

Council of Troyes, 878.

They made a *canon*, forbidding all *Christians* to marry a *second* wife while the *first* is living.

Cent. IX.

Council of COLOGNE, *anno* 877.
Revived the *canons* of *councils* againſt *unlawful* marriages.

Council of MENTZ.

Can. 10. Enjoins *clergymen* abſolutely to have *no woman* to cohabit with them.

Can. 26. Forbids that *widows* ſhall be eaſily admitted to the veil—if they embrace a ſingle life, it orders, that they be put into the monaſteries, where they ſhall live regularly with the nuns. If they violate their profeſſion, they ſhall be puniſhed *canonically*. They renew the canon of *Eleria*, made concerning *virgins* devoted to GOD, which violate their *virginity*.

Council of METZ, *anno* uncertain.

Can. 5. Prieſts ſhall have no women with them; no, not ſo much as their *mother* or *ſiſter*.

Can. 10. *Excommunicates* ſome perſons that had *gelt* a *prieſt*, who would oblige one of their kinſwomen to return to her huſband.

Council of VIENNA, *anno* 892.

Can. 5. *Prieſts* ſhall have *no women* with them.

Council of TRIBUR, *anno* 895.

Can. 5. He that kills a *prieſt*, ſhall do
five

five years *penance*. After this he may come into the *church*, but shall not communicate 'till *five* more years be expired.

Can. 12. *Baptism* shall not be administered but at *Easter* and *Whitsuntide*.

N. B. There are many canons to this purpose in the preceding centuries, but they always add—" *except in cases of necessity*."

Can. 23. Revives the laws against those who marry *virgins* consecrated to GOD.

Can. 33. Revives those *canons*, which exclude such persons from holy orders as have made themselves *eunuchs*.

Qu? If, as the *clergy* were condemned to *celibacy*, these were not the properest persons for *clergymen*?

Can. 40. Declares the marriage of a man and a widow *null*, who have committed *adultery* together in the life of the husband, under promise of marriage.

Can. 41. If an impotent person marry a woman, and his brother abuse her, they shall be parted, and she shall not have commerce with either of them; yet the *bishop* may permit her to marry again, after the *guilty* person hath done *penance*.

Can. 43. If a person commit fornication with a woman, who hath lain with his *son* or *brother* without his knowledge, and he deposeth upon oath that he is not conscious

conscious of any such thing, he may *marry*, after he hath done penance.

Can. 47. Allows him who is *godfather* to a man's child, to marry his *widow*, if she was not his *godmother*.

Can. 48. If a man by chance marry the *daughter* of his *godmother*, he may keep her, and live with her as his wife.

Can. 49. Forbids, that such as have committed *adultery* together should ever marry, dwell, or have society together. If they have any estate, it shall be kept for the *adulterous offspring*.

Can. 51. Repeats the prohibitions made to an *adulterer*, to marry the woman after her husband's death.

Can 54 and 58. Appoints *seven* years penance for *wilful murderers*. — Among other things — he shall not lie with his wife. See Gen. ix. 6.

Council of NANTES.

The canons which bear the name of this *council*, are a collection of constitutions made at different places.

Can. 3. Forbids a *priest* to have any woman with him, yea, those that are *accepted* by the *canons*. It forbids also *women* to approach the *altar*.

Can. 12. Allows a man to put away his wife for *adultery*, but not to marry another in her life-time. He may be reconciled

conciled to her, but on condition that *he* does *penance* with her.

Can. 13. *Three* years penance for *single* fornication.

Can. 14. *Seven* years penance on him that commits *adultery*, if married. *Five* on him that is not married.

Can. 17. Lays *fourteen* years penance on a *voluntary* and *public murderer*. *Five* years he shall be separated from the church; the rest of the time he may be at *prayers*, but without *offering* or *communicating*. See Gen. ix. 6.

The *bishops* of *Germany*, in a letter to *Pope* JOHN VIII. call *Rome*—" *the holy* " *apostolic see*—*the original of the* CHRIS- " TIAN RELIGION—*and the* source of " PRIESTLY DIGNITY."

Pope NICHOLAS I. *anno* 858.

Proves, by the *canons*, that those who have married *two sisters*, may not *marry* any more for the *future*.

That those who have *married* their relations, and are upon that account *divorced*, cannot *marry* as long as *both* of them live: but it is not forbidden when one of them dies.

That *marriage* ought not to be forbidden absolutely to such as have committed the crime of *sodomy*, provided they repent of their sin, and have left off that *cursed* habit.

CENT. IX.

N. B. This *curſed habit* is puniſhed leſs rigorouſly, than the having married *two ſiſters*.

Touching the *ceremonies* of marriage, he ſays, that, after *betrothing*, the *prieſt ought* to cauſe the perſons to come into the church with their offerings *(i. e.* to the *prieſt)* and there give them his *benediction* and the *veil*, which is not to be given in *ſecond* marriages. That, being gone out of the church, they ſhould wear *crowns* upon their *heads*. Theſe are the *ordinary* and *ſolemn* ceremonies; which, as the *Greeks* ſay of *theirs*, need not nevertheleſs be *always* obſerved. That *conſent*, according to the *laws*, might ſuffice, and that, if *that* be wanting, the reſt ſignifies nothing.

N. B. This article is very important—it contains an authentic record, even upon the teſtimony of a *Pope*, that in the *ninth century*, ſacerdotal *benediction*, or even *interpoſition*, or other ceremony of an *eccleſiaſtical* kind, were not neceſſary to the validity of marriage; but that *conſent* of the parties, according to the laws, both in the *eaſtern* and *weſtern* empire, was ſufficient.

He forbids marrying in *Lent*. Leaves it to the *biſhop*, or *prieſt*, to determine, after what *manner*, a man ſhould *live with his wife during that time*.

He expreſsly forbids a man to have *two wives* at a time. Permits all *believers* to make

make the *sign* of the *cross* upon the table, and to give a benediction thereon in the absence of the *priest*.

Pope JOHN VIII. 872,

Decides, that a man ought not to be parted from his wife, because he had *baptized* his child himself in a case of *necessity*.

That it is not permitted to *Christians* to marry their kindred, so long as they can make out *any relation*. That all those who are *so married*, and will *keep* their *wives*, or those that shall so marry for the future, to be subject to the church's *anathema* by APOSTOLIC authority, and forbids all *priests* to give them the *sacrament*, 'till they have done *penance*.

He also declares it unlawful to have *two wives*, or to have a *wife* and a *concubine* at the *same time*.

CENTURY X.

Du Pin opens this *century*, with an account of the quarrel between *Leo*, Emperor of the *East*, and *Nicholas*, the *patriarch* of *Constantinople*, who refused to marry *Leo* to a *fourth* wife. Having had *three* before, but no issue male by them, he, being desirous of a *son* to succeed him, married a *fourth* wife; but *Nicholas* refusing to marry him to this lady, whose name was *Zoe*, a *presbyter*,

CENT. X.

presbyter, whose name was *Thomas*, ventured to do it. *Nicholas* deposes *Thomas* for this, and excommunicates the *Emperor* himself.

Leo had recourse to the Pope *(Sergius)* for his approbation of the *marriage*, which, because such successive marriages were tolerated in the *West*, he easily obtained. But *Nicholas* the *patriarch*, continuing obstinate, would not acknowledge the *Emperor's* marriage as valid. The *Emperor* banished him, and placed *Enthymius* in his room. *Nicholas* wrote to the *Pope*, and stiffly maintained, contrary to the practice and opinion of the church of *Rome*, that to *marry* a *third* or *fourth* time, was absolutely unlawful. But the *patriarch*, receiving no answer from *Rome*, wrote another letter to *Pope* JOHN, wherein he offers, to observe a fair correspondence and union with the *holy see*, provided he would own, that a *fourth* marriage was not to be permitted to the *Emperor*, unless by way of *indulgence*, or consideration of his *royal person*, and that, *in itself* it was unlawful. The clergy were divided into two parties, one declaring for *Nicholas*, the other for *Enthymius*; but were re-united in the year 920; and made a treaty of union in an ecclesiastical *convocation*, by which (without disannulling any thing that was past) they *absolutely* prohibited for the future a *fourth* marriage, under *pain* of *excommunication*,

cation, to be inflicted on those who should contract such marriage, and to be in force during the continuance of such marriage. They likewise inflicted a penance, of *five* years, on such as should marry a *third* time, being above *forty* years old: and a penance of *three* years on such as should *re-marry*, after *thirty* years of age, if they had any children by their *former marriages*.

Anno 956.

On the death of the patriarch *Theophylact*, the *Emperor* constituted *Polyeucta* in his room. This *patriarch* had a warm dispute with the *Emperor Nicephorus Phocas*, who having married *Theophanes*, the widow of the Emperor *Romanus*, *Polyeucta* threatened to *excommunicate* him, unless he would renounce her. 1. Because this was the *second* marriage which *Nicephorus* had contracted, without submitting to the penance due to those who were guilty of *bigamy*. 2. Because it was reported, that *Nicephorus* had stood *godfather* to one of *Theophanes*'s children.—The *Emperor* proposed these questions to the *bishops* who were then in *Constantinople*, and to the chief of his *council*; who left him at liberty to keep *Theophanes* as his *wife:* and *Polyeucta* himself did not insist any more on the dissolution of the marriage, after the *Emperor* had assured him upon *oath*, that he had

never

never stood *god-father* to any of *Theophanes's* children.

Leo VII.

Declares that marriage between a man and his *god-mother* or *god-daughter* is *forbidden*.

Those *priests* who marry publicly, shall be deprived of their dignity; but their *children* shall not be endamaged thereby.

Atto, Bishop of Verceil,

Shews, that, by the *ecclesiastical* and *civil* laws, marriage is prohibited to those who had contracted a *spiritual affinity* by *baptism*; contrary to the advice of that *bishop*, who found fault that one who had married his *god-father's daughter*, was divorced from her, and excommunicated, 'till such time as he made his appearance in a court of judicature, before the *archbishop* and *bishops*.

Ambrose, a priest of *Milan*, writes to *Atto*, to tell him, that these sorts of marriages were likewise prohibited in his church. *Atto* writes to *ecclesiastics* in his own *diocese*, against those who kept company with lewd women, with whom they maintained a scandalous familiarity, and whom they kept and maintained out of the revenues of the church.

About the *end* of this *century*, Robert, King

King of *France*, being a *widower*, by the death of Queen *Lutgarde*, his *first* wife, had married *Bertha*, sister to *Radulphus* the *simple*, King of *Burgundy*, who was the widow of *Eudes*, first Count of *Chartres*. But forasmuch as she was his *kinswoman*, and he had formerly stood *godfather* to one of *her children*, though he had taken the advice of several *bishops* of his kingdom about it, yet the *Pope* opposed this marriage as *null*, and contracted between persons, who, *according to law*, could not marry together King *Robert* did what he could to confirm this marriage, and spake about it to *Leo*, the legate of *Gregory* V. in *France*; who *made him believe*, that he would obtain of the *Pope* what he desired, provided he would cause *Arnulphus* to be reinstated in the *archbishopric* of *Rheims*. In the mean time, notwithstanding the judgment which was passed in favour of the *Archbishop*, Pope *Gregory* V. held a *council* at *Rome*, anno 998, in the presence of the Emperor *Otho* III. at which assisted *Gerbert*, at that time *archbishop* of *Ravenna*, and twenty-seven *bishops* of *Italy*. In this council he declared, that King *Robert* ought to part from *Bertha*, whom he had married *contrary to the laws*, and do penance for *seven years* together, according to the *degrees* set down by the *canons*; and if he would not, he should be *anathematized:* that

Bertha

Cent. X.

Cent. X.

Bertha should submit to the same penalty; and he excommunicated *Archembold,* archbishop of *Tours,* who had celebrated that marriage, and the *bishops* of *France,* who had either *assisted* or *consented* thereto, 'till such time as they should come, and give the *holy see* satisfaction.

This sentence of the *Pope* made such an impression on the minds of men, that all the *king's domestics,* except *two* or *three,* abandoned him, and would no longer have any conversation with him, and even caused the vessels, out of which he had *eaten* or *drunk,* to be *burnt.* King *Robert* at last gave ear to the advice of *Abbo* the *abbot,* and parted with *Bertha,* two or three years afterwards. Leo IX. (as *Ives* of *Chartres* relates it) says, that they came to *Rome* with the *bishops,* to obtain their *absolution,* and get their *penance* mitigated.

The author of the life of *Abbo* does not say that *King Robert* went to *Rome*; but, that he confessed his fault both publicly and privately: that he asked pardon, and did penance for it. That which is most evident is, that the *marriage* was of no longer *force.*

Council of Coblentz, *anno* 922.

Can. 1. Forbids *marriage* between relations, to the *sixth* generation.

Council

Council of AUGSBURG, *anno* 952.

Can. 1. *Priests, deacons,* and *subdeacons* that marry, shall be deposed, according to chap. 25. of the council of *Carthage*.

Can. 2. Against those *clergymen* who keep *suspicious women* in their houses.

Can. 7 and 8. Forbid them to hinder *clergymen* and *canonesses* from embracing the *monastic* life.

Can. 11. Not only *bishops, priests, deacons,* and *sub-deacons* shall lead a *single life*, but also, the *other clergy* shall be obliged to live *continently* when they come to years of maturity.

General Council of ENGLAND,

Held by ST. DUNSTAN, Archbishop of CANTERBURY,

Ordained, that all *priests, deacons,* and *subdeacons* shall embrace a *regular* and *monastic* course of life, or retire. Accordingly, *St. Dunstan,* and *Oswald* and *Ethelwold,* bishops of *Worcester* and *Winchester,* turned the *old clergymen* out of most part of the churches, and put *monks* in their place, or else forced them to assume the monastical habit.

A certain very potent *earl* having married one of his *kinswomen, St. Dunstan* excommunicated him, and refused to take off

CENT. X.

off his *excommunication*, although the king *(Edgar)* had commanded him, and the *earl* had obtained a *brief* of the *Pope* for his reſtoration. At laſt the *earl*, in fear of thoſe *puniſhments* which the *divine vengeance* inflicts on *excommunicated* perſons, left his *kinſwoman*, did public *penance*, and threw himſelf down proſtrate before *St. Dunſtan*, in a council, *barefoot*, cloathed with a woollen garment, holding a *bundle* of *rods* in his hand, and lamenting his *ſin*; from which *St. Dunſtan* gave him abſolution, at the requeſt of the *biſhops* of the council. The arrogance of this proud *prieſt*, ſhews us to what a height of inſolence and tyranny *churchmen* were now arrived.

"*St. Dunſtan* was made *archbiſhop* of "*Canterbury*, anno 961. His ſkill in the "liberal arts and ſciences (qualifications "much above the *genius* of the age he "lived in) gained him firſt the name of a "*conjurer*, and then of a *ſaint*. He is re-"vered as ſuch by the *Romaniſts*, who keep "an *holy-day* in honour of him, yearly on "the 19th of *May*"—*(vide* alſo the *Pro-teſtant Kalendar.)*—"The *monkiſh* writers "tell us, that he was once tempted to "*lewdneſs* by the *Devil*, under the ſhape of "a *fine lady*; but inſtead of yielding to "her *temptations*, he took the *Devil* by the "*noſe* with a pair of red-hot tongs." See GREY'S HUD. *part* 2. *cant.* 3. l. 618. n.

ALFRIC,

ALFRIC, Archbishop of CANTERBURY, Successor of *St. Dunstan*—wrote a letter concerning the *monastic* life—and another against the marriage of *clergymen*.

CENT. X.

Few *councils* were held in this *century*. In most part of them the decrees were concerning *tythes*—against churchmen who keep *concubines*—and against marriage among *near relations*. The degrees of *consanguinity* were extended to the *seventh*, in which it was forbidden to contract marriage; and *spiritual* affinity took place, as well in the *eastern* as the *western* churches. Such as married with *these impediments* were * *divorced* without redress; neither were any *dispensations* granted, as it appears from the case of *King Robert*, and that of the Emperor *Nicephorus Phocas*.

Fourth marriages were absolutely prohibited in the *eastern*, but not in the *western* parts.

In the reign of *Edmund* king of *East-Anglia*, about *anno* 944, a time when *monks* and *priests* had gotten full possession of the understandings and consciences of mankind, a mixed *synod* or *assembly* was held, wherein *ceremonies* of *marriage*, and preliminary *securities*, which the *parties* were to give one another, were settled. See *Rapin*, vol. i. 214.

* See *Mark* vii. 9.

RATHERIUS,

CENT. X.

RATHERIUS, Bishop of VERONA,

A man of great repute in *Italy*. A most violent stickler for the *canons*. He wrote several treatises: in one of which, he declaims against the irregular lives of the *clergy* of his time, and falls upon their *immodesty*, which was then at such an height, that "one could scarce" (says he) "find a man fit to be ordained a *bishop*, or any *bishop* fit to ordain *others*." He reckons up several horrible stories, and charges them chiefly with an infamous commerce with *women*.

Another treatise is an injunction against the marriage of a clergyman's son of *Verona*, which was performed on a *Sunday in Lent*. He declares it *irregular*, and that no marriage ought to be celebrated during *Lent*, nor on *fast-days*, nor on *Sundays*, nor on *holydays*: and orders all those who commit such a *fault*, to fast forty days; that is to say, when others eat at nine o'clock, they should stay 'till *noon* ere they eat—when others eat at *noon*, they should fast 'till *three* o'clock. He *excommunicates* such offenders, as would not submit to this *penance*, and declares that GOD would consign them over to *eternal damnation*.

FULCUS, Archbishop of RHEIMS, *anno* 882.

This *archbishop* wrote to several *kings* and *princes*, among others, to *Alfrede* King of Britain,

Britain, whom he congratulates on the choice he had made of a worthy person to fill the see of *Canterbury*; because he heard, that, in his country, he advanced such sort of men, as permitted the *bishops* and *priests* to have *women* among them, and the *laics* to marry their *kindred*, as well as those *virgins* who were dedicated to GOD's service, and to have a *wife* and a *concubine* at the same time.

CENTURY XI.

ST. FULBERT, Bishop of CHARTRES,

Determines, that a woman who was engaged on oath to marry a man, could not marry another, 'till after his *death*, or *by his consent*. A woman, not being willing to live with her husband, and saying, she had rather live a *nun*, the husband desires he may have leave to marry another. *St. Fulbert* declares, that, 'tis his opinion, he could not have leave, 'till she were either *dead*, or *turned recluse*.

About the *middle* of this *century* the famous dispute concerning the *presence* of CHRIST's *body and blood* in the *eucharist* was revived.

Berenger, principal of the public school at *Tours*, and afterwards *archbishop* of *Angers*, a man of a most acute and subtle genius,

Cent. XI.

nius, and highly renowned both on account of his extensive learning, and the exemplary sanctity of his life and manners, (see *Mosheim*, edit. *Maclaine*, vol. i. p. 534.) had the *assurance* to deny the *bodily presence*; and to maintain, " that the *bread and wine* " were not changed into the *body and* " *blood* of Christ, but preserved their " natural and essential qualities, and were " no more than figures and external sym- " bols of the body and blood of the di- " vine Saviour."

This wise, scriptural, and rational doctrine was no sooner published, than it was opposed by certain doctors of *France* and *Germany:* but *Pope* Leo IX. attacked it with peculiar vehemence and fury, in the year 1050; and in *two councils*, one at *Rome*, the other at *Vercelli*, had the doctrine of *Berenger* solemnly *condemned*, and the book of Scotus, from which it was drawn, committed to the *flames*. This example was followed by the council of *Paris*, which was summoned the same year by Henry I. in which *Berenger*, and his numerous adherents, were menaced with all sorts of *evils* both *spiritual* and *temporal*.

These threats were executed in part against this unhappy *prelate*, whom Henry deprived of all his revenues. *Mosheim*, ibid.

Lanfranc, archbishop of *Canterbury*, was one of *Berenger*'s most formidable enemies.

He

He, and numbers of other confiderable churchmen, wrote againſt *Berenger*'s *heretical* doctrine. But one of the moſt curious, was GUITMOND, *archbiſhop* of AVERSE, who wrote books againſt that *heretic*, as *Berenger* was called; in one of which, *Guitmond anſwers* an objection made by *Berenger*, viz. " That the fleſh of JESUS
" CHRIST is *incorruptible*, but the ſacra-
" ments of the altar are *corruptible* if kept
" too long."

Guitmond's reply to this, contains ſuch a proof of the *ſize* of men's underſtandings, where they are retrenched by *prejudice* and *ſuperſtition*, to the ſtandard of *vulgar notion* and *popular opinion*, that I cannot forbear laying it before the reader, as the tranſlator of *Du Pin* now lays it before me. Cent. xi. p. 18.

" *Guitmond* replies—that, though the
" *conſecrated bread* ſeems to be corrupted, to
" the apprehenſion of corrupted men; yet,
" in reality, it is not changed at all; and
" that it does not appear *altered*, unleſs as
" a puniſhment of the infidelity and ne-
" gligence of men — that it cannot be
" *gnawn* by *mice*, and other *vermin*; and,
" if at any time it appears to be ſo, 'tis
" only to puniſh the negligence, or try
" the faith of men.

" Nor will he admit, that the *fire* can
" *conſume* theſe *myſteries*; and he ſays, that
" with veneration they commit it to this

Cent. XI.

"moſt pure element, to be carried up into *heaven*.

"Laſtly, he affirms, that, though the *euchariſt* may ſerve for *nouriſhment*, yet it does not turn to *excrement:* and as to that objection which might be made—that, *ſuppoſing a man ſhould eat nothing for ſome conſiderable time*, but *conſecrated bread*, he would *neverthelefs have occaſion to go to ſtool*—he anſwers, that, 'tis matter of fact which has never been yet experienced, and that it could never enter the heart of any *Catholic* to try ſuch an experiment.—That if any of *Berenger*'s party thought fit to do it, one ſhould not trouble one's head much, about what became of the *maſs* of thoſe *infidels*, which committed ſo great a *crime*; becauſe, ſays he, we do not believe that the *bread* and *wine* are neceſſarily changed into the *body* and *blood* of JESUS CHRIST, unleſs among thoſe who have *faith* to believe this myſtery, and that the words of JESUS CHRIST are *efficacious*.

"Laſtly, if any of them ſhould order a *Catholic prieſt* to confecrate one or more great loaves, to try the experiment, it is to be believed, that this loaf would not be turned into *excrement*; or rather, that GOD would permit theſe *hereticks* to be *deceived*, by ordering ſome *angel* or *ſpirit* to convey away this *conſe-*
"*crated*

" *crated loaf,* and to put an *unconsecrated*
" one in its *stead.*"

This *Berenger,* or *Beringarius,* as *Fox* calls him, was the first that was deemed an *heretic,* for denying *Transubstantiation.* See *Fox* Mart. vol. ii. p. 383.

LANFRANC, *Archbishop* of CANTERBURY.

In a letter to the *archbishop* of *York,* he very *clearly determines,* that it is not lawful for a *man* or a *woman,* divorced for *adultery,* to *marry again.*

Letter 21. To *bishop Herfast,* about a man whom he had ordained *deacon,* without having any order for it, who, besides, was a *married* man, and would not *turn off his wife.* He enjoins the *bishop* to depose the man from his *deaconship,* to give him, for the future, only the four *lesser* orders, and not to place him among the *deacons* unless he would *live single.* If he did that, then he should not confer the order of *deacon* upon him again, but only grant him a power of discharging his functions, by giving him the *gospels* in a synod or assembly of the *clergy.*

Council of PAVIA, under *Pope* BENEDICT VII.

Decr. 1. and 2. Prohibit the clergy from having any *concubines,* and from living with *women.*

Council of Rome, 1051.

Gregory bishop of *Verceil* was deposed for *adultery*, and several laws made against incontinent *clerks*.

D°, anno 1059.

Can. 11. No person shall marry a relation, to the *seventh* generation, so long as the *kindred* may be known.

D°, anno 1063.

Alexander II. held this council, consisting of above 100 *bishops*. They revived the decrees of Leo IX. and Nicholas II. against those who *married* their *kindred*, till after the *seventh* degree.

In two other councils held at *Rome*, *Alexander* condemned those who maintained, that the degrees of *consanguinity* ought to reach no *farther* than to *cousin-germans*, which he calls the *heresy* of the *Nicolaitans*.

Hildebrand, or * Gregory VII.

This *Pope's* decree against those *clerks* who either kept *concubines* or were *married*, removed, in *Germany*, *Italy*, and *France*, a

---

* For the history of this *miscreant*, see Fox, vol. i. 196.

great many *ecclesiastics* out of their places, who were found guilty of having *unlawful* commerce with *women*.

These men not only complained of this *yoke*, which the *Pope* would impose upon them, but they likewise inveighed against him, and accused him of advancing an insupportable error, and such as is contrary to the words of Our Saviour, who says, that *all men* are not able to live *continently*; and contrary to the words of the *apostle*, who enjoins those who cannot live *continently*, to *marry*.

They added, that this law, which he would impose on them, which obliged them to live like *angels*, by offering force to the ordinary * course of nature, would be the cause of great disorders: that, moreover, if the *Pope* persisted in his resolution, they had rather renounce the *priesthood* than mar-

---

* Qu? How much less is it contrary to "the or-"dinary course of nature" to compel men to live in a state of *celibacy* (for that is the fact) who cannot afford a *divorce* from *adulterous* wives, or who are under necessary, perpetual, and irrevocable *separation*, and, perhaps, bound by large penalties to abstain from all intercourse whatsoever with the women to whom they have been married? *Pope Gregory* had just as much right to impose *celibacy* on the *clergy*, as the *Protestant* powers have to inflict it on such as are above-mentioned. Such a thing was never heard of in the *Jewish law*, nor ever would have been thought of, unless *men* had abolished the whole *œconomy* of that most righteous *system* relative to *marriage*, and taken upon themselves that which belongs to God *only*.

CENT. XI.

riage, and let him fee if he could get *angels* to take care of their *flocks*, fince he would not make ufe of *men*. This was the language of thofe *corrupted* ecclefiaftics (fays *Du Pin*) according to the account of an hiftorian of that time.

But the Pope preffed the execution of his decree, and wrote very warm letters to the *bifhops*, to oblige them to take ftrict care of it.

The *archbifhop* of *Mayence* doing his utmoft therein, found how difficult it was to root out an *abufe*, fo inveterate, and fo general, as this was; and before he proceeded againft the refractory, he gave them *fix months* time to *reclaim*. Laftly, having called a *fynod* at *Erford*, he told them, that they were either to renounce their *pretended marriages*, or elfe their attendance on the *altar*.

When they found they could not, by their *prayers*, prevail upon him to alter his refolution, they withdrew from the council in great wrath, threatening either to turn the *archbifhop* out or to kill him. He, to pacify them, ordered them to be called back again, and promifed he would fend to *Rome*, and endeavour to work the *Pope* over to another mind.

The decree of *Gregory* met with no lefs oppofition in *France, Flanders, England,* and *Lombardy*, than it did in *Germany*; and this oppofition rofe fo high at *Cambray*, that

that they caused a man to be *burnt*, who had asserted that *married priests* ought not to celebrate the *mass*, or any *divine office*, and that no man ought to assist them therein.

All this did not *discourage Gregory* VII. in the *least*: on the contrary, he wrote several letters to the *princes* and *bishops* of these countries, whereby he enjoins them not to tolerate *clerks* that were *married*, or kept *concubines*. He then ordered an apology of his decree to be issued out, in the nature of a *manifesto*, wherein he very much exalts the authority of the *holy see*, and the *decretals* of his *predecessors*.

He afterwards decreed, that the *bishops*, who shall permit *priests, deacons,* or *sub-deacons* of their *diocese* to live *married*, shall be *suspended* of their *functions*.

During this *Popedom*, *Hugh* bishop of *Dia*, held a council at *Poictiers*, wherein it was decreed—

Can. 8. That the children of *priests*, and *bastards*, shall not be admitted into *holy orders*, unless they be *monks*, or live in a regular *convent*. But that they shall not hold any ecclesiastical preferments.

Can. 9. *Sub-deacons, deacons*, and *priests*, shall have no *concubines*, or any *other* suspicious women in their houses; and all they who hear a mass of a *priest* that keeps a *concubine*, shall be *excommunicated*.

William Duke of *Acquitain*, and Count of Poitiers,

CENT. XI.

Poitiers, having married one of his *relations,* the *legate* of the holy fee, and the archbifhop of *Bourdeaux,* called a fynod, to oblige him to *part* from her. However, the *duke,* of his *own* accord, *parted from his wife.* With this fubmiffion *Gregory* was highly pleafed.

Gregory determined that a *woman,* who had *married* one of her *kinfmen,* and was become a *widow,* ought not to receive any *dowry,* from any part of her hufband's revenue, nor to have any advantage of that marriage, which was in its *own nature null.*

Letter 48. He orders a man who had *killed his brother,* to be prevented *marrying* till he had done *penance.*

Letter 50. He determines, that one who is not born in *lawful* wedlock *(i. e.* fuch as the *canons* deemed *lawful)* cannot be advanced to the *epifcopacy*—becaufe it is contrary to the *canons.*

Council of MELPHI, under URBAN II. anno 1089.

URBAN II. renewed the decrees againft the fimoniacal, and concerning the *celibacy* of thofe who were in *holy orders.* He therein enjoins, that none fhall be admitted into *holy orders* but fuch as had led *chafte* lives, and had never been *married* to more than *one woman.* He declares the *fons* of *priefts* incapable of *holy orders,* unlefs they have

have taken upon them the monaſtical habit.

Council of BENEVENTO, *anno* 1091, under URBAN II.

Can. 4. *Laics* are forbidden to eat *fleſh* after *Aſh-Wedneſday*—and all the *faithful* of *both ſexes* are enjoined to put *aſhes* on their heads on that day.

It is likewiſe ordered, that *no marriage* ſhall be *ſolemnized*, from *Septuageſima Sunday*, till after the *octave* of *Whitſuntide*; and from the firſt Sunday in *Advent*, till after the *octave* of *Epiphany*.

Council of CLERMONT.

Can. 9, 10. Againſt thoſe clerks who keep *concubines*.

Can. 11. Prohibits promoting to holy orders the *ſons* of *concubines*, or the beſtowing any benefices upon them, unleſs they have embraced the monaſtical or *canonical* life.

Can. 25. The children of *prieſts*, *deacons*, and *ſub-deacons*, ſhall not be promoted to *holy orders*, if they be not either *monks* or *regular canons*.

Can. 29, 30. Thoſe who fly to *a croſs*, ſhall be as ſecure as thoſe who fly to a *church*. They ſhall not be delivered up to *juſtice*, 'till they are aſſured that no violence ſhall be offered to their lives or members.

CENT. XI.

Council of NISMES, *anno* 1096.

Can. 10. Thofe who marry their *relations* fhall be *excommunicated*.

In this *century*, there were violent controverfies between the *Latin* and *Greek* churches; and among other *curious* particulars of accufation againſt the *Greeks*, Cardinal *Humbert* charges them with permitting *married men* to wait at the *altars*, even at the time when they had to do with their *wives*: and charges *Nicetus* with being a *Nicolaitan*, becaufe he oppofed the *celibacy* of the *prieſts* and *deacons* He explains the *canons*, which prohibit *prieſts* from *parting* with their *wives*, of the care they ought to take of them, in looking upon them *ſtill* as *their wives*, though they have no carnal knowledge of them.

He produces the canon of the council of *Nice*, concerning *women* who live with *clerks*, and feveral *authorities of the Popes*, to prove that *prieſts* ought to live *chaſtly* (*i. e.* in *celibacy.)*

He charges the *Greeks* for not ordaining *prieſts*, till they had obliged them to *marry*, and concludes all with *anathematizing Nicetus*, who had written on thefe points againſt the *Latin church*.

Whoever has a mind to read as much *nonfenfe* and *abfurdity* as would reach from *Rome* to *Conſtantinople*, and *back again*, may meet with it in thefe famous *controverfies* between

between the *Latins* and *Greeks*. One charge againſt the *Latins* was, that, "*monks* might be permitted to eat *fleſh* and *bacon*."—Another—"that they were *guilty* of eating *cheeſe* and *eggs* in the *holy week*."

PETER DAMIEN, Cardinal Biſhop of OSTIA.

In a *letter* to his nephew *Damien*, (whom he exhorts to be zealous in the exerciſes of a *monaſtical* life) he reproves him for having gone from an *hermitage* to a *monaſtery*, and exhorts him to return thither again. In another, he reproves a *monk*, who delayed turning *hermit*, becauſe he could hardly perſuade himſelf not to *drink wine*.

This *Cardinal* wrote a treatiſe called the *Gomorrhean*, dedicated to Pope *Leo* IX. who approved of it, in a letter which is prefixed at the beginning. In this tract he proves that *clergymen* who have committed ſins of uncleanneſs, which modeſty does not permit to be named, ought to be deprived for ever. He rejects the *canons* of the *penitential books*, which impoſe *too light penances* for thoſe *ſorts of crimes*, of which he ſhews the enormity: he inveighs againſt thoſe perſons who are guilty of ſuch notorious offences, and exhorts them to a ſpeedy repentance, and to do ſevere *penance*.

N. B. How is it, that this *cardinal* did not ſee, that the *unnatural* wickedneſs, which

CENT. XI.

which he complains of, among the *clergy*, was the *natural* consequence of their *celibacy*, and being shut up together in *monasteries*, where *no women* must ever enter?

But so blinded was this *cardinal* to the *real source* of the evil, that, when he began to think the time of his dissolution drew near, he excused himself from going to *Mount Caffin* on a visit, " lest he should " die out of the precincts of a *monastery*."

In a tract dedicated to *John* bishop of *Cesena*, and to the *archdeacon* of *Ravenna*, he *confutes* the opinion of the lawyers, who restrained the *degrees* of *consanguinity*, in which one might contract marriage, to the *fourth degree*, and imagined that *grand-nephews* and *grand-nieces* may *intermarry*. He maintains, that *as far* as any *consanguinity* or *affinity* can be *discerned*, matrimony ought not to be contracted; which takes place to the *seventh degree*.

He also treats at large of *alms-giving*, and shews the usefulness of it, both for the *living* and the *dead*.

Treatise 17th, to Pope *Nicholas* II. he exhorts him to put a stop to enormities committed by *unchaste* clergymen, and to make use of the severity of the *canons* against them, in imitation of *Phineas*'s zeal.

His *eighteenth* treatise consists of three letters, which *shew, very evidently*, whom he ranked among *unchaste* clergymen; for

he

he shews that the *clergy* are obliged to lead a *single life,* and inveighs most bitterly against those who *married* or kept *concubines.*

In another letter, he recommends *chastity* to his nephew *Damien,* and persuades him to receive the *communion every day,* to be in a condition to preserve that virtue. Afterwards he gives him wholesome instructions to withstand the temptations of the *Devil.*

St. Anselm, Archbishop of Canterbury, 1089.

In a treatise of marriages between near relations, he enquires into the reasons of that prohibition, which he extends *only* to the *sixth* degree of *consanguinity.*

This *saint* was a great opposer of *priests' marriage.* Under his auspices a council was held, in which was decreed, " an or-
" der for priests to be sequestered from
" their wives, which before were not for-
" bidden (in *England*) according as the
" words of mine author do purport (says
" *Fox)* whose words be these. Ansel-
" mus *prohibuit uxores sacerdotibus* Anglo-
" rum *ante non prohibitas. Quod quibus-*
" *dam mundissimum visum est, quibusdam pe-*
" *riculosum, ne dum munditias viribus ma-*
" *jores appeterent, in immunditias horribiles*
" *ad* Christiani *nominis summum dedecus in-*
" *ciderent.* Henr. Hunt."—" Anselm pro-
" hibited

CENT. XI.
"hibited *wives* to the priests of the *English*, which were not prohibited before. Which thing appeared to some *most filthy*, to others *dangerous*, lest, while they earnestly endeavoured after greater *purity*, they should fall into *impurities*, so horrible, as to bring a disgrace on the *Christian* name. ANSELM did not attend to this, but made a canon for the *excommunication* of *sodomites*, which was never published." See *Thelyph.* vol. i. p. 177, n. first edit.—171, second edit.

"After this *council*, *Herbert*, bishop of *Norwich*, had much ado with the *priests* of his *diocese*, for they would neither *leave their wives*, nor *quit their benefices*: whereupon he wrote to *Anselm* for advice. *Anselm* required him (as he did others at the same time, by writing) to persuade the people of *Norfolk* and *Suffolk*, that, as they *professed Christianity*, they should subdue them as *rebels* against the *church*, and utterly drive both *them and their wives* out of the country, placing *monks* in their rooms.

"The like business had also *Gerard*, archbishop of *York*, in depriving the *priests* of his *province* of their *wives*: which thing, with all his *thunderings* and *excommunications*, he could hardly bring about.

"Upon this ruffling of *Anselm* with married priests, were rhyming verses
"made,

" made, to help the matter withal, when
" reafon could not ferve; which verfes,
" for the folly thereof, I thought here to
" annex.

> " O male viventes, verfus audite fequentes;
> " Uxores veftras, quas odit fumma poteftas,
> " Linquite propter eum, tenuit qui morte trophæum,
> " Quod fi non facitis inferna clauftra petetis.
> " CHRISTI fponfa jubet, ne Prefbyter ille miniftret,
> " Qui tenet uxorem, Domini qui perdet amorem:
> " Contradicentem fore dicimus infipientem:
> " Non ex rancore loquor hæc, potius fed amore."
> See Fox. Mart. vol. i. p. 216.

I ftand not to comment on the falfe *profody* in thefe verfes—their *quality*, not their *quantities*, are moft to the purpofe; the *Englifh* reader may be acquainted with the *former* by the following tranflation—

> " O ye evil-livers, hear the following verfes;
> " Your wives, which the SUPREME POWER hateth,
> " Leave for his fake, who triumphed in death;
> " Which if ye do not, you WILL GO TO HELL.
> " The fpoufe of CHRIST commands, that the Prefbyter
>   fhould not minifter,
> " Who keeps a wife, who will lofe the love of the Lord.
> " He that contradicts this, we fay, is foolifh:——
> " I fpeak not this out of rancour, but rather from love."

We may obferve, that *now* the feeds of oppofition, and contempt of the *word*, and *ways*, and *will* of GOD, concerning marriage, in this *kingdom*, were growing up, from the *planting* of *Auftin* the *monk*, anno 597, to the *watering* of his fucceffor *St. Anfelm*, who died *anno* 1109, towards that maturity, to
which

CENT. XI.

which they will be found to have arrived, before we have finished our enquiries upon the subject.

Some years after the above verses had been sent forth, they met with an answer, from the pen of *Walter Mapes*, archdeacon of *Oxford*, in the reign of *Henry* II. This same *Walter* seems to have been a very merry fellow, and to have indulged a vein of pleasantry in all his compositions; some of which I have seen, and among others the following *drole* on the prohibition of *clerical* marriage, which I will here insert for the entertainment of my *learned readers*; and if any of them will favour me with a suitable translation of them, it shall make its appearance in the next edition of this *volume*, that my *unlearned* readers, as well as they, may find a little entertainment in the midst of this dry and barren desart of *Popish* quotation.

Part of the account which I find of this man, in an old book, intitled, " *Remaines* " *concerning Brittaine*"—printed *anno* 1629, runs thus—

" *Walter de Mapes*, arch-deacon of *Ox-*
" *ford*, who, in the time of K. *Henrie* II.
" filled *England* with his merriments, when
" the *Pope* forbad the *clergie* their wives,
" became proctor for himself and them,
" with these verses; desiring only for his
" fee, that every *priest*, with his *sweet-heart*,
" would say a *pater-noster* for him."

Prisciani

Prisciani regula penitus cassatur,
Sacerdos per hic & hæc *olim declinatur* ;
Sed per hic *solummodo nunc articulatur,*
Cum per nostrum præsulem hæc *amoveatur.*

CENT.
XI.

 Ita quidem presbyter cœpit allegare,
Peccat criminaliter qui vult seperare
Quod DEUS *injunxerat, fœminam amare:*
Tales dignum duximus fures appellare.

 O quàm dolor anxius, quàm tormentum grave,
Nobis est dimittere quoniam suave!
O Romane Pontifex, statuisti pravè,
Ne in tanto crimine moriaris, cave.

 Non est * *Innocentius, imo nocens verè,*
Qui quod facto docuit, studet abolere,
Et quod olim juvenis voluit habere,
Modo vetus Pontifex studet prohibere.

 Gignere nos præcepit vetus testamentum,
Ubi novum prohibet nusquam est inventum:
Præsul qui contrarium donat documentum,
Nullum necessarium bis dat argumentum.

 Dedit enim DOMINUS *maledictionem*
Viro qui non fecerit generationem;
Ergo ibi consulo, per hanc rationem,
Gignere ut habeas benedictionem.

 Nonne de militibus milites procedunt?
Et reges a regibus, qui sibi succedunt?
Per locum a simili omnes jura lædunt,
Clericos qui gignere crimen esse credunt.

 Zacharias habuit prolem & uxorem,
Per virum quem genuit adeptus honorem;
Baptizavit enim nostrum SALVATOREM :—
Pereat qui teneat novum hunc errorem.

 Paulus cælos rapitur ad superiores,
Ubi multas didicit res secretiores:
Ad nos tandem rediens, instruensque mores,
Suas (inquit) habeat quilibet uxores.

 Propter hæc, & alia dogmata doctorum,
Reor esse melius, & magis decorum,
Quisque SUAM *habeat & non proximorum,*
Ne incurrat odium, & iram eorum.

* *Nomen Papæ.*

Proximorum fœminas, filias, & neptes,
Violare nefas est, quare nihil disceptes:
Vere TUAM *habeas, & in* HAC *deleƈtes,*
Diem ut sic ultimum tutius expeƈtes.
  Ecce jam pro clericis multum allegavi,
Necnon pro Presbyteris plura comprobavi:—
PATER-NOSTER *nunc pro me quoniam peccavi,*
Dicat quisque PRESBYTER *cum* SUA SUAVI.

Synod of ARRAS, *anno* 1025.

News being brought to *Gerard*, bishop of *Cambray* and *Arras*, that there was a sect of *heretics* arrived from *Italy*, who taught, that "*marriage* was condemned by "the ordinances of the gospel," the bishop summoned a *synod* at *Arras*, wherein this, and some other errors, were refuted, and the heretics brought to subscribe a *recantation*.

Council of BOURGES, *anno* 1031.

Can. 5. *Priests* who *cohabit* with their *wives*, shall only be *readers* or *chanters* for the future. *Deacons* and *sub-deacons* shall not be suffered to keep their *wives* or *concubines*.

Can. 6. The *bishops* shall oblige them to take an *oath* to *that purpose*, at their ordination.

Can. 7. All who are employed in *ministerial* functions, shall have ecclesiastical *tonsure*—*i. e.* their beards shaved, and the *crown* made on their heads.

Can.

Can. 8. The *sons* of *deacons* or *sub-deacons* shall not be admitted into the *clergy*.

Can. 10. Such shall be deemed *sons* of *clergymen*, as were born after their fathers quitted the *ecclesiastical* state, and returned to that of *laics*.

Can. 11. Bishops shall declare, at the time of ordination, that they *excommunicate* those who shall presume to present to them *sons* of *clergymen* to be ordained, and that such as have got their ordination by surprize shall be deposed.

Can. 16. Those who leave their wives, except upon account of *adultery*, shall not marry others, as long as the former are living, nor the women other husbands in like cases.

Can. 17. No man shall take to wife a relation, to the *sixth* and *seventh* degree of consanguinity.

Can. 18. None shall marry, in like manner, his *kinsman's* wife.

Can. 19. No man shall give his daughter in marriage to any *priest*, *deacon*, or *sub-deacon*, or to their *sons*.

Can. 20. None shall marry the daughters of the *clergy*. After the session of this *synod*, *Aimo* the *archbishop* declared, that *St. Martial* should be styled an *apostle* in all the church offices.

CENT. XI.

Council of LIMOGES, *anno* 1031.

The same question was debated, and after many arguments, the *apostolical dignity* was conferred on *St. Martial*.

For the nonsensical disputes about this *St. Martial*, between the *priests* and *monks*, see MOSHEIM, *edit. Macl.* vol. i. p. 540—1.

The *canons* against *incontinent* clergymen were *revived*.

The bishop of *Puy en Valay* reported, that the *Count* of *Clermont* being *excommunicated*, for leaving his lawful wife to *marry* another, made a journey to the *court* of *Rome*, where he obtained *absolution* of the *Pope*, who had no notice of the *sentence* passed against him. That the *bishop* having made a complaint, the *Pope* returned for answer, that he ought to blame himself for what had happened, as he did not inform him that the *Count* was *excommunicated*. The *Pope* added, that, if he had known it, he would have confirmed the *bishop's sentence, because* he makes profession to assist his brethren in *every thing*, and not oppose them: therefore he abrogated and made void the *penance* and *absolution* granted to that *excommunicated* person, who ought to expect nothing but a *curse*, 'till he has made *satisfaction*, and has been *duly absolved* by his *diocesan*.

Councils held in FRANCE, 1040.

It was ordained in all thefe *councils*, that the people fhould abftain from eating *flefh* on *Fridays* and *Saturdays*, and from drinking *wine* on *Fridays*; and that, in confideration of this *abftinence*, offenders fhould be difcharged from other *penances*, provided they bound themfelves by *oath* to obferve it.

A great number of bodies of *faints*, and *abundance* of *relics*, were brought into thefe councils; and it was *generally* believed, that many *miracles* were wrought therein.

Council of RHEIMS, *anno* 1049.

The bifhop of *Langres* was accufed by one of his *clerks*, for that he, the faid *bifhop*, *took away the wife* of him, the faid *clerk*, and after having *abufed* her, made her a *nun*. The *bifhop*, not appearing, was *excommunicated*: as were all thofe *prelates*, who, being fummoned to this *council*, and did not appear. *N. B.* Here is a precedent of *excommunication* for non-appearance on *citation*.

Can. 11. No man fhall take to wife any of his *near relations*.

Laftly. All thofe perfons were *excommunicated*, who fhould protect, or hold correfpondence with, the new heretics of *France*, the *fodomites*, and certain *lords* who had

CENT. XI. had contracted *forbidden marriages*, and assaulted some *bishops* and other *clergymen*.

Council of TOURS, 1060.

Can. 9. Those men who marry their *kinswomen*, or those women who keep an unchaste correspondence with their *kinsmen*, and refuse to leave them, or to do *penance*, shall be *excluded* from the communion of the faithful, and turned out of the *church*.

NORMANDY.

Council of ROUEN, *anno* 1050.

Can. 1. The articles of faith, comprized in the *creed* of the *catholic* and *apostolic* church, ought to be *firmly* adhered to.

Qu? What was become of the *scriptures*?

Council of LISIEUX, *anno* 1055; and that of ROUEN, *anno* 1063.

The *archbishop* of *Rouen*, under whom the preceding council was held, was deposed *anno* 1055, in another council convened at *Lisieux*: — that which chiefly brought on him this condemnation, was the displeasure of duke *William*, his *nephew*, who was incensed against him, because he had *excommunicated* that *prince*, upon account of his marriage with the princess *Matilda*,

Matilda, his *kinswoman*, the daughter of *Baldwin* count of *Flanders*.

This prelate published a *confession of faith* against *Berenger's erroneous* opinions. See before, 113.

Council of ROUEN, *anno* 1072.

Can. 14. No marriages shall be solemnized *privately*, nor after meals. The *bridegroom* and *bride*, being *fasting*, shall be *blessed* by a *priest*, in like manner *fasting*. Before he proceed to *marry* them, enquiry shall be made, whether the parties be not *relations*, in the *seventh* degree of *consanguinity*.

Can. 15. *Priests, deacons*, and *sub-deacons*, who are married, cannot enjoy any church revenues, nor dispose of them by themselves or by others.

Can. 16. A man cannot marry a *widow*, with whom he is *suspected* to have *conversed* scandalously, in her husband's life-time.

Can. 17. A man, whose wife is veiled a *nun*, cannot take another as long as she is living.

GERMANY.

Council of SELINGENSTADT, *anno* 1023.

Can. 1. Abstinence from eating flesh shall be observed fourteen days before the *festival* of *St. John*, and before *Christmas*; on the *vigils* of the *Epiphany*, of the *festivals*

vals of the *apostles*, of the assumption of the *Virgin Mary*, of *St. Lawrence*, and of all the *saints*.

Can. 2. Fixes the *Ember* weeks.

Can. 3. Denotes the time when the solemnization of matrimony is *forbidden, viz.* from *Advent* 'till after the *Epiphany* (five weeks) and from *Septuagesima* 'till after *Easter* (nine weeks) making together above a quarter of a year; as also on the *above-specified days* of abstinence. *N.B.* Let the reader add all these together, and he will be at a loss to conceive when marriage could be solemnized.

Can. 11. The first degree of *consanguinity* shall be reckoned from the *cousins-german*.

The Council of MENTZ, *anno* 1069.

Sigefroy, or *Sigefrid,* archbishop of *Mentz,* held this *council,* in which the *emperor* HENRY IV. made a proposal to *divorce* his *wife,* because he could have no issue of her body. *Sigefrid* inclined to this opinion; but *Peter Damien,* the *Pope's legate,* being arrived, prevented the *divorce.* The *archbishop* wrote to *Alexander* II. that " he had " prohibited the *emperor* from divorcing " his wife under pain of *excommunication;* " but that this *prince* having alledged, that " he could not have *carnal copulation* with " her, and the *empress* having owned her " *impotency,* he found himself obliged to
" consult

"consult the *Holy See* about so extraordinary a case; that he was unwilling to pass judgment on the affair in a *council*, which was called upon *that* occasion, 'till he received his answer, and entreated him to send his *legates*, to examine and decide the matter in *Germany*."

How this matter ended is not said, but, it is to be supposed, in favour of the *divorce*; and that the *emperor* married again: as we find *him*, with his *empress* and his *son*, afterwards waiting, bare-legged and bare-footed, at the gates of *Canusium*, three days and three nights, in the depth of winter, before he could be admitted to have an audience of Pope *Hildebrand*, who had excommunicated him. See *Fox*, vol. i. 202.

ENGLAND.

The Council of AENHAM, *anno* 1010.

King *Ethelred* called a council, in which *Elphegus*, archbishop of *Canterbury*, and *Ethelred*, archbishop of *York*, assisted, and made several constitutions and rules, that ought to be followed by the *clerks* and *monks*—concerning the celibacy of *priests*, and other *clergymen*—against *superstitious* practices and *incontinency*—about the rights of churches, particularly *St. Peter*'s pence —the *great festival* of the *Virgin Mary*— the *Ember weeks*—concerning the time in which marriages are forbidden to be solemnized

Cent. XI.

lemnized—about the interval to be obſerved by *widows* before they marry again, which is a year.

Council held at LONDON, *anno* 1075.

Superſtitions were *forbidden,* and the *celibacy* of the clergy was *ſtrictly* enjoined.

D° *anno* 1102*.

Can. 4. Revives the conſtitutions about *celibacy*.

Can. 12. Declares promiſes of marriage, made without witneſſes, to be *null,* if denied by one of the parties.

Can. 14. Prohibits marriages to the *ſeventh* degree of conſanguinity.

Can. 16. *Sodomy* is forbidden under very ſevere penalties, and this caſe is reſerved to the cognizance of the *biſhops*. Theſe conſtitutions were confirmed by the ſee of *Rome*.

In the year 1108, *St. Anſelm* held another council at *London*, in which he made *ten* very *rigid canons* againſt *prieſts and deacons,* who *married,* or *lived incontinently*.

* *N. B.* This Council rather belongs to *Cent.* XII. but I ſet it down as I find it in *Du Pin*.

SPAIN.

Spain.

Council of COYACO, *anno* 1050.

Can. 3. *Priests* and *deacons* shall not keep any *women* in their houses, unless their *mother, sister, aunt,* or *mother-in-law.*

Can. 4. Persons guilty of *murder, adultery,* or *any sort* of *uncleanness,* shall be obliged to do *penance;* and if they refuse to do it, they shall be *separated* from the *church* and the *communion.*

Can. 12. Those who have taken *sanctuary* in a *church,* nay even within *thirty paces* of it, shall not be taken from thence by *violence.*

Du Pin, in his observations on this *eleventh century,* says, that *marriage,* and *concubinage* of *clergymen,* had their career, at last, quite stopped, by the means of a vast number of decrees; that the sentences of *excommunication* were so *frequent* as to become *contemptible.* They extended even to the *third* generation of those who conversed or corresponded with the *excommunicate.*

The use of the *disciplining whip,* unknown to all antiquity, began in the end of *this* century—the custom of doing *penance* for *another,* was likewise introduced at *that time.*

CENTURY XII.

Ivo, Bishop of CHARTRES,

Was a great writer; *Du Pin* mentions 287 letters of his, yet extant.

Letter 99. Is the resolution of a question proposed by *Gualon*, abbot of *St. Quintin* in *Beauvais*, viz. "If children under *six* years of age can be contracted or married with one another; and in case there be only a contract between them, and one of the parties die, whether the surviving party may marry the *brother or sister* of the other?"

"Answer. None can actually *marry* 'till the age of *fourteen*, but that children may *promise* marriage to each other, as soon as they are at years of discretion, which he determines to be at *seven* years of age; and that a *contract* agreed on at that age, shall hinder either party, if one of them die before they are compleatly *married*, from *marrying* with the *brother* or *sister* of the deceased."

Letter 122. To *Volgrin*, archdeacon of *Paris*, asserts, that a *Jewish* woman, marrying a *Christian* husband, and afterwards returning to *Judaism*, is not *freed* from her *conjugal vow*, nor, though she leave him, can the man *marry* with another *during her life*.

In Letter 123. To *Gaultier*, library-keeper of the church of *Beauvais*, he gives his opinion on a *difficult case*, which he had consulted him upon—viz.—" how he " should proceed against a *priest*, who had, " in a profane manner, made use of other " *ceremonies* and *words* than are prescribed " in the *form* of *marriage?*" *Ivo* tells him, that " he had never yet heard of *so* " *foul a sacrilege*, nor was there *any* provi- " sion against it in the *canons*; and there- " fore, this being a *crime* wholly *new* and " *unparalleled*, some more than *ordinary* " punishment ought to be inflicted on the " author of it: however, not to deal *too* " *severely*, without warrant and authority " from scripture, or the *ecclesiastical* laws, " he thinks it sufficient, that such punish- " ment be laid on him, as the *canons* or- " der to be inflicted upon those that vio- " late the *sacraments* and *holy things*."

On the above we may observe, that *marriage* was getting more into the hands of the *priests*—that the *church* had increased its *ceremonies* since the time when the *priest* only attended to give a *benediction*—that they were very * jealous of any disrespect to these *ceremonies*—but that *marriage* was not yet a *sacrament*.

Letter 155. To *Odo*, archdeacon of

---

* As well they might be, for they hung by the *slender thread* of *human invention*.

CENT. XII.

Orleans, Ivo treats of this question, "If a woman who has committed *fornication*, and is great with child, may marry? and concludes, that, in strictness, no *great-bellied* woman ought to have *carnal knowledge* with any man— but, considering the infirmity of the flesh, *St. Paul* advises men to *use their own wives*, for avoiding *fornication*, although they are *with child*, and therefore, by consequence, a man may marry a woman in that condition."

N. B. Here we may suppose what they meant by *fornication*, namely, the man and woman *coming together* without a *priest:* this, as we shall find, was not brought to its perfection 'till the next *century*.

Letter 158. He acquaints *Hugh*, archbishop of *Lyons*, that King *Philip* and his son are resolved to make the marriage void, of *Constance*, the king's *daughter*, and *Hugh* earl of *Troyes*, because of their being too nearly *related*; and desires the *archbishop* to send speedily to all the *bishops*, summoned to court on this occasion, the *genealogy* of *both families*.

Letter 161. He asserts, that a man, who promises *marriage* to a woman, and afterwards *marries* another, ought to be divorced, and to return to his first * engagement.

* See this, the *ecclesiastical* law of *England*, vol. i. p. 30, 1st edit.—p. 31. 2d edit.

Letter 167. He writes to the *bishop* of *Mans*, to hinder the marriage of one who had already engaged himself to another woman.

Letter 174. He assures *Mathilda*, Queen of *England*, that he will pray for the soul of her brother *(Edgar*, King of *Scotland*, who died without issue *anno* 1107;) for though he doubts not but his soul is in *Abraham's bosom*, yet, since we cannot be certain of the state of souls in the other world, it is a piece of commendable devotion to pray even for those in *heaven*, that their *happiness may be augmented*, and for those in *purgatory*, that their *sins may be forgiven* them.

Letter 187. He admonishes the *Countess* of *Chartres*, to leave troubling the *abbot* and *monks* of *Bonneval*, on account of the *murder* of *Hugh* the *black*. Qu? If *Hugh* the *black* had *murdered* the *abbot* and *monks*, whether this good *bishop* would have been so *merciful?*

Letter 202. He admonishes *Daimbert*, archbishop of *Sens*, to correct two scandalous abuses in his church; one, of the *chaunter*'s holding another preferment, contrary to his oath; the other, in one of the *chapter*'s keeping in his house *two women* of *ill fame*.

Letter 205. Is written to a *knight*, who suspected his wife to be *with child* by *another*, because he had been absent from her

CENT. XII.

her *seven days* longer than is usual, between the times of *conception* and *bringing forth*, and because the person, whom he suspected of being too familiar with her, had been *burnt* in passing the trial of *ordeal*. As to the computation of time, *Ivo* tells him, *that* ought not to sway him, since many women go much longer with child; and for the trial by *fire*, no heed is to be given to it: so that these two reasons prove nothing against the *honesty* of his *wife*; whose *oath*, and the good word of her neighbours and acquaintance, ought fully to suffice in *vindication* of her.

Letter 218. He writes to *Gualon*, bishop of *Paris*, that the *canon* of that church, who had lately been *married*, ought to lose his preferment, and be *degraded* from being a *clergyman*, but that his *marriage* must remain *good* and *valid*.

Letter 221. To *John*, bishop of *Orleans*, concerning a *freeman*'s having married a *slave*, without knowing her to be so. *Ivo* says, that by the *civil* law, the marriage is *void*, and he may quit her, and marry another woman; but that, by the laws of * GOD and *nature*, they ought to keep together, or at least, if he *put her away*, he may not *marry* again.

Letter 222. To the clergy of *Autun*, he enquires, if a woman, who has been

* Qu? When the *civil* law contradicts the laws of GOD and *nature*, which is to be followed?

guilty

guilty of *adultery*, muſt neceſſarily be *divorced* from her huſband ? and concludes, that, in ſtrictneſs, ſhe *ought*; but by the *wiſdom* of the *goſpel*, ſuch a temper was preſcribed as may reconcile her to her huſband.

Letter 242. To *Owen*, biſhop of *Eureux*, he explains himſelf concerning his having given his opinion that a freeman, who had married a ſlave, without knowing her to be ſuch, ought to be *divorced* from her; and adds, that this is not diſſolving a *lawful* marriage, but only declaring that it is unlawful for them to live together any longer, their marriage being *null* by *law*—*i. e.* the *civil* law. See before, p. 144.

Letter 145. To *Hugh*, earl of *Troyes*, who having liſted himſelf for the *holy land*, deſigned to *put away* his *wife*, and live in *celibacy*—he *commends* his reſolution.

Letter 246. He declares, that it is not allowable for a man to marry *two ſiſters* ſucceſſively, though the marriage with the former was never *conſummated*.

Letter 162. To *Pontius*, abbot of *Cluny*, he ſhews him the reaſon, why, in the conſecration of the *cup*, at the *Lord's ſupper*, the words " *myſtery of faith* " are added, which were not uſed by OUR SAVIOUR, at the inſtitution of the *ſacrament*; and ſays, that this is done, becauſe we judge of the *greatneſs* of the *myſtery* contained in it, not by the *ſenſes*, but by *faith*.

N. B. To believe what contradicts the *senses*, is not *faith*, but *folly*.—See *Locke,* Hum. Und. b. iv. c. 18.

The Contents of the XVII. parts of the DECRETAL.

VII. Is of the retirement and single lives of *monks* and *nuns,* and of the penance to be undergone for the breach of the *vow* of *continency.*

XV. Of *penances,* and *commutations* of *penances.*—*N. B.* See *Thelyph.* App. to chap. X.

Pope PASCHAL II.

Held a second *Lateran council,* in the which he made an oration to the *bishops* there assembled, *anno* 1116, on the *infallibility* of the church, and to prove that it had never been guilty of *heresy,* nor, as it should seem, ever could.—It is for *this church,* said he, that the *Son of* GOD prayed, just before His *passion,* when he said—*Peter, I have prayed for thee, that thy faith fail not.*—*N. B.* It is to be remarked, that these people seldom quote scripture, but, as the *Devil* did, to abuse it.

Council of RHEIMS, *anno* 1119.

Here Pope *Calixtus* II. published *five* canons.

Can. 5. Against the *priests, deacons,* and *sub-deacons,* who had *wives* or *concubines.*

LATERAN Council, *anno* 1123.

Can. 3. Renews the prohibitions made by the *laws of the church*, against *clerks* having *wives* or *concubines*, or to live with *women*; excepting such as are exempted by the council of *Nice*.

Can. 5. Renews the prohibition of marriage among *relations*.

Can. 21. Does again prohibit the *marriages* of the *clergy*, and declares the *marriages* which they have contracted *null*. This is *the canon* (says *Du Pin*) which expressly pronounces the *nullity* of the marriages of such persons as are in *holy orders*.

The *Pope* wrote to the clergy of *Terrouane*, that they ought not *suffer* any *married* clergy among them.

ST. BERNARD.

William, Duke of *Guienne*, having quarrelled with the bishop of *Poictiers*, refused to be reconciled to him: to surmount his obstinacy, *Saint Bernard* took the *blessed sacrament*, and carrying it to the place where the *duke* was, conjured him in the name of *Jesus*, and with such *terrible words*, that the *frightened duke* fell flat upon the ground, and was forced to be reconciled to the bishop of *Poictiers*. Among other things, *St. Bernard* assured the *duke*, that the Son of GOD was come *in person*

CENT. XII. *perſon* * to him. This ſaint was a great *hero* in *monkery*, and at his death left behind him near 160 *monaſteries* of his order, *founded* by him.

Pope EUGENIUS III.

Writes to *Hildegarda*, abbeſs of *Mont St. Rupert*, commending her *ſpirit* of *prophecy*, adviſing her to preſerve, by her *humility*, GOD's grace granted unto her, and always to make uſe of *prudence*, in the *unfolding* of thoſe *myſteries* which GOD had revealed to her.

In this *century* various ſects of *heretics* aroſe, ſome of which maintained, that " the *forbidden fruit* was *Adam*'s carnal " knowledge of *Eve*," and that " no " perſon could be *ſaved* in a married ſtate." Theſe called themſelves *Cathari*, or *Puritans*. Abſurd and unſcriptural as theſe *hereſies* were, yet they were as defenſible as *Jerome's*—*Coïtus præmium mors*—the *celibacy* of the *clergy*—and *monkery*. The only very material difference between the *Catharists* and their *oppoſers*, ſeems to have been, that the latter had the *authority* of the church to maintain their *errors*, while the former were unprotected by *prieſtly* power *in theirs*. Thus—

> *Little villains muſt ſubmit to fate,*
> *That great ones may enjoy the world in ſtate.*
> GARTH.

* Is it poſſible, that, when *St. Bernard* told this *ſwinger*, he could believe it himſelf?

Peter

Peter ABELARD.   CENT. XII.
The history of this unfortunate man is well known. I will only observe, that all the miseries he underwent, were wholly occasioned by the enormous and wicked institution of clerical *celibacy*. His story is told at large in *Du Pin,* Cent. 12. chap. 7.

One of the *errors* imputed to this *father,* is, that he maintained, the *bread* and *wine* at the *altar,* to remain *the same* in *substance* after *consecration,* as before it.

Pope ALEXANDER III.
Letter 23. Inveighs against *clandestine* marriages, that were contracted without the *benediction* of a *priest.* See *Thelyph.* vol. ii. 149 —156, 1st edit.——p. 141—149, 2d edit.

HILDEBERT Bishop of MANS. Afterwards *Archbishop* of TOURS.
Letter 7. He determines that a *virgin,* betrothed before she was *marriageable,* whose husband died without knowing her carnally, cannot marry the *brother* of her former *husband,* because *marriage* does *not* consist in *carnal copulation,* but in the *consent* of the *parties.*

Letter 34. He declares, that he refused to approve the intended marriage of a *count,* with one of his *kinswomen;* although it might put an end to a war, which was carried on between him and his future *father-in-law.*

Letter 51. Is a large refutation of a person, who revived the *error* of *Vigilantius,*
viz.

viz. "That the *invocation* of *saints* was *unprofitable*, becaufe they do not hear our prayers, and have no knowledge of tranfactions on earth."—This man gave out, that *Hildebert* was of his mind; which obliged him, not only to difown that opinion, but alfo to *fhew*, by the *teftimony of the fathers*, that the *faints* hear our *prayers*, and that they make *interceffion* for us with GOD.

ERNULPHUS, Bifhop of ROCHESTER,

Wrote to *Waquelin*, bifhop of *Windfor*, in anfwer to a queftion, which that *bifhop* propofed to him in a conference at *Canterbury*, viz. "Whether a woman, committing *adultery* with her hufband's *fon* by a former wife, ought to be *divorced* from her hufband?" He maintained the *affirmative*; the *bifhop*, to whom he wrote, the *negative*. In this treatife, he *fhews*, that all the paffages of fcripture in which 'tis forbidden to *part man and wife*, ought only to be underftood of a voluntary feparation, between perfons who are not guilty of *adultery*; and afterwards confirms his opinion, by making it appear, that the *bifhops*, to prevent diforders, have often condemned *adulterers*, to abftain for ever from the ufe of *marriage*; that it is the *ufual cuftom of the church*; that *this punifhment* is ordained in the *penitential books*; and that a *divorce* is juftly allowed on account of *fpiritual alliance* (as being *god-fathers* and *godmothers,*

mothers, either at baptism or confirmation, and the like) although it be not expressed in scripture as *adultery*. He adds, that 'tis not unjust, that a husband should be divorced from his wife, although he be innocent of the crime committed by her; and that there are *many other causes*, for which a husband is obliged to *put away his wife*.

PETER of BLOIS, Archdeacon of BATH.

Letter 83. Advises the *bishop* of *Exeter* to declare the *marriage null*, that was contracted between *Robert* and *Ismenia* his *kinswoman*; according to the *express order* he had received from the *Pope*.

HUGH Archbishop of ROAN, *anno* 1130,

Wrote a discourse on the dignity of the *clergy*—of the manners of *clerks*—of the *celibacy* which they are obliged to observe—of the *vow of chastity*.

PETER LOMBARD,

Called *master of the sentences*. He was esteemed the chief of all the *school-divines*, and his writings were in greater repute than the *Bible*. (See *Mosheim*, edit. *Maclaine*, vol. i. p. 600. n.) This man found out that there were *seven sacraments* under the *new law*, of which *marriage* is one. He wrote a book on the *holy sacraments*, in which he treats of the *antiquity* of the *sacrament of marriage*—He enquires of what marriage consists—

CENT. XII.

consists—distinguishes a promise of *future marriage*, from marriage contracted by the *present consent* of the *parties*—gives an account of the *conditions* that ought to be annexed to such a *consent* as is *necessary for consummation of marriage*—explains the advantages of marriage, which are, *fidelity*, the *lawful* procreation of children, and the *benefit* of the *sacrament:*—he discourses of matters relative to the continency of married persons at certain times—relates divers considerations of the *fathers*, with respect to the *polygamy* of the *patriarchs:*—he treats of the *impediments*, that render persons incapable of contracting marriage, and which make their marriage *void* and of *none effect*. See *Thelyph*. vol. ii. 147, 1st edit.—p. 139, 2d edit.

He shews that a man may be divorced from his wife for *adultery*, and that they may be afterwards reconciled—that he who has committed *adultery* with a woman, may marry her after her husband's death, provided he were not accessary to his death, and did not promise to marry the wife in his life-time.—He treats of the impediment which arises from the difference of age and condition between the parties contracting.

He discourses of the injunction of *celibacy* observed by *bishops*, *priests*, *deacons*, and *sub-deacons*, and of Pope *Calixtus'* ordinance, declaring such marriages *null*.

This great *Doctor* taught, that, if the first man had not *sinned*, those who are now *damned*, would not have been brought forth into the world; and that *St. Benedict* had as clear a knowledge of God in *this world*, as the *blessed spirits* have in *heaven*.

" The *book of sentences*, which rendered
" the name of *Peter Lombard* so illustrious,
" was a compilation of *sentences*, and pas-
" sages, drawn from the *fathers*, whose
" *manifold contradictions*, this *eminent pre-*
" *late* endeavoured to *reconcile*. This *work*
" was the *wonder* of the 12th *Century*, and
" is little more than an object of *contempt* in
" ours." *Mosheim*, Macl. vol. i. p. 598. n.

Council of London, *anno* 1125.

Clerks are prohibited to cohabit with strange women.—Marriages are prohibited between relations to the *seventh* degree.

Council of Cassel, in Ireland, 1172.

Can. 1. All the *faithful* in *Ireland*, shall be obliged, not to intermarry with their near relations, but to contract *lawful* marriages.

Council of Avranches, 1172.

Can. 10. Forbids an husband to turn *monk*, whilst his wife remains in a *secular state*, unless both are too *old* to have children—the same with respect to the *wife*.

Can. 13.

CENT. XII.

Can. 13. Relates to *perquisites* claimed for the *benedictions* of *marriages*.

N. B. After *marriage* was determined to be a *sacrament*, the *church* was at no small trouble, how to reconcile the taking *money* for the *administration* of it. However, *Stephen Langton, archbishop* of *Canterbury,* Cent. XIII. made the matter easy by the following *injunction*.

"We do firmly injoin, that no sacra-
"ment of the *church* shall be denied to any
"one, upon the account of any sum of
"money, nor shall matrimony be hindred
"therefore: because, if any thing hath
"been accustomed to be given by the *pious*
"*devotion of the faithful*, we will that
"*justice* be done thereupon to the *churches*
"by the *ordinary* of the place afterwards."
See *Burn's* Eccl. Law, tit. *Marriage.*

Council of LONDON, *anno* 1175.

Can. 1. They who have entered into *holy orders*, and keep a *concubine*, whom they refuse to expel, shall be deprived of *office* and *benefice*.

Clerks below a *sub-deacon*, and are *married*, shall not be *divorced* from their *wives*, but shall no longer enjoy their *spiritual livings*.

Sub-deacons, and those in *superior orders*, who contract marriage, shall be *compelled* to *part with their wives*. The *sons* of *priests*
shall

shall be incapable to succeed their *fathers*, in the churches possessed by them.

Can. 18. *Clandestine marriages* are *forbidden*.

Can. 19. Prohibits marrying children that are not come to age of *maturity*, unless in case of *necessity*, or for promoting *peace*.

Synod of York, *anno* 1195.

Can. 4. More than *three* persons shall not be required to stand as sureties at the *baptismal font*, viz. *Two god-fathers* and one *god-mother* for a *boy*; or *two god-mothers* and one *god-father* for a *girl*.

N. B. The *rubric* of the *Protestant* church of *England*, confirmed by *act* of *parliament*, has adopted this *wise* regulation.

Can. 12. Renews the prohibitions so *often made*, that *clergymen* should keep *unchaste* correspondence with *women*, and regulates the manner of trying those who are accused of that *crime*.

Second General Council of LATERAN, 1139.

Can. 6. *Sub-deacons*, or those in *higher orders*, if they *marry*, or keep *concubines*, shall be deprived of their *offices* and *benefices*.

Can. 7. Prohibits hearing *masses* of *priests* who are *married*, or keep *concubines*—declares the *marriage* of *priests* to be *null*; and

and ordains that those who have *contracted* it, shall be *divorced* and put to *penance*.

Can. 8. Regulates the same things, with respect to *virgins* consecrated to God, if they *marry*.

Can. 17. Re-enforces the laws against marrying *relations*.

Third General Council of LATERAN, anno 1179.

Can. 7. Condemns abuses, which passed into a custom, of exacting *money* for the *benediction* of *marriages*.

Can. 11. Renews the prohibition, *so often reiterated*, with respect to the *clergy* companying with *women*; condemns *sodomites* to very severe punishments; and forbids ecclesiastical persons to frequent the monasteries of *nuns*, unless upon some *emergent* occasion.

Ivo bishop of *Chartres*, on being asked, Whether it was lawful for a man to marry his *concubine?* answered — That some *laws* forbid it, *others* have *permitted* it; and leaves the whole matter to the discretion and judgment of the *bishops*.

CENTURY XIII.

Pope Innocent III.

In a letter to the bishop of *Marsi*, he decides the following case, viz. A man married a woman, with whom he had before been *carnally* acquainted: after that, he married *another*, by whom he had had *children*. The *first woman* demands, either that he may *live* with her, or else that she may have leave to *marry another*. The *Pope* answers, "That if this man married the
" former by *verba de præsenti*, he then
" ought to return to her; but if *per verba*
" *de futuro*, they must then *both* have a *pe-*
" *nance* injoined them, and the woman be
" at liberty to marry whom she would."

N. B. By this time, the *reader* must be supposed to see, *how*, and by what *degrees*, *marriage*, and all that belonged to it, was taken out of GOD's hands, into the hands of men, and *how* the word of GOD began to be of no avail in the matter.—But to proceed.

Letter 45. He determines that *women* may come into the *church*, in a short time after their *lying-in*; but yet, if they think to *stay away* out of *respect*, their devotion is not to be *condemned*.

Letter 92. Is against the *incestuous* marriage of the *king of Castile's* daughter, with
the

CENT. XIII.

the king of *Leon*. He charges Cardinal *Rainier* to *excommunicate* them if they did not *part*.

Letter 102. He tells the chapter of *Spoletto*, that the marriage of a man, with a *concubine*, which he kept while his *wife* was *alive*, is *valid*; except it could be proved, that *one* of them had a hand in her death.

Letter 326. He gave leave to the *bishop* of *Faience* to remove to the bishopric of *Pavia*. There are very *pretty* things in this *letter* (says *Du Pin*) about the *spiritual* marriage of a *bishop* with the *church* his *spouse*. What is said in scripture of the *indissolubility* of a *carnal marriage*, he presumes may be as *well* applied to the *spiritual*. He adds, that it should seem, then, as if it were not in the power of the *Pope* to *break* the *spiritual marriage* of a *bishop* with his *church*:— and yet CUSTOM, which is the INTERPRETER OF THE LAWS, and the HOLY CANONS, always gave full power to the *holy see*, to which *alone* belong the *placing*, the *deposing*, the *translating* of bishops: wherein, he saith, the *Popes* do not exercise *human* authority, but that of JESUS CHRIST, whose *vicars* they are. Lastly, he declares that he consents to this *translation*, *merely* for the *good* which would ensue to the church of *Pavia*.

Letter 362. He decides the case of a man who was accused of *adultery* by his *wife*, thus; that judgment could not be given upon an information that was made *lite non contestata*; and all that could be done, was to *excommunicate* the man for *refusing* to make his *appearance*.

N. B. We may observe whence *ecclesiastical* courts took cognizance of *matrimonial* causes, and whence the dreadful *engine* of *excommunication* proceeded, for *contempts* of their *usurped* authority.

Letter 380. He declared a marriage *null*, because the *woman* had, *before* they were *married*, been *god-mother* to a natural son, which the man had by *another* woman.

Letters 28, 29, 30. Are about a *crooked* man, that had married a *widow*, being chosen *bishop* of *Cambray*. — He declares the election *null*.

Letter 455. A religious *vow*, made before the year of *probation*, is *valid*. That the *vow* of a *married* person ought not to be accepted, except *she* likewise, to whom he is *married*, makes a *vow* of *perpetual continence*.

Letter 458. He confirms the sentence given in favour of the church of *St. Paul*, about the *privilege* of having a *font*, and *baptizing*; which was disputed by the church of *St. Mary* of *Cervaro*, near *Monte-Cassino*.

Letter 514. Determines, that the marriage of *infidels* with such as were *akin* to them, could not be dissolved when they turned *Christians*.

Letter

CENT. XIII.

Letter 50, Book 2. Though the marriage between *infidels* be *diſſolved*, when one of them is converted to the faith, yet it is not the ſame thing of thoſe who were married while they were *believers*, when one of them becomes an *heretic* or *Pagan*.

Letter 66. He determined, that not only thoſe, who have contracted *two valid* marriages, are to be accounted *bigamous*, but thoſe too who have contracted ſuch as were *nulled*; becauſe, that although they were not in *facto bigamiſts*, for want of the SACRAMENT, yet the intention of being ſo was the ſame; and there was a *fault* committed beſides, therefore he would not have a *diſpenſation* granted to *ſuch*, as there is to *other bigamous* perſons.

Letter 178. From the *archbiſhop* of *Dioclia* and *Antivari* to the *Pope*; in which he preſents him with the orders made by the *legates* of the *holy ſee*, about the celibacy of the *clergy*—the *degrees* of *affinity* within which it is not allowable to *marry*—Laſtly—A prohibition from putting the *children* of *prieſts*, or *baſtards*, into *holy orders*.

Letter 229. *Clergymen* not to be allowed to have any *women* live with them, except they be of their *kindred*.

Letter 232. He declared, that a woman, who had taken upon her a *vow* of *chaſtity*, to avoid being *married*, but upon condition of tarrying in her own houſe, and had afterwards *married* a man, by whom ſhe had

children,

children, ought to take her *religious* habit again, and *observe* her *vow*.

Letter 261. To the bishop of *Rossano*, in which he answers divers questions. 1. That the *kindred* of a *woman* might *marry* the *kindred* of her *husband*. 2. That although *husband* and *wife* are *god-father* and *god-mother* to a child, yet they do not thereby contract any such *compaternity*, as can hinder them from *living* as *man* and *wife*. 3. The *Latin* priests might neither have *wives* nor *concubines*. Lastly—that the chaplains of *Rossano* had nothing to do with the *validity* or *invalidity* of *marriages*. —Qu? *Who* or *what*, but GOD and his *word*, have any thing to do either with the *one* or the *other?*

Letter 7, Book 5. He determined, that the *son* of a *god-father* could not marry the *daughter* of the *god-mother* to the *same* child, although he was born before they baptized the child. That if *these* two persons had *married*, they ought to be *parted*; and that *whosoever* knew of any *such thing* they ought to discover it.

Letter 48. To the *archbishop* of *Rheims*, about the design of *Philip* King of *France* to get himself *separated* from his *wife*. He wrote also to that *prince* upon the subject: he talks with him about his complaining of harder usage than other *princes* had met with on the like occasion, seeing that King *Lewis* his father, the Emperor *Frederic*, and,

CENT. XIII.

and, very lately, * *John* King of *England,* had been *separated* from their *wives,* by the judgment of their *prelates* and *estates,* which the *holy see* had, without any *scruple,* confirmed. The *Pope* answers — "They "were his *legates* who *separated* the Em- "peror *Frederic;* and that King *Lewis,* and "the *King* of *England,* were *parted* by "their *prelates,* but that was because "there had been no complaint made to "the *holy see;* which was the very reason "why the judgment was not *revoked,* "because no body protested against it: "but the matter now in hand had been "laid before the *holy see;* Pope *Celestin* had "revoked the sentence of *divorce,* and had "sent his legates into *France,* who per- "haps might have put an end to the "affair, if he had not eluded their judg- "ment: that it was in the *power* of the "*holy see,* not only to *annul* the sentence, "but likewise to use censures against those "that had given it: as Pope *Nicholas* had "done against *Gontierus* archbishop of *Co- "logn,* and *Tetgaudus* archbishop of *Treves,* "for having divorced King *Lotharius* of "*Tetberge.*"

Letter 128. Is to *William* Earl of *Mon- pellier,* who had, by the *archbishop* of *Arles,* desired the *Pope* to legitimate his children. *Innocent* proves first of all, that the legiti-

* See Rapin, vol. i. p. 262. fol. edit.

mation

mation of the *holy see* is *valid*, not only in what concerns the *spirituals* but the *temporals* too: and, becaufe this *Earl* alledges the example of the *King* of *France's* children, which *Philip* had by a wife which he took after having left *Ifemburga*, to obtain the fame favour for thofe whom he had by a wife that was married in the *fame manner*, *Innocent* tells him, there is a great deal of difference. 1. Becaufe the King of *France* by his lawful wife had a fon who was prefumptive *heir* of the crown—whereas he had no fon by his lawful wife. 2. Becaufe the King of *France* had no more from the *holy fee* than what concerned the *fpirituals*—whereas he defired it both for *fpirituals* and *temporals*. 3. Becaufe the King had not left his wife 'till divorced by the *archbifhop* of *Rheims*, and had thefe lawful iffue by the *other wife*, before the *holy fee* had forbidden him to live with her—whereas he had obferved no form nor law in the matter. 4. Becaufe the *King*, acknowledging no fuperior in *temporals*, had fubmitted himfelf to the *holy fee* in this cafe, though perhaps he could have given himfelf this difpenfation as to *temporals*;—but as for him (the Earl) who depended upon other *fovereigns*, this difpenfation could not be granted him, without incroaching upon their right, and he could not grant it to himfelf.

About the end, he begins to eftablifh the power,

CENT.
XIII.

power, which he had, not only over the temporality of *St. Peter's* patrimony, but over that of other states.

"This audacious prelate *had the honour*
"of introducing and establishing the use
"of the term *transubstantiation*, which was
"hitherto absolutely unknown. He also
"placed, by his *own* authority, among the
"*divine laws,* that of *auricular confes-*
"*sion* to a *priest.*" *Mosheim. Macl.* vol. i. p. 683.

"About the conclusion of this century
"Boniface VIII. added to the public rites
"and ceremonies of the *church*, the famous
"*jubilee*, still celebrated at *Rome*, at a stated
"period, with the utmost profusion of
"pomp and magnificence." *Mosh.* ib.

Pope INNOCENT IV. *anno* 1243.

Letter 10. To his legate in *Cyprus*, determines, that *married* priests, having the care of souls, ought not to be hindered from taking the confessions of penitents, to enjoin penances, and to act in their name.— That *fornication soluti cum soluta* was a *deadly* sin—(Qu? If his *holiness* meant any thing more by *fornication*, than the act of those who came together without the *sacrament* of marriage, as it was now called?) — that the Greeks ought not to condemn all *third* and *fourth* marriages—that the priests should not give their blessing upon *second* marriages—that they should not *marry*, so as they did,

did, within the *fourth* degree—that those *Greeks* who acknowledged that the souls of those who died, not wholly *cleansed*, might exist after death, and be *eased* by the *prayers* of the *living*, were obliged to call the place where they are—PURGATORY.

GREGORY the TENTH, *anno* 1271.

Among his other *letters*, there is one to the bishop of *Liege*, who was *deposed*, in the council of *Lyons*, for his *incontinency*.

MANUEL CHARITOPULA Patriarch of CONSTANTINOPLE.

Institut. 1. Women, forsaken by their husbands, of whom they have heard no news for *five* years together, may afterwards *marry*.

The bishop of *Pella* asks, what *penance* ought to be inflicted on *priests*, by whose negligence it happens, that the consecrated bread is eaten by *rats*? and what ought to be done, when, the priest being at the *altar*, a *mouse* happens by chance to eat the consecrated host?

We may remember, that some time ago, a *father* of the *Latin* church declared against *Berenger*, that neither *mice* nor other *vermin* would *touch* it. See before p. 113.

Qu? 4. *Laics* above 40 years old, and that have been married *twice*, and have children, may not marry again.

Qu? 6. What punishment those *priests* deserve,

deserve, who celebrate marriages in *Lent*, and what one ought to think of such marriages? Ans. Those *priests* who did it out of ignorance and simplicity, ought to bear less punishment than if they did it *wilfully*; but *such* marriages are *valid*.

Council of PARIS, *anno* 1212.

Can. 4. Prohibits the *clergy* from having *women* in their houses.

Can. 21. Forbids *monks* to lie *two* in a bed. That the *nuns* lie *single*.

Can. 14. The *abbots* not to suffer *young women* to come into *monasteries*.

Can. 20. To extirpate that *crime* which is *odious* to name.

Can. 21. To punish that disorder severely, according to the *rule* made in the *Lateran* council.

Fourth LATERAN Council, *anno* 1215, under INNOCENT III.

Can. 50. Repeals the prohibition of marriage in the second and third *degree* of *affinity*, and between children issuing from a *second* marriage and the relations of a *former* husband; and restrains the *degrees* wherein marriages were *unlawful*, to the *fourth* degree of *consanguinity*.

Can. 51. Prohibits *clandestine* marriages, and orders that the *priests* shall publish *banns* in *churches*, that so such impediments as are lawful may be objected against them.

Penalties

Penalties are also inflicted on those who countenance or authorize *incestuous* or *clandestine* marriages.

N. B. By *incestuous*, are here meant, such *marriages* as are not within the *degrees* allowed by the *canons.* The *Bible* is out of the *question.*—N. B. The origin of *banns.*

Council of OXFORD, *anno* 1222.

Can. 19. Prohibits *rural deans* from taking *cognizance* of *matrimonial* causes.

Can. 42. *Advocates,* who shall dispute the *validity* of a *marriage,* which shall be declared good by the sentence of a *judge,* shall be suspended for a year.

Council of MENTZ, *anno* 1225.

Can. 1, 2, 3. Against clerks who keep *concubines.*

Can. 5. Declares legacies of church goods, by *clerks,* to their natural children, or *concubines,* null.

Council of CHATEAU GONTHIER, *anno* 1231.

Can. 1. Prelates ought not to tolerate *clandestine* marriages, and to proceed without *delay* and without *excuse,* to the *divorcing* of those who had *contracted* them. Comp. Mat. xix. 6. and Stat. 26 Geo. II. c. 33.—the *marriage-act.*

Can. 34. Prohibits, under pain of *excommunication,* the *contracting* of marriage till

till after the *banns* have been published; that so an engagement to *marry* may be *granted,* and given in the face of the *congregation.*

Council of ARLES, *anno* 1234.

Can. 3. *Heretics* to be rooted out.

Can. 6. Condemned to perpetual imprisonment—those who will *recant*, to be delivered up to the *secular power*—every *Sunday* an *excommunication* shall be published against *heretics* and their *favourers.*

Council of L'ISLE en PROVENCE, *anno* 1251.

Can. the last. Against *clandestine* marriages.

Council of TOURS, *anno* 1236.

Can. 8. Declares those who contract *two marriages* at a time *infamous,* and to be *whipped.*

Council of LONDON, *anno* 1237.

Can. 1. Concerns the *dedication* of churches, and implies, that it derived its original from the *Old* and *New Testaments,* and has been observed by the *holy fathers* under the *New.* That it ought to be solemnized with greater dignity and care, since then they only offered sacrifices of *dead beasts,* whereas now they *offer* on the altar,

altar, by the hands of the *priest*, a living and true *sacrifice*, namely, the only *Son* of God; therefore the *fathers* have with reason ordered, that so sublime an office should be celebrated only in consecrated places, &c.

N. B. How one *lye* begets another, and how they travel on from *generation* to *generation!*

Can. 15. To prevent some marriages, which some *clerks* contracted *clandestinely*, to save their benefices, declares the children born of such marriages incapable of holding benefices.

Can. 16. Renews the ecclesiastical statutes against *clerks* who keep *concubines*.

Can. 17. Prohibits children of *clerks* from possessing the benefices of their *fathers*.

Can. 23. Care shall be taken to place able *judges*, especially in *matrimonial causes*; and that the judges of *abbots* who are in possession, shall not pass a definitive sentence, 'till after they have consulted the *bishop* of the *diocese*.—Qu? Who placed *matrimonial* causes in the hands of *ecclesiastical* judges?

Council of Cognac, *anno* 1238.

Can. 9. The *bishops* shall see that the sentences of *excommunication*, issued out by their *colleagues*, be *duly executed* in their *dioceses*.

CENT. XIII.

Can. 10. That none shall be commissioned to try *causes* of *matrimony*, but able and discreet persons.

Can. 11. Excommunicates *lay-judges,* who oblige *ecclesiastics* to plead before them.—*N. B.* How gloriously was the power of *churchmen* now increased!

> Here we may see, whate'er we see beside,
> The *laymen* bridled, and the *clergy* ride.

Council of SAUMUR, *anno* 1253.

Can. 11. Prohibits the admitting any *canon,* who is not born in *lawful wedlock:* i. e. according to the laws of the *church*.

Can. 27. Prohibits *clandestine marriages.*

Council of ALBY, *anno* 1254.

Can. 41. Prohibits *priests* from keeping *women* within the *inclosures* of the *church*.

Council of ARLES, *anno* 1260.

Can. 4. None shall contract marriage without leave of the *church.*—*Bravo!* This is *speaking out.*

Council of COGNAC, *anno* 1260.

Can. 5. Prohibits curates from marrying of *women* of *another parish,* without the *consent* of their *curate.*

Council of BOURDEAUX, *anno* 1262.

Can. 5. Those who shall contract *clandestine marriages*, both the *ministers* and *witnesses*, shall be *excommunicated*, and suspended *ab officio & beneficio*. Those *marriages* shall be reckoned *clandestine*, which are not contracted by the proper *curate* or *pastor* of the husband or the wife, with the consent of the other *curate*.

Council of LONDON, 1268.

Can. 3. Churches shall be *consecrated*.

Can. 14. Against those who obstruct the *celebration* of *matrimony*.

Can. 15. Relates to *wills* and *testaments*, and obliges the *executor* to renounce the right which he hath to plead in his jurisdiction.

Council of LANGEIS, *anno* 1276.

Can. 3. Against *clandestine marriages*.

Can. 4. Against *priests* keeping in their houses *children* born of their *concubines*, and from *bequeathing* any thing *to them*.

N. B. See 1 Tim. v. 8.

Council of BUDA, 1279.

Can. 26. Prohibits clerks from keeping in their houses the *children* which they have had whilst in *holy orders*, and declares those *children* to be the *vassals* of the *church*.

Can. 39. Reserves the cognizance of *matrimonial*

CENT. XIII.

matrimonial caufes to prudent and difcreet perfons.

Can. 4. Prohibits *ecclefiaftics* from keeping *concubines*.

Council of RAVENNA, *anno* 1286.

Can. 8. Againſt *clandeſtine marriages*.

Council of BOURGES, 1286.

Can. 2. Prohibits *clandeſtine marriages*.

Can. 3. Prohibits *ecclefiaftical* judges from cognizance of *matrimonial caufes* out of their *jurifdiction*.

Can. 24. Prohibits women inhabiting in the houſes of *monks*.

SYNODAL CANONS of PETER, Biſhop of EXETER,

Contain an inſtruction to his *clergy* about the SEVEN SACRAMENTS, and about the *celebration* of *marriage* — appeals — *queſtors*—the *relics* of ſaints—laſt *wills* and *teſtaments*—*excommunications*, &c. &c. *cum multis aliis, quæ nunc præfcribere longum eſt.*

Council of L'ISLE in PROVENCE, *anno* 1288.

Can 14. Againſt thoſe who give *poiſon* or *phyſic* to cauſe *abortion*.—Mark, reader, this horrid evil, and from whence it ſprang; even from leaving the *laws* of GOD and *nature*, for the *doctrines* and *commandments* of men!

Council of SALTZBURGH, *anno* 1291.   CENT. XIII.

Can. 1. It is ordered, that to remedy the abuse of *marriages clandestinely contracted*, there shall be *six* honest and creditable persons, of the neighbourhood or parish of the *contractors*, who shall be present, and serve as *witnesses* of the *marriage*.

The same *canon* issues forth the penalty of *excommunication, ipso facto*, against those who shall transgress this order, or shall be present at *clandestine marriages*, or shall *suffer* them to be contracted in their *houses*.—N. B. What wicked pains did these *fellows* take to bring grist to their *mill!*

WALDENSES or VAUDOIS, and ALBIGENSES.

Amidst all the darkness, superstition, and folly of *Popery*, GOD did not leave himself without witnesses of his truth. These poor people, though persecuted with all the malice and cruelty that *Hell* or *Rome* could invent, nobly stood in defence of GOD's word against the *Popish* encroachments. Their tenets were called *heresy*, and their persons *heretics*, because they opposed the *doctrines* of the scriptures to the *inventions* of men.—Among other things, they condemned the *ceremonies* used in the celebration of marriage, as having no foundation in the word of GOD—they taught—" that the
" consent of a willing couple, without the
" formality

CENT. XIII.

" formality of *sacerdotal benediction*, made a *lawful* marriage."—They did not acknowledge the *spiritual* alliance [as between godfathers and godmothers] nor the impediments of *affinity* and *consanguinity* appointed by the *church*—no more than those of public *order* and *decency* [i. e. the throwing marriage into the hands of *priests*, and the *ceremonies* invented and used thereon] thus casting a blemish on the SACRAMENT of *marriage*. That women needed no *benediction* after their lying-in [this we call *churching* of women.] That the church was wrong in prohibiting the *clergy* from *marrying*.—They *invocated* no *saints*, but worshipped GOD alone—they despised the *canonizations, translations,* and *vigils* of the *saints*—they taught, that the doctrine of JESUS CHRIST and the *apostles* is sufficient to salvation, without being obliged to observe the *laws of the church*, and that the *tradition* of the church is the tradition of the *Pharisees*—that the church of *Rome* is not the *church* of CHRIST, but a *church* of *wicked men*; and that it has ceased from being the *church* of CHRIST ever since the time of *Pope Sylvester*—*(Du Pin* calls him *St. Sylvester)*—when the *poison* of *temporalities entered* into the *church*:—they denied *purgatory*, and *transubstantiation* by the hands of a priest.

These, and other as great *heresies*, did these excellent *reformers* teach. For which an open war was carried on againſt them, under the general name of *Albigenſes*, which, after the utmoſt exertions of *cruelty*, and of the moſt barbarous *maſſacres*, ended in their *deſtruction*.—See *Moſheim, Macl.* vol. i. p. 700. Theſe might well be numbered among the champions for the word of GOD—*of whom the world was not worthy.* Heb. xi. 38. *Du Pin* ranks them among thoſe *heretics*, who ſubverted the *fundamentals* of the *Chriſtian religion*, by openly oppugning the *authority*, the *ſacraments*, the *ceremonies*, and the *diſcipline* of the *church*.

THE INQUISITION.

It may perhaps lead me for a while from the immediate and particular ſubjects of this *book*, but I cannot help obſerving here, that, in this century, appeared that *monſter* of all *monſters*, that moſt horrible, iniquitous, helliſh *tribunal*, the *Court of Inquiſition*, the moſt formidable engine of *church power* that ever was invented. It was generated between the *eccleſiaſtical courts*, and the *great whore*, mentioned Rev. xvii. 1. 5. xix. 2. and it may be truly ſaid, that of all the *abominations* of which *ſhe* has been the *mother*, this has been the moſt dangerous and deſtructive to the perſons, lives, and properties of mankind; and ſtands as a melancholy proof of the aſcendency which *prieſtcraft* and *ſuperſtition* are capable of gaining over the human mind, when creatures,

CENT. XIII.

tures, endowed with reason, could so lose all sense of *self-preservation*, as not to arise with *one consent*, and *strangle* it in its *birth*.

But the comparatively petty *tyranny* of *ecclesiastical* courts, which, from the days of *Constantine*, had been gradually subjugating the understandings of men, more and more, under the assumed and ungodly power of *churchmen*, had paved the way; and therefore we are told by *Du Pin*—Cent. xiii. p. 154. Eng. transf.—

"The *Pope* and the *Prelates*" (he might have added the *Devil*, and made it a sort of *triumvirate*) "perceiving that the *former*" [i. e. those *notorious heretics* the *Albigenses*] "contemned the *spiritual* power, and that "excommunication, and the other *ecclesiasti-* "*cal* penalties, were so far from *reducing* "them, that they rendered them the more "*insolent*, and put them upon *using vio-* "*lence*" [i. e. defending themselves when they were most inhumanly and unjustly attacked, and standing for their lives and properties] "were of opinion, that it was "lawful to make use of *force*, to see whe- "ther those who were not *reclaimed* out of "a sense to their *salvation*, might be so by "the *fear* of *punishments*, and even of *tem-* "*poral death*.

"There had already been several in- "stances of *heretics* condemned to *fines*, "*banishments*, *punishments*, and even to "*death* itself; but there had never yet been
"any

" any *war* proclaimed againſt them, nor
" any *croiſado* preached up for the *extir-*
" *pation* of them. *Innocent* III. was the
" *firſt* who proclaimed ſuch a war againſt
" the *Albigenſes* and *Waldenſes*, and againſt
" *Raymond*, count of *Thouloufe*, their *pro-*
" *tector*. War might ſubdue the *heads*,
" and reduce whole *bodies* of people; but
" it was not capable of altering the ſenti-
" ments of particular perſons, or of hin-
" dering them from teaching their doc-
" trines *ſecretly*.

" Whereupon the *Pope* thought it ad-
" viſeable to ſet up a *tribunal* of ſuch per-
" ſons, whoſe *buſineſs* it ſhould be to make
" *enquiry after heretics*, and to *draw* up
" their *proceſſes*. For this purpoſe, he
" made choice of the *Dominican* and *Fran-*
" *ciſcan fryars*, who were *newly* eſtabliſh-
" ed; to whom he gave commiſſion to
" make *exact enquiry* after *heretics*, and to
" draw up *informations* againſt them : and,
" from hence, this *tribunal* was called THE
" INQUISITION.

" By degrees the authority of thoſe *in-*
" *quiſitors* increaſed; and whereas, at the
" firſt, they only drew up the proceſs of
" *heretics*, and ſolicited the *ordinary judges*
" to condemn them, they afterwards had
" power granted them of trying the *crime*
" *of hereſy* conjointly with the *biſhops*.

" The emperor *Frederic* II. approved
" of this *tribunal*, took the *inquiſitors* into
" his

CENT. XIII.

"his *protection*, and attributed to the *ec-clesiastics* the taking cognizance of the *crime* of *heresy*; leaving only to the *secular judges*, the power of inflicting the punishment of *death* on those who were condemned.

"This *tribunal* of the INQUISITION was at first set up at *Thoulouse*, and in the other cities of *Languedoc*, where the *heresy* of the *Albigenses* and *Waldenses* had the *deepest rooting*. The *Popes* likewise set it up in *Italy*, from whence it passed, a long time after, into *Spain* and *Portugal*; but it was banished *France*, and could never be introduced into *Germany*."

CENTURY XIV.

Council of COMPEIGNE, *anno* 1304.

Can. 1. *Excommunicate* persons, and such as have contracted *clandestine marriages*, with *all* persons that procured them, or were present at them, shall not be admitted to the divine service of the *church*, nor allowed *Christian burial*.

Council of PRESBURG, *anno* 1309.

Renews the decretal of Pope *Benedict* XI. against such *clergymen* as keep *concubines*, and deprives such as are beneficed, of a *fourth* part of their *benefice*, if they observe it not.

Council

Council of COLEN, *anno* 1310.

Can. 9. Confirms the punishments on *clerks* that keep *concubines*.

Can. 10. Forbids that *clergymen* should do *public penance*.

Can. 22. None shall be present at *clandestine marriages*, but the banns of all *marriages* shall be *published*.

Council of RAVENNA, *anno* 1311.

Can. 19. That the banns of *marriages* shall be published, that the *curates* may know whether there be no impediments. *Marriages* shall not be *celebrated* from the first *Sunday* in *Advent*, till after the *octaves* of the *Epiphany*—from *Septuagesima Sunday*, till the *octaves* of *Easter*—from the day before the *Ascension*, to the *octaves* of *Pentecost*.

Council of NOGAROL, *anno* 1315.

Can. 2. Declares the children of such as have contributed to *lay taxes* upon the *clergy*, incapable of receiving *holy orders* to the *fourth generation*, and deprives their family of *Christian burial*.

Council of VALLADOLID, *anno* 1322.—
Of TOLEDO, *anno* 1323.

Can. 6. Forbids all *clergymen* to be present at the marriages of their *children* and *nephews*.

CENT. XIV.

Can. 7. Against *clergymen* who keep *concubines.*

Anno 1324. Can. 20. A *clergyman* shall not go out at night without a *candle.*—*N. B.* This must be to prevent *deeds of darkness.*

Council of SENLIS, *anno* 1326.
Can. 6. Forbids *clandestine marriages.*

Council of ALCALA, or COMPLUTUM, *anno* 1326.
Can. 2. Against clergymen who keep concubines *openly.*

Council of NARBONNE, *anno* 1374.
Can. 22. Against *clandestine marriages.*

Council of PALENZA, *anno* 1388.
Can. 3. *Married clerks* to wear the clerical crown and tonsure, if they will enjoy the privileges of their *priesthood.*
Can. 7. Against *adulterers,* and such as keep concubines *publicly.*

ENGLAND.

Council at LONDON, *anno* 1328.
Can. 8. Marriages shall not be solemnized without the publication of *banns.*

Council of LAMBETH, *anno* 1330.

Can. 5. Priests shall not celebrate marriages, which are *clandestine,* or without *publication* of *banns.*

Council of YORK, *anno* 1367.

Can 9. Against clandestine marriages, and such as are without *publication* of *banns.* See *Thelyph.* vol. ii. p. 147, n. 2d edit.

LOLLARDS.

The sect of the *Lollards* spread throughout *Germany,* and had for their leader *Walter Lollard,* who began to disperse his *errors* about 1315. *Du Pin*'s charge against them consists of many particulars—among the rest—that they despised the *sacraments of the church* (i. e. *five of Peter Lombard's seven,* of which one was *marriage* by *priests)* and derided her *ceremonies* and her *constitutions*—observed not the *fasts* of the *church,* nor its *abstinences,* and acknowledged not the *intercession* of *saints.* *Trithemius* says, that *Bohemia* and *Austria* were *infected* with them, that there were above 24,000 persons in *Germany* who held these *errors,* and that the greater part defended them with *obstinacy,* even unto *death.*

N. B. Error and *heresy* are two *ecclesiastical scare-crows,* and signify, usually, any thing which the *ruling powers* chuse to call by those names. These, with the word

CENT. XIV. word *schism*, have done special service in their day. See Index to *Thelyph*. vol. ii. tit. LOLLARDS.

CENT. XV.

CENTURY XV.

THOMAS WALDENSIS.

So called from being born at *Walden* in *Essex*. Studied at *Oxford*. Was chosen *confessor* to Henry V. King of *England*, with whom he went to *France*, and died at *Roan*, November 3, 1430.

This learned and famous Doctor stoutly opposed the *errors of Wickliffe*. He wrote a great book—intituled—" *A Doctrinale of* " *the Antiquities of the Faith of the Catho-* " *lic Church*," against the *Wickliffites* and *Hussites*, divided into three *tomes*. In tom. 2. he lays down the doctrine of the *church*, about the (seven) *sacraments*—*proves* the *real presence*, and *transubstantiation*. On the sacrament of *orders* he *proves*—that the *celibacy* of the *clergy* is according to the *spirit* and *genius* of the *holy scripture*, and agreeable to the practice of the *antient* church.

On *marriage*.—He shews that this *sacrament* may subsist between persons that observe *continence*—that it ought to be contracted according to the *forms prescribed by the church*—and with the *benediction* of the *priest*; and distinguishes between *marriages* which are *lawful* and which are *unlawful*.

This

This book is said to be the *fountain* from whence many writers of controversy, since, have drawn their arguments against *heretics* of *later* times.

ALPHONSUS TOSTATUS, Bishop of AVILA,

A most voluminous writer.—He left behind him *twenty-seven volumes folio*. He wrote a book against *Concubinary Priests*—A Treatise of *Five* Laws—of the Law of *Nature*—of the Law of *Moses*—of the Law of *Pagans*—of those of *Mahomet*—and of the * *Laws* of *Christians*.

He died *anno* 1454, aged 40 years, and was interred in the church of *Avila*, with this *epitaph*.

Hic stupor est mundi qui scibile discutit omne.
i. e.
Here is the wonder of the world, the discusser of all that is *knowable*.

ÆGIDIUS CARLERIUS, Dean of CAMBRAY,

Wrote many learned *treatises*; among others—a Treatise on the perpetual *Virginity* of the *Virgin Mary*—against the Opposers of *Images*—of the *Celibacy* of *Ecclesiastics*—and of the *Ecclesiastical Hierarchy*.

* By this it should seem, that " the *laws* of *Christians*" were supposed to be as distinct from the " *law* of *Moses*," as from the " *law* of *Mahomet*!" This is *audax* JAPETI *genus* with a witness!—See before, p. 68, n. After all, what were these " *laws* of *Christians*," but the arbitrary impositions of *fathers, popes, councils,* &c. on the rest of mankind?

Council of OXFORD, *anno* 1408.

Can. 4. Nothing shall be taught about the *sacraments*, but what is agreeable to the *doctrine of the church*.

This council, which was held under *Thomas Arundel*, archbishop of *Canterbury*, made thirteen regulations, to put a stop to the progress of *Wickliff*'s errors.

Council of SALTZBURG, *anno* 1420.

Can. 6. Excludes *bastards* from the order of the *clergy*.

Council of COLLEN, *anno* 1423.
Can. 1. Against *concubinary clergymen*.
Can. 8. Concerns *public concubinaries*.

Council of PARIS, *anno* 1429.

John of *Nanton*, archbishop of *Sens*, forbad the *licences* dispensing with the *banns* of *matrimony* to be granted easily.—With us they are *easily granted* to all who can afford to *pay* for them.

N. B. There was a council held at *Bourges, anno* 1438, but as *Du Pin* does not mention it in its place, the reader will find it, as in *Du Pin*, under the next *century*, art. 1.

Council of ANGERS, *anno* 1448.
Can. 12. Forbids *clandestine marriages*.

Council of TOLEDO, *anno* 1473.
Can. 16. Forbids to *celebrate marriage*

at any other time than what is permitted by the *laws* of the *church*, and condemns those *clergy* to be fined, who give the *nuptial blessing* at the times forbidden. See canon 62 of the church of *England*.

Can. 17. Against *clandestine marriages*.

Council of SENS, *anno* 1485.

The archbishop of *Sens* assembled a synod at *Sens*, wherein he confirmed the constitutions made in a *synod* held twenty-five years before, for the *celebration of marriages*.

One of the *errors* imputed to *Wickliff*, was, his saying, " that the causes of *di-*
" *vorce*, on account of *confanguinity* and
" *affinity*, as established by the *church*,
" are *human* constitutions, and ground-
" *less*."

One *Lailier*, a licentiate in *theology* at *Paris*, was severely persecuted, for saying,
" 1. You ought to keep the commands of
" GOD and His *apostles*; and, as to the
" commands of the *bishops*, they are no
" better than chaff, for they have de-
" stroyed the *church* by their *reveries*.
" 2. Saying *St. Francis* was rather in *hell*
" than in *heaven*. 3. I am not bound to
" believe a man is a *saint* because he is
" *canonized*, since he is *canonized* for *mo-*
" *ney*, and none are *canonized* but those
" who give *something for it*. 4. If a
" *priest* marry *clandestinely*, and come to
" me

CENT. XV.

"me and confess it, I would not enjoin him *penance*. 5. The priests of the *eastern* church do not *sin* in marrying, and I believe that neither should we *sin* in the *western* church, if we should marry. 6. 400 years ago the *priests* were forbidden to marry, by a *Pope or a butterfly*—[D'un *pape* ou un *papillon*]— I don't know whether he could do it. 7. I would give two *blancs* to him, that will produce any passage in *scripture*, whereby we are obliged to fast in *Lent*."

The faculty condemned these propositions as *heretical, erroneous, schismatical, rash*, &c.; for which *Lailier* was *excommunicated*, and would probably have fared much *worse*, if the poor man had not been put into the hands of an *inquisitor* and a *bishop*, who frightened him into a recantation.

This *century* was disgraced with the burning of *Sir John Oldcastle, John Huss, Jerome of Prague*, and other champions for the religion of the *Bible*, as *heretics*—hereby giving a deadly proof of the sad consequences to mankind, when the *ecclesiastical* and *secular* powers unite, for the maintenance of *error* and *superstition*, and of course to destroy those who dare to discover and oppose them.

CENTURY XVI.

We are now coming to the moſt remarkable *period* in all the annals of *Europe*. In *Germany* LUTHER riſes, ſees the *papacy* diſowned in *Saxony, Brandenburgh, Heſſe, Pomerania,* the greateſt part of the territories that belong to the houſe of *Lunenburg,* and moſt of the free cities. In *Sweden* and *Denmark* his doctrine is abſolutely and quietly ſettled.

In *England*, HENRY VIII. takes away the *Pope*'s power, pulls down *monaſteries,* and ſcatters the ſworn defenders of the *papal hierarchy*. His ſon *Edward* VI. builds upon his foundation, and goes on with that *reformation* which his father had begun. All this was firſt occaſioned by the preaching of *Luther*, a private *monk,* whom his enemies would have *cruſhed* with an high hand, and deſpiſed till it was too late.

Having ſeen, during a long ſucceſſion of ages, the church of *Rome* gradually riſing into its plenitude of power—all matters relative to *marriage* taken into the hands of *men,* and regulated as they thought moſt conducive to the advancement of *eccleſiaſtical intereſt* and *authority*; inſomuch that GOD's *word* was entirely aboliſhed, as having any ſhare in the *laws* which were made concerning it—one might

might expect to find, that the *reformation* would have totally changed the *face* of things, in this respect—that *marriage* would have been restored to its *antient simplicity*, and, instead of being suffered to remain on that *papistical* plan, where *Popes, councils*, and *fathers* had placed it, and as our *reformers* found it, we should have seen the *Bible* made the only rule of *faith*, in this respect, as in others, perhaps of inferior consequence to the present and eternal interests of mankind.—Whether we have reason to complain of *disappointment*, will appear in the *sequel*.

Council of BOURGES, *anno* 1438.

Referred to by *Du Pin*, Cent. XVI. c. i.

Art. 20. Against such *clergymen* as kept *concubines publicly*. It deprives them of the profits of their benefices, and declares them incapable of being promoted to any honours, dignities, and benefices, without a DISPENSATION from their SUPERIORS; and if they relapse after such DISPENSATION, they shall be out of hope of ever having *another*.

It also orders how such *superiors* shall be proceeded against, who are not careful to punish them: and as to those who ought to be deposed by the *Pope*, the *provincial councils* or their *superiors* may inform

inform against them, or send informations to the *holy see*.

It is declared, that a person who keeps *concubines publicly*, is not only he that is so declared by a sentence of *law*, or by his own confession made judicially, or by the notoriety of the fact, which cannot be concealed; but he that keeps a suspicious, or infamous woman in his house, and, being admonished by his *superior*, doth not put her away. The council also decrees the punishment of those *ecclesiastical* judges, who shall *commute* with those that keep *concubines*, or that suffer, or neglect to punish them. It enjoins *superiors* to force their *inferiors* to cast off their *concubines*, and forbids *secular judges*, yea, KINGS THEMSELVES, to hinder the proceedings of *ecclesiastical* judges against them. It also advises the *laity* to *marry*, and not live in *concubinage*.

N. B. *Concubinage* brought in no *grist* to the *Pope's* mill—for by *concubinage* we are to understand *cohabitation*, independently of *priestly* ceremony; which *cohabitation*, in process of time, grew into a *mortal sin*, though such *concubinary* parents, as they were called, might get their *marriage ratified*, and their *issue legitimated*, by a proper sum of money, and attending while a *priest* performed the *mass*, or *office of matrimony*. See *Reynold*'s Historical Essay, p. 71. See *Thelyph.* vol. ii. 155—6, 1st edit.———p. 148, 2d edit.

CENT.
XVI.

In

CENT. XVI.

In short, the *ecclesiastical* powers had now got full possession of the ordinance of *marriage*; it was now numbered among the *sacraments*; its *nullity*, except administered according to the *rites* and *ceremonies* of the church, inculcated; and we find its " *essence* made to consist, in the " *contract and in the sacrament,* not in *one* " without the other. This was said to " be the opinion of *councils, fathers,* and " *divines,* and the most *judicious* of the *ca-* " *nonists.*" See *Du Pin*, cent. xvi. p. 143. Eng. Transf. fol.

From hence arose the doctrine—" *No* " *priest no marriage*"—if no *marriage* no *obligation*—if no *obligation,* no *security* whatever to the *seduced:*—hence was derived that inundation of *whoredom* and *prostitution,* which *has been, is,* and *will be,* the *disgrace* and *curse* of this, and every other *Christian* country, where this *Popish lye* is adopted; which is so *bare-faced,* as not to *dare* to appeal to a single text of scripture for its defence and support.

On their part, the *lawyers* defined marriage to be " a *lawful* and perpetual union " of man and wife, in order to the pro- " creation of children, which includes a " partnership of life and goods."

This definition looks fairly, but the *grass* which conceals the *snake* is in the word *lawful*; and on due examination we shall find, that the *civil* and *ecclesiastical* laws,

laws, which, from the days of *Conftantine*, were entering into an *alliance* for the fupport of *church power*, againft the natural rights and liberties of mankind, both agreed to define that to be *lawful*, which was made fo by the legiflative contrivances of *human power* and *policy*.

What is *lawful* according to the fcripture, and in God's fight, would have been a dangerous queftion to their whole *fyftem*, and muft have laid their *Popes, councils, divines, canonifts,* and *cafuifts,* under the moft unfurmountable difficulties to maintain their *plan*. They feem to have feared and dreaded the teftimony of the *pure* fcripture, as a *thief* would dread the *teftimony* of a *witnefs* that could *hang* him.— They feldom mention that of the holy fcripture, but they couple it with *tradition* and the fathers; which *two laft* they introduce, as the people in *Bengal* are faid to introduce their *interpreters* before the *European* judges, in order to miflead them by falfe interpretations of what the witneffes depofe.

As for this country—we cannot eafily forget can. 4. of the *council* of *Oxford*, *anno* 1408, by which it was decreed, that " nothing fhall be taught about the *facra-* " *ments*, but what is *agreeable* to the *doc-* " *trine of the church*." Here was a ftop put to all enquiry upon the fubject, on the footing of *divine revelation*; and thus the

the *man of sin* placed *himself in the temple of* GOD, *exalting himself above all that is called* GOD, *or worshipped.* See 2 Thess. ii. 4.

MARTIN LUTHER.

At length, *Martin Luther* arose—He opened his *Bible*—by the light of this, he enabled *numbers* to see, as he did himself, the monstrous iniquity, that, for so *many ages*, had been deceiving the *Christian* world. He had, at first, in a manner, *all the world* against him, and he was persecuted with all the malice that could be poured out upon him. He was an instrument, every way fitted for the work he had to do —vehemence of temper—unshaken courage —invincible resolution—were in his composition—these, with *truth* on his side, proved too hard for all the efforts of, what was then called *legal authority*;—the *Pope* —the *Emperor*, with other *kings* and *princes* of the earth, in vain opposed; he fairly set them at defiance, and, in the face of *difficulty, danger,* and, as it were, of *death* itself, was the great instrument, in the hands of Providence, to break off the yoke of *papal* power, and to loose the bands of *ignorance, error,* and *superstition*, from the necks of many countries.

He was wonderfully preserved, from the time when he published his first thesis against *indulgences* at *Wittemberg, anno* 1517,

1517, 'till his *death*, which happened at *Isleben*, anno 1546, a space of 29 years.

It would be beside my present purpose, to enter farther into *Luther's* history, than is necessary to elucidate the subjects of this book; but we may learn this useful lesson from it—that *intrepidity* in the cause of *truth*, however offensive *to them that live in error*, and to those who chuse their own *delusion to believe a lye* (see 2 Pet. ii. 18. and 2 Thess. ii. 11.) is not to despair of meeting with success in the end.

Three of *Luther's* noble and scriptural positions, with respect to *marriage*, which were censured by the divines at *Paris*, held at the *Mathurins*, anno 1521, were as follow: " 1. That * *matrimony* is not a *sacrament* of " CHRIST's institution, but invented by " *men*." " 2. That the union between " the *man* and *woman* ought to hold, al-" though it be made contrary to *human* " laws." " 3. That the priests ought to " approve all marriages contracted against " the *ecclesiastical* laws, with which the " *Popes* can dispense, except the *mar-*" *riages* of those that are expressly for-" bidden in scripture."

All the *doctors* in the assembly determined *Luther's* doctrine " to be proper

---

* Meaning, doubtless, that execrable *farce*, which the *priests* had been acting since the days of INNOCENT III. and which was *now* called—" THE FORM " OF THE SACRAMENT."

" only

CENT. XVI.

"only to *deceive simple people*—injurious
"to all the *doctors*—derogatory from the
"*power* of the *church*, and *hierarchical*
"*order*—openly schismatical—contrary
"to the scripture, whose sense it cor-
"rupts—blasphemous against the *Holy*
"*Spirit*—pernicious to the *Christian* com-
"monwealth—and so it ought to be sup-
"pressed, the writings which contain it
"to be burnt, and the *author* forced, by
"all *lawful* means, to recant—for that
"*all his doctrine* contained detestable *errors*
"both in *faith* and *manners*."

Never was man who experienced more *abuse* than M. *Luther*.—The *Popish* rulers saw, very plainly, that the *doctrines* which he had set forth in his *writings*, were too well founded on the authority of the scripture, to be shaken by fair and plain argument. They therefore essayed two modes of refutation, which, backed by the credit they themselves were in with the ignorant vulgar, they imagined would answer the purpose which they despaired of from fair argument.

One of these was, devising scandalous and opprobrious terms for the *writings* themselves, which implied great mischiefs to the *church* from the consequences of *Luther*'s "damnable and antichristian "errors," as they called the doctrines which he set forth.

The other was, raking together all the personal

personal scandal they could, in order to vilify and blacken the author in the estimation of mankind, and thus shake the credit of his *writings* in the public opinion.—In what manner this is set forth in the canon of *St. Victor*, may be seen in the *Gen. Dict. Hist.* & *Crit. Art.* LUTHER. See before vol. ii. 164, n. 1st edit.—154, n. 2d edit.

However powerful such methods as these may prove, in vulgar, weak, low, ignorant, and malicious minds, yet what do they amount to in the eyes of dispassionate, moderate, and considerate men? *These* will always reflect, that the merit or demerit of any writing, is to be demonstrated by *itself*, and to be gathered by a sober, attentive, unprejudiced, and deliberate perusal of it; not from this or that *epithet*, which malice, prejudice, and ignorance may have bestowed upon it; this, perhaps, from mere report of those who have never red a line of the book in question, and who owe, very probably, their opinions to the reports of others as ignorant as themselves.

The meanest, and lowest, and most wicked of all, is, the *second* experiment, which was tried on *Luther*'s personal character. This doubtless had its effect with many empty and ignorant professors, who had not recollection enough to make them reflect on its total *inconclusiveness*, with respect to the *truth* or *falshood* of the doctrines which *Luther* had advanced. His attack on the villainous traffic of *indulgences*—on the doctrine of *purgatory*—the worship of the *Virgin Mary* and the *saints*—the merit of *works*—the papistical schemes of *celibacy* and *matrimony*—&c.—had little to do with all they could say against *Luther* himself. The truth or falshood of what he said, did not in the least depend on the *man*, but on the *word of* GOD, on which he rested the whole evidence of what he published.

Luther full well knew the truth of these observations in his own mind, and therefore all that was said against *him* and his *writings,* was treated with deserved contempt.

He still had a friend in the *Elector* of *Saxony;* who, foreseeing that the *Emperor* was about to make a bloody edict against *Luther,* and that he could protect him no longer after that, nor suffer him in his countries, without bringing trouble upon himself from the *Emperor,* resolved to have him taken, and put into a *castle,* where he might lie concealed, and no man know where he was; which was accordingly done. For when *Luther* went to *Eysenac, May* 3, and was passing through a forest in his way to *Wittemberg,* he was set upon by some horsemen in disguise, who threw him down, and took him, as it were by force, to carry him into the

castle

castle at *Wittemberg*, where he lay concealed nine months.

While *Luther* was shut up in his *castle*, which he called his *hermitage* and his *Patmos*, he composed several books, to maintain his opinions, and to destroy the *discipline of the church*, threatening the *Pope* and the *bishops*, if they did not change their customs, after they were warned by his writings, GOD would permit others to oblige them to it.

It is not to be wondered at (says *Du Pin*) that *Luther*'s doctrine, which was so favourable to *concupiscence*, should meet with many followers—that the *monks* left the *cloysters*, and dispensed with the observation of their *vows*; that the *priests married*, and the *people* were pleased, to see themselves discharged of all that was *penal* by the laws of the *church*, as *fasting, confession, penance,* &c. and embraced greedily these *novelties: Caroloftadius* was one of the first, that gave the *priests* an example of *marrying*. *Justus Jonas*, provost of *Wittemburg*, and *Bernard Veltkirck*, pastor of *Kenbergen*, did the same, as also *John Buginhagius*, who had been a schoolmaster at *Treptow* in *Pomerania*, but then settled at *Wittemburg*. *Veltkirck* was accused of the matter before the *Elector of Mentz, Archbishop of Magdeburgh*, and *Veltkirck* made an apology to him, to *justify* what he had done.

CENT.
XVI.

Luther fcrupled not to defend his doctrines in many writings, in which he feverely attacked the *Pope* and the *bifhops*; he accufes the latter of *ignorance, debauchery,* and *tyranny*—of being enemies to the *gofpel,* and the *truth*—of being *idolaters,* becaufe they followed the *traditions* of men, and worfhipped their idol the *Pope.* He faid that *monafteries, cathedral* and *collegiate churches,* are the *gates of hell,* and *fhops* * *of ufelefs ceremonies.* He declaims againft *celibacy* and *vows*—" hiding his
" *malignity* (fays *Du Pin*) under an ap-
" pearance of *zeal* for the truth, and cit-
" ing feveral texts of fcripture to fhew,
" that the doctrine and behaviour of the
" bifhops of his time, were oppofite to
" thofe which *St. Paul* requires in a *bi-*
" *fhop.* Laftly, he fays his defign is to
" perform the office of a public herald,
" to make it manifeft every where, that
" the *bifhops,* which govern the greateft
" part of the world, are not of GOD's ap-
" pointment, but by the delufion of *Sa-*
" *tan,* and by error and traditions of men,

---

* It would have reflected great honour on the *reformation,* if all *thefe fhops* had been *fhut up* entirely, and their revenues, which are *immenfe,* been properly appropriated to the poor parochial *clergy;* the indigence of many of thefe is a *fcandal* to the *nation,* but hardly a greater, than, that *others* have to fay—

Nos numerus fumus, fruges confumere nati. HOR.
But we, mere cyphers in the book of life,
Born to confume the fruits of earth. FRANCIS.

" and,

"and, in one word, the *nuncios* and *vicars*
"of the *devil*."

There lived in the *sixth century* one *Gildas*, furnamed the *Wife*, who was made *abbot* of *Bangor*; this man was born in *England*, anno 520, and by his writings we find, that, from his time to *Luther's*, *churchmen* were no *changelings*; for of the *clergy* of *England* *Gildas* writes — "*England* has
"*bishops* enough, but they are either *fools*,
"or *ministers* to the paffions of the great,
"or unchafte men — it has *clergy* enough,
"but, for the moft part, they have only
"the *name* of *paftors*, and are, at the bottom, *wolves* prepared to kill the fouls
"of their *sheep*; they never think of doing good to the people, but *only* how to
"*fill their own bellies*. — They feek for
"*churches*, but it is *only* out of a defire of
"*filthy gain* — they teach the people, but
"at the fame time they give them bad examples — they very feldom offer facrifice,
"and never go to the altar with a clean
"heart — they flatter the people in their
"crimes, and feek only to fatisfy their
"paffions — they very feldom fpeak the
"*truth* — they defpife the poor, and make
"court to riches — they canvafs for and
"purchafe *ecclefiaftical* offices, &c. He
"concludes with a prayer to GOD, to
"preferve the fmall number of good paftors that was left." See *Du Pin*, cent. 6. tit. *Gildas*.

CENT. XVI.

Luther's writings gave great offence, and raised up many *answerers;* among the rest he had a *royal* adversary, Henry VIII. King of *England*, who, for the book which he wrote against *Luther*, was honoured by the *Pope* with the title of *defender of the faith*, which has ever since been given to our *kings*.

However, nothing could daunt *Luther's* truly heroical spirit; he found, that all the calumny and abuse from his enemies, and with which they loaded him in their attacks upon his writings, tended to little else than to expose the nakedness of their cause, and but badly supplied the place of rational and scriptural arguments, he therefore was no more troubled at them, than at the whistling of the wind.—His pen was kept constantly at work: and in *anno* 1522 the *Pope* sent his *nuncio Cheregatus* to the *diet* of the *empire*, held at *Nuremburg*, to declare, that though he was
" comforted to think that *Luther's* doc-
" trine was so visibly *bad*, that he could
" not believe it would be *tolerated*, yet
" this *poisonous* plant had taken root—that
" it appeared strange, that so large and re-
" ligious a nation as *Germany*, could be
" seduced, in so great a part of it, by a
" *wretched fryar*, who had *apostatized* from,
" and left the way, which our LORD, the
" *apostles, martyrs,* and so many illus-
" trious persons for *doctrine* and *holiness*,
" and

"and laſtly, their *anceſtors*, had followed
"to that very time—that *Luther* ſtill con-
"tinued to teach and put out *books* full of
"*errors*—that he takes the ſame methods
"to ſeduce the people that *Mahomet* uſed;
"for, as *Mahomet* allowed men to have *ſe-*
"*veral wives*, and divorce them when
"they pleaſed, ſo *Luther*, to draw *monks*,
"*nuns*, and laſcivious *prieſts* to him, he
"allowed them to *marry*.

"That having repreſented theſe things
"to them, he exhorted the *princes, pre-*
"*lates*, and *people*, to rouſe up themſelves
"to oppoſe the injuries which the *Lu-*
"*therans* do to God and to *religion*—that
"the *Pope*'s ſentence and the *Emperor*'s
"edict ſhould be executed—that *Luther*
"ſhould not be allowed to *defend* what he
"hath taught about matters of faith, be-
"cauſe moſt of the *truths* which he op-
"poſeth, have been determined by *general*
"*councils*, and ſuch things ought never to
"be called in queſtion, as have been *once*
"*approved* by thoſe *councils*, and *all the*
"*church*."—N. B.

The *diet* anſwered the *Pope* very reſpect-
fully—at the ſame time giving him to underſtand, that they did not chuſe to enter
upon the violent meaſures, with reſpect to
the *Emperor's edict* and the *Pope's ſentence*
againſt *Luther*, which *his holineſs* had recommended—" As to the advices which
"the *Pope* had deſired, that, they did
"not

"not mean to treat only about the bu-
"finefs of *Luther*, but alfo concerning
"the extirpation of many other errors,
"abufes, and vices, *rooted by cuftom and
"time*, and maintained by the *ignorance*
"of fome, and *malice* of others.

They then fpeak of taking away the *liberty* of the *prefs*, that "*Luther*, and his
"followers, might not write, print, or
"put any thing out in public—that the
"*magiftrates* fhould appoint men, of *pro-
"bity* and learning, to licenfe *new books*,
"and without this, no *new books* fhould
"be *publifhed*; and thus things would be
"*kept quiet*, till a free *council* could be
"called, with confent of the *Emperor*, in
"fome convenient place in *Germany*.

" As to the priefts which are *married*,
"and the *monks* who have left their *con-
"vents*, they fhould be punifhed by their
"*ordinaries* according to the *canons*, by
"deprivation of their benefices, or the
"like, fince the *civil* laws had declared
"nothing againft them."

The *Nuncio*, in his reply, faid, "that
"for the future, they fhould put in exe-
"cution the decree of the *council* of *La-
"teran*, by which it is forbidden to *print*
"any *book* about *matters of religion*, that
"had not been allowed by the *ordinary*."
About the matter of *married priefts*, he
faid—" the anfwer of the *diet* did not dif-
"pleafe him, if it had not this claufe at
"the

"the end, That the *breakers* of their *vows*, if they committed any crime, should be punished by the *secular magistrates*, pretending that it was contrary to the liberties of the *church*, and that the judgment of such persons belonged to the *ecclesiastical* judges."

After this the *diet* sent a *memorial*, of "an hundred grievances," to the *Pope*. Some of which were, about *constitutions*—they complained, that there was too great a number of *human constitutions*, about things which are neither commanded nor forbidden by the *commandments* of GOD; among others, "the hindrances of *kindred* and *affinity, legal* and *spiritual*—about *marriage*, abstinence from *meats*, &c. which they *dispensed* with for *money*; by which means, they got great sums out of *Germany*, besides the *scandals* and other evils which this multitude of laws caused."

They also complained of the incroachments of *ecclesiastical* judges, in *laymen's* causes, and the malversations which they committed in their *judgments*—of the exactions of the *clergy* for the *sacraments*, and also for *licences* to keep a *concubine*.— Also of the faculties given to the *Pope's legates* and *Nuncios* to legitimate *bastards*, &c. &c.

They told the Pope, that, "if he gave them not satisfaction, they were resolved

CENT. XVI.

"solved not to suffer these charges, nor those of *indulgences*, which freed men from *punishment* for *money*; they would seek means to release themselves from them."

This resolution of the *diet* of *Nuremberg*, was made into the form of an *edict*, and published *March* 6, 1523.

Luther's exhortations were soon followed with effects. The same year *Leonard Coppen*, a *burgess* of *Targaw*, took away *nine nuns*, on a *Good Friday*, among which was *Catherine Bora* (whom *Luther* married *two years* after) from the nunnery of *Nimptschen*, and carried them to *Wittemberg*. This action (says *Du Pin*) *Luther* dared to extol, in a book in the *German* language, where he has the impudence to compare that deliverance, to that of the souls which CHRIST delivered by his *death*.

Luther, desiring utterly to ruin the *monastic* orders, and mix them with the public, made a kind of *manifesto* in the *German* tongue, which he intitled, "The Common Treasury;" in which he affirms, that there ought to be a *treasury* made out of all the revenues of the monasteries, *bishoprics*, and *chapters*, and in general out of all *ecclesiastical benefices*, and be given partly to the *pastors and preachers*, and other parts to different beneficial and charitable *uses*.

Zuinglius made no less progress in *Switzerland*, than *Luther* did in *Saxony*. He taught

taught that *marriage* is allowed to all the world, and no man is obliged to make a *vow* of *chastity*, and that *priests* are not at all obliged to live unmarried.—That the power which the *Pope* and *bishops* assumed to themselves, is a piece of pride, which hath no foundation in the scriptures.—That the *character* which the *sacraments* are said to impress, is a modern invention, of which the scripture makes no mention.

John Faber, chief vicar of the *bishop* of *Constance*, who opposed *Zuinglius* at the conference of *Zurich*, maintained, that where a doctrine had long been settled in the *church*, and authorized by the practice of all nations, such customs *ought not to be abolished by any allegations out of the scriptures*, or *pretences that they are contrary to them.*—*Zuinglius* replied, that we ought not to regard how long a thing has been, or has not been in use; but observe only whether it be agreeable to the *truth*, or *law* of God: to which custom could not be opposed.—N. B.

August 23, 1522, *Zuinglius* presented, in his own name, and in the name of many of his followers, a petition to the *bishop* of *Constance*, to intreat him to *allow*, at least to tolerate, the *marriage* of *priests*. He wrote also a letter, against such *impediments* of marriage, as were thought to be made by *spiritual affinity*.

CENT. XVI.

The *Pope's legate*, not satisfied with the decrees of the diet of *Nuremberg*, held an assembly at *Ratisbon*, with some *princes* and several *bishops*, where it was decreed, that there should be *no alterations* in the celebration of the *mass, administration* of the *sacraments*, and other *ceremonies* of the *church*, or in other *antient usages*—that the *marriages* of *monks* and *priests* should be hindered, and those *punished* that should do the *contrary*—that *printers* should not commit any book to the *press*, till it had been *examined* and *approved*—that no *prince* should entertain a *Lutheran* in his dominions—that *priests*, who keep *concubines*, shall be severely punished—that *marriages* shall be *celebrated* in a *full congregation* in the *church*, unless there be a necessity to ask the *bishop*'s consent, except in *Lent*, the last weeks of *Advent*, at the feast of *Easter*, *Whitsuntide*, and the *Nativity*, and their *octaves*, and the *Rogation* days—that *monks* and *priests* which *marry*, shall be proceeded against, and if the ordinaries neglect to do it, the *Pope* shall appoint *judges* to punish the *guilty*.

About this time arose great troubles in *Germany*, greatly owing to the disputes and controversies among the *Protestants* themselves. Still *Lutheranism* increased, and settled itself in several cities. The *Elector* of *Saxony*, the *Landgrave* of *Hesse*, the *Duke* of *Brunswick*, professed it; the city of *Strasburg* received it; and the *Senate* of that city maintained the *married clergy*, in opposition to the *bishop*.—In almost all the states of the *Empire*, *Lutheranism* was preached, and gained many followers.

In the same year 1525, *Luther* married *Katherine Bora*, a person of quality, who had been a *nun*, and was taken (as before is mentioned) out of the *nunnery* of *Nimptschen*, in 1523; he defended the fact, without *blushing*, in the face of all the world, and had the *boldness* to advise the *archbishop* of *Mentz* to do the like.

Diet of Augsburg, 1530.

The *Emperor* published the decree of the Diet, which ordered, " that the doc-
" trine of *justification by faith* should be
" rejected — that the *sacraments* of the
" church should be preserved in the same
" *number* and manner as formerly—that
" the *ceremonies* and other usages of the
" *church* should be observed—that married
" *priests* and *clerks* should be deprived of
" their benefices, unless they would leave
" their wives."

Henry VIII. King of *England*.

We must now go back a little, in point of time, in order briefly to state the beginning and progress of *reformation* in this *country*.

Henry VII. married his eldest son *Arthur,* prince of *Wales*, to *Katherine* the
daughter

Cent. XVI.

daughter of *Ferdinand,* king of *Arragon*—*Nov.* 14, 1501. *Arthur* dying in a few months after, it was promised that *Katherine* should be married to *Henry* duke of *York,* the king's *second son.*

But because this could not be done without a *dispensation, Pope* Julius II. was sued to for one; who granted it, by his *Bull,* bearing date *December* 26, 1503, wherein he recites—" That *Katherine* had
" been married to *prince Arthur,* and that
" perhaps this marriage was consum-
" mated—that nevertheless, *Arthur* being
" dead, *Henry* his brother and she desired
" to be married together; whereupon, to
" preserve peace among *catholic kings* and
" *princes,* he *dispensed* with the *impediment*
" of *consanguinity* in *Henry* and *Katherine,*
" all *ordinances* and *apostolic constitutions*
" *notwithstanding;* he allowed them to
" *marry,* and, if they were already *married,*
" he confirmed it."—See *Lev.* xviii. 16.

After this *dispensation, Henry,* who was still under age, was married to his *brother's wife.*—See *Thelyph.* vol. ii. 1st edit. p. 76, n. —p. 70, 2d edit. and p. 13, n.

Tis not known upon what account his father obliged him to enter a *protestation* against this marriage, *June* 27, 1505, before *Fox,* bishop of *Winchester;* " that,
" being of age, he now revoked the mar-
" riage, which he had made with his *bro-*
" *ther's widow;* that he thought it *null,* and
" would

"would have it *legally dissolved.*" Nevertheless it remained still as it was.

Henry VII. dying *April* 7, 1509, the young *king* caused the validity of his marriage to be examined by his *council*; and *Warham*, archbishop of *Canterbury*, was hardly brought to approve it; but the contrary opinion being the stronger, the *king* married *Katherine* publicly, *June* 25, 1709. This *princess* was with *child* several times, but either *miscarried*, or the issue lived but a little while, except one daughter, *Mary*.

Henry lived with *Katherine* till 1525, without any scruple about his marriage, for he did not think of the divorce till 1526. What moved him to begin is not certainly known. He only pretended *conscience*. The distaste which he took to *Katherine*'s infirmities did contribute to it, but the love which he entertained for *Anne Boleyn* fixed his resolution more than all the rest, to require a *divorce* from *Katherine*, that he might marry *Anne*.

Cardinal Wolsey, out of revenge for some treatment he had received from the emperor *Charles* V. nephew of queen *Katherine*, resolved to make king *Henry* an irreconcileable enemy to the *emperor*, confirmed *Henry*'s scruples about the lawfulness of his marriage; well knowing, that as *Katherine* was sister of *Joan* of *Arragon*, the mother of *Charles* V. it would be an horrid affront, that would fall upon the whole

whole family, to have her defpoiled of her quality of *Queen*, her daughter *Mary* thereby declared illegitimate, and incapable of inheriting the *crown* of *England*.

The whole affair may be feen in *Du Pin*, and *Burnet* Hift. Ref. at a much greater length than it is at all to my purpofe to mention here. I would only obferve, that after much chicanery and difputation, among divines and cafuifts, in almoft all the countries of *Europe*, the queftion was decided againft the poor *Queen*, and a fentence of divorce pronounced by *Cranmer*, archbifhop of *Canterbury*, as *legate of the Holy See*, May 23, 1533. Five days after which, king *Henry*'s marriage with *Anne Boleyn* was confirmed, fhe came to *London* in triumph, May 29, made a magnificent entrance, and was proclaimed *Queen* on the 30th, and the *King* commanded all his fubjects not to give *Katherine* the name of *queen*.—He alfo caufed her to be importuned not to ftand on the validity of the *marriage*, but all in vain.

News being carried to *Rome*, whither *Katherine* had appealed, incenfed that court againft *Cranmer*; the *Pope* made all his proceedings void, denouncing *excommunication* againft the *King* and *Anne Boleyn*, if they did not appear at *Rome* before the end of *September*, or if they parted not before that time.

Few

Few among the Protestants favoured the king's cause, or approved of his divorce from *Katherine*. *Melancthon*, and the other *Lutheran* divines, held that the marriage with her was *valid*. *Oeclampadius*, *Zuinglius*, and *Calvin*, asserted the nullity of the marriage, grounded on the prohibition in *Leviticus*. Several books were put out, for and against the marriage of *Henry* with *Katherine*, and the question was hotly disputed between the *divines* and *casuists*.

At *Rome* the affair was debated in a consistory, May 23, 1534, and of twenty-two *cardinals*, nineteen were of opinion, that the *marriage* of *Katherine* with *Henry* was good, and the *divorce null and void*.—He was enjoined to take her again for his wife, and forbidden to continue his separation from her any longer.

This proceeding laid the foundation of abolishing the *Pope*'s power in *England*, and occasioned many *acts of parliament* for that purpose; but *Popery* still remained, and some of its most horrid cruelties placed in the power of the *king*. They also settled the succession of the crown upon the children that should be born of *Anne Boleyn*; and the princess *Mary*, the daughter of *Katherine*, was excluded.

Anne Boleyn did not long enjoy her dignity: the *king*, being enamoured with *Jane Seymour*,

Cent. XVI.

Seymour, found a means to get rid of his wife *Anne*, by accusing her of *adultery*; for which she was condemned to *death*.

Before this sentence was *executed*, she was forced to declare, before the *archbishop* of *Canterbury*, and the *ecclesiastical court*, that, before she married the *king*, there was a promise or contract of marriage between her and the lord *Percy*, who was then become earl of *Northumberland*; and, upon this declaration, *Cranmer* passed a *sentence*, by which her marriage with the *king* was declared *null*, and her daughter *Elizabeth* declared illegitimate, as *Mary* the daughter of *Katherine* had been. *Anne* was beheaded, May 19, 1536.

The next day after her *death*, *Henry* married *Jane Seymour*, with whom he was passionately in love. The *princess Mary* was received into favour, after acknowledging in writing that the *king* was *supreme head* over the church of *England*, and that the marriage of her mother was *null* and *incestuous*.

In the following *parliament* a very severe law was made, *anno* 1536, against those who should acknowledge the power of the *Pope*.

The *convocation* of the *clergy* agreed on several matters, by which the Popish doctrines were established, as *transubstantiation*, auricular confession, and that the *ceremonies* are to be retained as good and commendable;

able; with many other matters of the like fort. Thefe were all confirmed by the *king*.

Neverthelefs he did not fpare the *abbies* and *nunneries*, but diffolved them all, and * feized their revenues.

In 1539 he caufed fix articles to be drawn up, and to be eftablifhed by the parliament. One among which was, that it is not lawful for thofe in *holy orders to marry* —the marriages of *priefts* declared void, and thofe ordered to be punifhed with *death* who fhould *marry*, as well as thofe who, by preaching, writing, or open difcourfe, fhould declare or maintain it *lawful* for them fo to do.

Jane Seymour, the third wife of *Henry*, dying in 1537, two days after her delivery of *Edward* (afterwards *Edward* VI.) the *king*, by the *advice* of *Cromwell*, whom he had made his vicegerent in *fpiritual* affairs, and *lord privy feal*, and had lately created earl of *Effex*, married *Anne of Cleves*; but the *king* took a diftafte to her, and, immediately after his marriage, endeavoured to break it. Poor *Cromwell* was difgraced— accufed of *herefy*, and other offences, for which he was beheaded, July 28, 1540.

---

* I have been told, that the only one that efcaped, was the little *convent* of *St. Katherine's* near the *Tower*, which ftill confifts of a *Superior* (now called the *Mafter*) and of *Brothers* and *Sifters*.

He was no sooner condemned, than the *king* sought to dissolve his marriage with *Anne of Cleves*. The causes alledged for it were, that she had been before contracted to the *marquis* of *Lorrain*—that the *king*, having married her against his inclination, had never consummated the marriage. Upon these reasons, the *parliament* declared the marriage *null*, and *Cranmer*, and the rest of the *clergy*, were of the *same opinion*, and so sentence was given *July* 9th.

The *queen* consented to it, and remained ever after in *England*. The *king*, soon after, married *Katherine Howard*, whom he *loved passionately*.

The *commissioners*, whom the *king* had appointed for *ecclesiastical* affairs, drew up a long instruction, in which they owned all the *Catholic doctrines* except the *Pope's supremacy*. They regulated all the *ceremonies and rites* then in use, according to the practice of the *primitive church*. They also held *free-will*, and the *merit* of *good works*.

Doctor Barnes, and some others, having preached against these doctrines, were condemned to death as *heretics*. In short, *Henry* punished with death, *Lutherans*, and the defenders of the *Pope's supremacy*, alike.

Katherine Howard was discovered to lead a loose life; which being proved against her, she was beheaded, *February* 12, 1542.

King *Henry*'s sixth wife was *Katherine Parr*, the widow of *Nevil lord Latimer*, whom he married in *July* 1543. Though she favoured the *Protestants*, yet the *king* did not stop the execution of the *Lutherans*, or *Sacramentarians*. *Henry* to his death continued in the same judgment, as to his *religion*, but would never return to the church of *Rome*, and in this disposition he died, January 27, 1547, being fifty-six years old, having reigned thirty-seven years and nine months, and having passed many laws, which made him a *Pope*, and the *archbishop of Canterbury*, and the rest of the *bishops* and *clergy* in *convocation*, so many *Popes* under him.

Diet of RATISBON, *anno* 1541.

Before we proceed any farther in the affairs of religion in *England*, it will be necessary for us to return to the *Continent*, in order to acquaint ourselves with those transactions, which may be said to have had so great an effect with regard to religion in general, and particularly afterwards in *England*.

The diet of *Ratisbon* was attended by the emperor in person, and by all the *princes* of the *empire*, either in *person* or by *deputies*. The *Pope* sent to it cardinal *Contaremus*, a man famous for *wisdom* and *profound learning*.

CENT. XVI.

At this *diet* there was a conference appointed, between the *Catholic* and *Protestant* divines, nominated by the *emperor* for this purpose. He chose for the *Catholics*—*Julius Pflugius*, *John Eckius*, and *John Groppen*:—And, for the *Protestants*—*Philip Melancthon*, *Martin Bucer*, and *John Pistorius*.

A book was delivered to the *collocutors*, thought to be drawn up by *Groppen*, which contained 22 articles.

Art. 15. Is about the *sacrament* of *marriage*, and tells us, " That it is *appro-*
" *priated* to *Christians*; that it is grounded
" upon the words of CHRIST, when the
" inseparable union of *male and female* is
" commanded, and the outward conjunc-
" tion of them is the *element*, and the *vir-*
" *tue* consists, in acknowledging that *man*
" *and wife* are joined together by the *au-*
" *thority* of GOD, and have received a
" *grace* which makes their *union lawful*."

Art. 21. Concerns the *ecclesiastic* discipline of the *clergy*, and it is said, " That
" if the latter *canons*, which obliged *priests*
" to live *unmarried*, be retained, the an-
" tient censures against *priests* that keep
" *concubines*, ought to be revived." Some of the antient rules, concerning the *continence* of *priests*, are here set down.

These, and others of the *articles*, were objected to by the *Protestants*. The *Pope*'s legate gave an answer which they did not like;

like; this provoked the *Protestants*, displeased the *emperor* and the *Catholic princes*; but the *legate* said, that the *articles* should be generally referred to the judgment of the *Pope*, and the *Apostolical See*, in a *council*, to which he remitted that business entirely.

While the *emperor* and king of *France* were waiting for the calling of a *general council*, they consulted the *divines* of the *University* of *Louvain*, which was one of the most famous in *Europe*, who drew up 32 articles against the *innovators*, Nov. 6, 1544.

Art. 18. *Marriage*, lawfully *contracted*, and *consummated*, among *Christians*, cannot be dissolved, though it happens to either of them, who are so joined together, that they commit *adultery*, or become *barren*, or be *heretics*.

Art. 19. It was never allowed to a *Christian* man to marry again after a *divorce*, so long as the *woman* from whom he was *parted* be *alive*.

Art. 20. That *marriages* contracted against the *canons*, which have laid down the invincible impediments, are *null*.

Art. 32. That it is good to make *monastic* and other *vows*, and that being made they are obligatory before GOD.

The divines of *Paris*, by the *king's* order, *March* 10, 1542, composed 25 articles of faith.

Art. 11. It is not to be doubted but the

the *saints* in heaven and earth work miracles.

Art. 12. It is a pious thing, and agreeable to GOD, to pray to the *virgin Mary*, and to the *saints*, that they would be our *advocates* and *intercessors* with GOD.

Art. 15. That if any one prays to the *virgin Mary*, or to some saint, rather than to GOD, he doth not sin.

Art. 20. It is certain we ought to believe many things, which are not mentioned in scripture, but received by the *tradition* of the *church*.

Art. 25. That *monastical* vows of *chastity*, *poverty*, and *perpetual obedience*, oblige in *conscience*.

That the constitutions of the *church* oblige in *foro conscientiæ*.

There were several *provincial councils* held in *France* and *Germany*, before the *council* of *Trent*, against the *new heresies*.

Council of BOURGES, anno 1528.

Can. 1, 3. The *heresy* of *Luther* having been condemned by the *holy see*, no person shall *print*, *sell*, or *keep* any *books*, in which the said *heresy* shall be diffused.

Can 12. Injoins the *curates* not to suffer certain ridiculous *ceremonies* any longer to be used in the *administration* of the *sacraments* of *baptism* and *marriage*.

Can. 18. No *school-masters* shall read such

such books to their *scholars*, as may make them averse to the *ceremonies* of the *church*.

Council of the *Province* of SENS, held at PARIS, *anno* 1528.

Can. 1. Is about the *unity* and *infallibility* of the *church*. It is there declared, that it cannot fall into any error about *faith* and *manners*; and he that doth not *depend* on its authority, both in *doctrine* and *manners*, is *worse than an infidel*.

Can. 3. He that resists the authority of *general councils*, ought to be accounted an *enemy* to the *faith*.

Can. 4. It belongs to the *church* to interpret the scriptures; and those who do not follow the *canons* of the council of *Carthage*, *Innocent*, and *Gelasius*, and refuse the *sense* which the *holy* fathers have put upon them, are *schismatics* and *heretics*.

Can. 5. Establishes the necessity and validity of *traditions*, and tells us, that such things as are derived to us *that way*, ought to be *believed*, and *observed*, and whosoever refuseth to accept any truth, for *this reason only*, "because 'tis not *clearly delivered* to "us in *holy* scripture," ought to be esteemed an *heretic* and *schismatic*.

Can. 6. Concerns the obedience due to the *constitutions* and *canons* of the *church*, and condemns those that *despise* them.

Can. 7. They are pronounced *accursed*, who

Cent. XVI.
who do not observe the *Lent fast*, and other *fasts*, and times of *abstinences* commanded by the *decrees* of the *church*.

Can. 8. Numbers those among *heretics*, who teach that *priests, deacons,* and *sub-deacons,* are not obliged to live a *single life*, and so leave them at liberty to *marry*.

Can. 9. Against those who count *perpetual* vows unlawful, and especially *monastical* vows. They *prove* the obligation of them, and order those to be punished according to the *canons*, who say that it is *lawful* to *break* them.

Can. 10. Condemns such as lessen the *number* of *sacraments*, or deny that they have a power to *confer grace*—that *marriage* is a true *sacrament*, by which the persons joined together receive a *celestial blessing*.

Lastly. All those that acknowledge not the seven *sacraments* are to be esteemed *heretics*.

In another set of *canons*—It is ordered, that all shall attend the *parochial mass* on *Sundays*, and inform the *officers* of the *ecclesiastical courts*, of those who are absent three *Sundays* together.

Can. 39. *Marriage*, being a *sacrament*, ought to be received with reverence, and all persons shall forbear laughter, and merry talk, while the *office* is *celebrating*, and the *marriage-blessing* is pronouncing—that the persons *espousing*, shall prepare themselves

for

for this *sacrament* by *fasting* and *penance*—that none shall be *married* for the future 'till after *sun-rising*, and not immediately after *midnight,* as has been usual; which has been the occasion of many *clandestine* marriages, from whence many very great scandals have arisen; and therefore all such as *contract* or *favour* them, are excommunicated *ipso facto.*

Can. 40. No new *miracle* shall be published, without the express licence of the *bishop.*

First *Provincial* Council of Cologne, anno 1536.

This *provincial* council was called in the time of Paul III. and of the *Emperor* Charles V. by *Herman de Meurs,* archbishop of *Cologne;* who afterwards embracing the *new doctrine* of Luther, sent for Bucer and Melancthon to preach it in his *archbishopric;* and whose engagement to this *new doctrine* was so strong, that he rather chose to leave his *archbishopric* than renounce it; and so he died in 1552, in the *heresy* which he had embraced.

Art. 32, 33. Contain an advice to such as have *several benefices,* especially with the *cure of souls,* not to satisfy themselves, that they have gotten the *Pope's* (*hodie* the *archbishop of Canterbury's*) dispensation for it; but to examine themselves, and see *whether they*

CENT. XVI.

they have one * *from* GOD: neverthelefs, for fear they fhould injure their own confciences, they are ordered to fubmit their *difpenfations* to the *bifhops,* that they may judge impartially whether the pretences be juft.

In the *fecond* part of the council are 32 articles.

Art. 25. It were to be wifhed that *clergymen* would not be prefent at *weddings.*

Art. 40—47. Speak of the *facrament* of marriage, and wifh that the good cuftom of *fafting* and receiving the *communion* before *marriage,* were again reftored. It enjoins *curates* to *marry* none, unlefs the *banns* were publifhed *three times;* as alfo not to *marry* any ftrangers without certificate from the place of their abode, to teftify that they are not already *married,* and without a *licence* from their *curates* that they may be married by another. And if there be any degrees of *confanguinity* between the perfons, who are to be joined in *marriage,* and if they have obtained a *difpenfation* from the Pope, to examine it, and if they find the copy is not true, to declare their *difpenfation* null: as alfo to forbid thofe fports at church, which are ufual after the *celebration* of *marriage,* with the new-married couple.

It is alfo forbidden to eat *flefh* in the *holy* time of *Lent,* upon account of weaknefs, without licence from a *curate.*

* Qu? If this *advice* can ever be *unfeafonable?*

Council

Council of MENTZ, *anno* 1549.

Determines that the marriage of children, without the consent of their parents, is *null and void*; and orders, that all marriages shall be celebrated in the *church*, with the *usual ceremonies*, and after the *banns* have been *thrice* published. See Stat. 26 Geo. II. c. 33.

Divines of PARIS, assembled at MATHURINS, May 6, 1518.

They gave their judgment on two propositions concerning *indulgences*. The first was—"Whosoever shall put into the *crusade*-box a *testoon*, or the value of it, for a soul that is in *purgatory*, he shall free that soul immediately, and it shall infallibly and directly go to *paradise*. Item. If he cast in ten *testoons* for *ten souls*, or a *thousand testoons* for a *thousand souls*, they shall go immediately and certainly into *paradise*."

This, the *Paris* divines, alarmed with what *Luther* had published about *indulgences*, were afraid to approve of; however, they approved of a *second* proposition, which softened the *first*, by saying—"We must leave it to GOD to apply the treasure of the *church* to such *souls* as He *pleaseth*."

On May 16, 1526, The *faculty* passed a general censure on *Erasmus's Colloquies*, as a work wherein the *fasts* and *abstinences* of the *church*

CENT. XVI.

church are little efteemed, *prayers* to the *virgin* and *faints* laughed at, and *virginity* is fet below *marriage*.

There is alfo another *cenfure*, April 30, 1530, on the two following propofitions, viz.

Firft. That the fcriptures can't be well underftood without a knowledge in the *Hebrew* and *Greek* tongues.

Second. That a preacher can't explain the *epiftles* and *gofpels* aright without the faid *tongues*.

The *firft* is condemned as rafh and fcandalous—the *fecond* as falfe and impious, and which difcourages *Chriftian* people from hearing the word of GOD. They add, that both of them render their *authors* fufpected of *Lutheranifm*.

N. B. One precedent, at leaft, of that *neglect*, and indeed, of that *contempt*, among *Chriftians*, of the *original* fcriptures.

How would it *found* to the *ears* of *common-fenfe* and *right reafon*, to be told of a *people* who *cultivate* the knowledge of moft *other* languages, and *defpife* the attainment of *thofe*, in which the *only* foundation of their *religion* is contained ?—We fhould be ready to fay—" Surely, *ignorance* is the mother " of that *people*'s devotion"—yet in fo faying we muft reproach ourfelves.

It is to be remarked, that whenever men have fought dominion over the minds and confciences of their fellow-mortals, they have

have ever wished to keep them in ignorance; this is by no means to be confined to the *church of Rome*; the leaders among the *fanatical* sectaries in the *last century,* decried all *human learning* as *heathenish, antichristian,* and *profane.*—Dr. *South* (Sermons, vol. iii. p. 500) observes, that all
" *learning* was then cried down, so that,
" with them, the best preachers were
" they that could not read, and the best
" divines, such as could not write."—
" *Latin,*" says he (Sermon intitled *Christian Pentecost)* " unto them was a mortal
" crime, and *Greek,* instead of being the
" language of the *Holy Ghost* (as in the
" New Testament it is) was looked upon
" as the *sin* against it: so that, in a word,
" they had all the confusion of *Babel*
" among them, without the diversity of
" tongues."

> *What's Latin, but the language of the beast?*
> *Hebrew and Greek is not enough a feast:*
> *Han't we the Word in English, which, at ease,*
> *We can convert to any sense we please?*
> *Let them urge the original, if we*
> *Say 'twas first writ in English, so't shall be.*
> *For we'll have our own way, be't wrong or right,*
> *And say, by strength of faith, the crow is white.*
> See GREY; HUD. vol. i. 280, n. 3d edit.

The great and learned Mr. *Selden* was a member of the assembly of divines, anno 1643; and sometimes, when they had cited a text

CENT. XVI.

a text of scripture to prove their assertion, he would tell them—" *Perhaps in your* " little *pocket-Bibles* with *gilt leaves*" (which they would often pull out and read) " *the* " *translation may be thus*, but the *Greek* or " the *Hebrew signifies thus and thus*;" and so would totally silence them. *Whitlocke*, 71.

ERASMUS.

This great and learned man was born at *Rotterdam*, anno 1464 or 1465. *Du Pin* relates a curious anecdote relative to him. His father *Gerard* had two sons, by *Margaret* the daughter of a physician of *Tergoes*, to whom he had made a *promise* of *marriage*; the eldest of these sons was named *Peter*, and the younger *Erasmus*. *Gerard* was resolved to have married *Margaret*, but his father and brothers would not suffer him to do it; therefore he stole away out of that country and went to *Rome*, leaving *Margaret* great with child of her *second* son. She went to *Rotterdam* to lie in there, where *Erasmus* was born.

His father was at *Rome*, where he got his bread by writing, when he was informed that *Margaret* his spouse-elect was dead. He had always entertained hopes, that she should at last become his *wife*, and was so sensibly touched with the news of her death, that he gave over all thoughts of *marriage*,

marriage, and entered into *priest's* orders. Yet the news proved false; for when he returned into *Flanders*, he found her still alive, with his *two* sons, whom she was forced to provide for. Now, though he was no more in a condition to *marry*, or to live with her, yet he always loved her, and, so long as he lived, he took care of the two sons he had by her. As for himself, he was a man of good learning, had a talent for preaching, and in that employed himself the rest of his life.

Erasmus entered into the order of the *canons regulars* at *Stein*, when he was about nineteen years of age, but disliking the way of life, he left it, and, at his intreaty, JULIUS II. gave him a *dispensation* from his *vows*. This great man had a soul too enlarged, and a mind too well cultivated, to relish the wretched *school-divinity* of his day; he wrote many treatises, and brought much controversy upon himself, from men who seemed to have become his *enemies*, because he wished to tell them some *truth*. At the request of the *Pope*, the *Emperor*, the King of *England*, the *Cardinals*, *Prince George of Saxony*, and his own friends, he at last attacked Luther's book " *de Servo Arbitrio*," which engaged him in a long controversy with *Luther*. However, he was suspected in some points of *Lutheranism*, and some propositions were

CENT. XVI.

presented to the *parliament of Paris*, in 1523, which were censured as *erroneous and schismatical*, by *Natalis Bedda*, syndic of the faculty.

Erasmus wrote an Apology, in which he detected *Bedda*'s disingenuousness, and refuted his censures; however, a decree against *Erasmus* was published at *Paris* 1532.

The offence which *Erasmus* gave, by speaking too freely against the *monks*, the *school-divines*, and against some *superstitions*, occasioned him many bitter enemies among the *school-divines* and *monks*, who charged him with *error*, *heresy*, and *impiety*. The freedom with which he reproved them, the prejudices they were possessed with against every thing that appeared *new*, their *bigotry* in adhering to some common opinions and customs, were the causes of all that trouble which he suffered from them.

In short, *Erasmus*, notwithstanding his early prejudices for the church of *Rome*, declaimed openly against those, who, neglecting those sacred fountains of truth the *holy scriptures*, spent their time about questions of no moment, and who, neglecting the duties of *true religion*, too much confided in *ceremonies*.—He longed for a reformation of manners among the clergy, as the best way of putting an end to those disorders and confusions, which had been occasioned

by

by the handle they had given to their opponents the *Lutherans*. Inftead of this being taken in good part, they felected pieces of his writings, lame and imperfect fentences, detached from what *went before*, and from what *followed after*, and thns they obtained the *decree* againft him as before mentioned. His maxim was—" *I defire to do good to all* " *mankind, without offending any man*,"—but he found, as every man will, that this is impoffible.

He died, however, a true *Catholic* (after refufing a *Cardinal*'s hat) at *Bafil*, where he was *rector* of the *univerfity*, anno 1536.

In one of his epiftles he fpeaks of *Tertullian*, and feems to endeavour to foften many errors of that *father*, wherein he mentions the *antients* as againft *fecond* marriages, and that they even enjoined *celibacy*.

In another, to the bifhop of *Rochefter*, he tells him, that, on *one* fide, he had the *monks* and *divines* to encounter with, and they defigned his ruin; and, on the *other*, the *Lutherans*, who fretted at him, becaufe he retarded their triumphs, as they pretended, and would not openly profefs *Luther*'s doctrine. He fays, there were fome things in that doctrine which he did not underftand —fome which he doubted of—and fome which his confcience would not allow him to maintain: and he wished that the disorders which *Luther* had raised, might be as a bitter and violent potion, which might purge the *church*.

In an epistle to *Franciscus a Victoria*, he mentions an horrid saying of *St. Jerome's* on the subject of *marriage*, viz. " *What kind of good can that be, that is only approved of, in comparison with something that is more sinful?*"

Erasmus wrote a book intitled—" The institution of a *Christian marriage*."—In the *preface* he observes, that, " Of all things in this life, marriage is of the greatest importance — the *Pagan philosophers* have written of it, with all the prudence that reason could suggest to them. There have been an infinite number of *laws* made for the durableness and sacredness of *marriages*.

" It seems the *antient Christians* were more *negligent* of *this*, than of other things, because the *greatest* part of them were, by a fervent zeal, wonderfully inclined to *celibacy* and *perpetual virginity*. This is the reason that so many of them have made panegyrics on *virginity*, and have prescribed rules to *widows* and *virgins* how to live devoutly, and that *few* or *none* of them have done the same to *married* persons."

He defines *marriage*, with the *lawyers*,

to be "A *lawful* and perpetual union of
" *man* and *wife*, in order to the procreation
" of children; which includes a partner-
" ſhip of life and goods. That *procreation*
" being the end of *marriage*, it cannot
" properly be ſaid that *marriages*, between
" perſons not capable of having chil-
" dren, are *true marriages*, yet he is ſatis-
" fied that the *church* doth approve of
" them, and that they are in themſelves
" *lawful*.

" He ſpeaks occaſionally of the *cere-*
" *monies* of *antient Pagans* in their *marri-*
" *ages.* He treats very fully of the mar-
" riage between *Jeſus Chriſt* and his *church*,
" of which, marriage among *Chriſtians* is
" a *ſacrament* or *ſign*."

He ſays, " That ſome *antient divines* con-
" ſidered *marriage* only as a ſign, and did
" not acknowledge that it conferred *grace*,
" and therefore did not place it in the rank
" of thoſe that are properly called *ſacra-*
" *ments* of the *New Teſtament*; in which,
" the *ſigns* are efficacious by virtue of the
" covenant, in which GOD has declared his
" will. But that the more plauſible opi-
" nions of *modern divines* had prevailed,
" who taught, that in *marriage, lawfully*
" *ſolemnized*, there is conferred, as in other
" *ſacraments*, a ſpecial gift of the *Holy*
" *Ghoſt*; by which the man and the woman
" are confirmed in their reſolutions to live
" together

"together in perpetual agreement—but, as in the other *sacraments*, we do incur the displeasure of Heaven, if we do not receive them as we ought to do, so the same thing happens in *marriage*."

He confesses, "that the primitive *Christians* had so great a veneration for *virgins*, that their *glory* did obscure the *glory* of *marriage*. He does not think that every consent makes a true and lawful *marriage*. It is necessary, that the consent be given by *verba de præsenti*: that it be free and voluntary, and according to the *laws*."

He relates "many subtle questions of *lawyers* concerning this consent, and treats very fully of the obstacles of marriage, as well of those which make it *void*, as of those which make it *unlawful*, and would have the obstacle of spiritual relation altogether suppressed.

"That parents should instruct their children, at about *three* years of age, to bow at the name of *Jesus*, and to kiss the *crucifix*, &c."

Erasmus was of opinion that *St. Paul* was *married*, and he translated γνησιε συζυγε, Phil. iv. 3. by *Germana conjunx*, by which, he believed, *St. Paul* meant his *wife*, because the person here spoken to, was to minister to the necessities of the *female saints*.

GAUFRIDUS

GAUFRIDUS BOUSSARDUS,

Wrote a treatise concerning the *celibacy* of the *clergy*. Upon that question, " Whether the *Pope* can permit a *priest* to *marry*"—he lays down *seven* propositions, viz.

1. It is, and always has been, permitted in every place, as well in the *Eastern* as in the *Western* church, for the *clergy* that are in *lesser* orders to *marry*.

2. That it was allowed, as well in the *Eastern* as in the *Western churches*, from the very first beginning of the *church*, 'till the times of *Pope Siricius* and *Innocent* I. to promote *married* men to the higher orders, including that of the *priesthood*; and the *priests*, as well as others, were allowed to *live* with their *wives*.

3. Since the times of the above *Popes*, it seems it had never been allowed, in the *Western church*, that *married* men, who *lived* with their *wives*, should be promoted to *deacon's* or *priest's* orders; or that those who were promoted to those *orders* should have *wives*—or, if they had any, they were obliged to promise that they should live in *continency* with them. But 'till the times of *Pope Gregory*, married men might be ordained *deacons*, without *obliging themselves* to *continence*.

4. Since the time of *Pope Gregory* I. it has never been allowed in the *Western church*

Cent. XVI.

to ordain any *deacons*, but those who promise solemnly to live in *continence*.

5. It is and always has been allowed, in the *Greek* and *Oriental* churches, that those who are *married*, may be advanced to *orders*, even *priest's orders*, and that they may *live* with their *wives*.

6. It is not, nor ever was, allowed, that those who are already in *holy orders* (*priests, deacons*, or *sub-deacons*) should *marry*.

7. The *Pope* may, in some cases, grant a *dispensation* to a man that is in *holy orders* to *marry*.

Cardinal Cajetan.

In a treatise on marriage he teaches, that a marriage solemnized by *proxy* is not a *sacrament*, if it be not afterwards ratified by the parties present—That *clandestine marriages* may be sometimes permitted—That it is *absolutely unlawful* to converse together as *man* and *wife*, before they receive the *benediction of the church*—That the *priesthood* does not make a *priest* absolutely incapable of marrying, and that it does not make void a marriage already contracted—That the *priests*, when they enter into orders, take upon them the *vow* of *virginity*, but the *Pope* may *dispense* with it. He may also *dispense* with the *law*, which obliges them to live *unmarried*—That the *Pope* may *dissolve* a *marriage* contracted, but not consummated, and that he may do this not only

only when either of the parties, or both, are to enter into a *monastery*, but also for *other reasons*; because the only reason why the *sacrament* of *marriage* is not *dissolvable* is, that it is the sign of the union of JESUS CHRIST with his *church*; but marriage is not a compleat sign of that *union*, 'till it be *consummated*. That the *Pope* can dispense with the *vow* of *chastity*, but not with the vow of *living unmarried*. He maintains the validity of *Henry* VIII.'s marriage with his *sister-in-law*.

CORNELIUS AGRIPPA,

In his treatise of the *sacrament* of marriage, extols that *sacrament*, for the *antiquity* of its institution, for its *generality*, and for its being *indissoluble*, because, that, by *marriage*, the *man* and his *wife* become *one flesh*, and that a man cannot part with his *own flesh*; yet he excepts the case of *fornication*.

He was greatly censured, for saying "that marriage was dissolved by *adultery*." He held, that *Adam*'s sin, "was nothing "else, but the carnal knowledge of *Eve*" —Et "*serpens Evam* tentans, *Adami* vere- "trum."

JOHN FISHER, Bishop of ROCHESTER.

He maintained, that JESUS CHRIST has taught, and appointed *many things*, that are not written in the *four gospels*, and that the
Holy

CENT.
XVI.

Holy Ghoſt might teach the *church* ſome truths, which JESUS CHRIST had not taught before. He cenſures *Luther*'s arrogance, in deſpiſing the laws, cuſtoms, opinions, and faith of the *church:* and exhorts all *Chriſtian princes* not to give ear to his *groſs impieties*; and to employ the ſame force againſt *Luther*'s hereſies, as they would againſt *Turks, Saracens,* and *Infidels.*

Fiſher was one of thoſe who refuſed to put King Henry VIII. in the *Pope's* place, by acknowledging *his Majeſty ſupreme head* of the *church* of *England,* and taking the appointed *oaths*—for which he was *beheaded,* June 17, 1535.

JACOBUS LATOMUS.

He was *doctor and profeſſor* of divinity at *Louvain,* and a great controverſialiſt againſt *Luther* and his doctrines.

In a treatiſe *on Marriage,* he begins with laying down ſome principles concerning that *ſacrament.* To prove that a marriage *contracted* and *conſummated* can only be diſſolved by death, he lays it down—

1. The *ſacrament* preſuppoſes the *contract,* and if a ſtop be put to the *contract,* the *ſacrament* is *null*; as if, in *baptiſm,* the *water* were hindered from touching the body, then there would be no *baptiſm.*

2. When the *contract* is *valid,* and made according to the *laws,* then, neither the *contract*

tract nor the *sacrament* can be made void by the sins of the *contractors*.

3. Marriage is *indissoluble* by the law of GOD, founded on this divine oracle—*They two shall be one flesh—what God hath joined together, let no man put asunder.*

4. It is contrary to the *law of the gospel*, to say, that a marriage contracted, and *consummated*, can be *dissolved* during the *lives* of the parties; which he proves by the authorities of *St. Austin, St. Jerome, St. Ambrose, St. Chrysostom*, and some *other fathers*.

From these principles he concludes, that a marriage contracted and *consummated*, can never be dissolved, in the case of *adultery*. But he maintains, that, when it is not *consummated*, it is dissolved if either of the parties do enter into a *religious* order, because the person that does so, is *civilly dead*.

FRANCISCUS DE VICTORIA,

Professor of divinity at *Salamanca*, where he died anno 1546.

In a *lecture* on *marriage*, which he composed on occasion of the divorce of the *King of England*, he says—

1. Marriage is an indissoluble contract between *man* and *wife*; and there are two ends of it; the one is, the procreation and education of children; and the other is, the mutual assistance that they ought to give one

one another; that the *consent* of *husband* and *wife* is absolutely necessary to *marriage*, and to be plain and express *per verba de præsenti*.

2. That *princes*, as well as the *church*, have power to determine obstacles that break marriages; but that it is in the *power* of the *church* to take that power from them, and to discharge them to take the concerns of marriage under their cognizance.

3. The obstacles of marriage mentioned in *Leviticus*, are not *all* of perpetual obligation, by the *laws* of GOD and of *nature*.

JOHANNES COCHLÆUS,

A great writer against the *Lutherans*.— He declaimed boldly against the *impudence* of those, who allowed *priests and monks* to *marry*, and all sorts of people to carry away the *spouses* of JESUS CHRIST.

Council of TRENT, begun Dec. 13th, 1545, ended 1563.

This *council* may be said to have finally settled and fixed the *canon* of *Popery*—to have collected together all the *Popish* doctrine relative to the *sacrament* of marriage, *celibacy of priests, polygamy, clandestine marriages,* and *marriage ceremonies,* &c. and to have formed the whole into one connected *system,* which, receiving the *Pope's* approbation, became the rule of *faith* touching these matters,

matters, and remains so in the church of *Rome* to this day.

It would extend this work beyond all reasonable bounds, to set down the various arguments, *pro* and *con*, on the several subjects relative to *marriage*, which were solemnly treated at this famous *synod*; they may all be found in *Brent*'s translation of "The History of the *Council of Trent*, written in *Italian* by *Pietro Soave Polano*."—Let it suffice that I transcribe the *canons* formed and published on the occasion, as I find them in my author, p. 784.

" The doctrine of the *sacrament* of *mar-*
" *riage* did contain; that *Adam* did pro-
" nounce the *bond* of *matrimony* to be *per-*
" *petual*, and that ONLY *two persons* may
" be joined therein; a thing more *plainly*
" declared by CHRIST, who also by his
" passion hath merited *grace* to confirm it,
" and to sanctify those that are joined;
" which is intimated by *St. Paul*, when he
" said that, " this was a great *sacrament* in
" CHRIST and the *church*." Whereupon
" matrimony in the *evangelical law*, ex-
" ceeding the *antient marriages*, by addi-
" tion of *grace*, is justly numbered among
" the *sacraments* of the *new law*. There-
" fore the *synod*, condemning the *heresies*
" in this matter, doth constitute the ANA-
" THEMATISMS.—N. B.

" 1. Against him that shall say, that ma-
" trimony is not one of the *seven sacra-*
" *ments*

CENT. XVI.

CENT. XVI.

"*ments* instituted by CHRIST, and doth not
"confer *grace*.

"2. Or that it is lawful for *Christians* to
"have *many wives* at once, and that it is
"not forbidden by any law of GOD.—N. B.

"3. Or that only the degrees of *affinity*
"and *consanguinity*, expressed in *Leviticus*,
"may nullify the marriage, and that the
"*church* may not *add others*, or *dispense*
"with some of *them*.

"4. Or that the *church* cannot consti-
"tute *impediments*, or hath erred in con-
"stituting them.

"5. Or that one of those who are *mar-
"ried* may dissolve the matrimony for
"heresy, troublesome conversation, or vo-
"luntary absence of the other.

"6. Or that *lawful* matrimony, *not con-
"summated*, is not dissolved by a solemn
"religious *vow*.

"7. Or that the *church* hath erred in
"teaching, that the matrimonial bond is
"not dissolved by *adultery*.

"8. Or that the *church* doth err in sepa-
"rating those who are married for a de-
"terminate or indeterminate time, in re-
"spect of carnal conjunction or cohabi-
"tation.

"9. Or that the *ecclesiastics* of holy or-
"der, or professed *regulars*, may *marry*, as
"also all those who find they have not the
"gift of *chastity*, in regard that GOD doth
"not

" not deny the gift to him that doth de-
" mand it.

" 10. Or that shall prefer the state of
" marriage, to *virginity* and *chastity*.

" 11. Or that the prohibition of *marri-*
" *age*, in certain times of the year, is *su-*
" *perstition*, or shall condemn the *benedic-*
" *tions* and other *ceremonies*.

" 12. Or that matrimonial causes do not
" belong to *ecclesiastical judges*.

" The decrees of the *reformation* of *mar-*
" *riage* did contain,

" 1. That, howsoever it be true, that
" *clandestine marriages* have been *true* and *law-*
" *ful*, so long as the *church hath not dis-*
" *allowed them*, and that the *synod* doth *ana-*
" *thematize* (i. e. curse) him who doth not
" hold them for such; as also those who
" affirm, that *marriages* contracted without
" consent of parents, in whose power the
" married persons are, are void, and that
" the fathers may entirely approve or dis-
" approve them, yet the *church* hath ever
" forbidden and detested them.

" And because prohibitions do no good,
" the *synod* doth *command*, that the *matri-*
" *mony* shall be denounced in the *church*,
" *three festival days*, before it be contracted,
" and, no impediment being found, shall be
" *celebrated* in the face of the *church*, where,
" the parish *priest*, having interrogated the
" man and the woman, and heard their con-

Vol. III.   R   " sent,

"sent, shall say—*I join you in matrimony,*
"*in the name of the Father, Son, and Holy*
"*Ghost,* and shall use other words ac-
"customed in the province.

"Notwithstanding, the *synod* doth re-
"fer it to the will of the *bishop* to *omit*
"the *banns*, but doth declare those to be
"incapable of *marriage* who attempt to
"contract it without the presence of the
"*parish priest*, or another *priest* of equal
"authority, and of *two* or *three* witnesses,
"making *void* and *nullifying* such con-
"tracts, and *punishing* the transgressors.

"Afterwards it exhorts the *parties* not
"to dwell together, before the *benediction*,
"and commands the *parish priest* to have a
"book, in which marriages, so con-
"tracted, shall be written.

"It exhorts the parties that are to be
"married to *confess*, and communicate,
"before the *contract*, or *consummation* of
"the marriage.

"It reserveth the *customs* and *ceremonies*
"of every province, and will have this
"decree to be of force, within *thirty* days
"after it shall be published in every
"parish.

"2. Concerning the *impediments* of
"*marriage;* the *synod* doth affirm, that
"the multitude of *prohibitions*, did cause
"great *sins* and *scandals:* therefore it doth
"restrain that of *spiritual cognation*, to that
"which the *baptized*, and their parents,
"have

"have with the *god-fathers* and *god-mo-*
"*thers*, and the number of thefe to one
"man and one woman only. Ordaining
"the fame about the kindred, which doth
"arife by the *facrament* of *confirmation*.

" 3. It doth reftrain the *impediment of*
"*honefty*, which hath its beginning from
"contracts, to the *firft degree* only.

" 4. That of *affinity* by *fornication* to
"the firft and fecond.

N. B. The *Albigenfes*, about the year 1175, taught—that, "the confent of a
"*willing* couple, without the formality
"of *facerdotal benediction*, made a *lawful*
"*marriage*."

The *Lollards*, cent. 14, laid it down as *found doctrine*, that, " if a man and woman
"came together with an *intention* to live
"in *wedlock*, this *intention* is fufficient,
"without paffing through the *forms* of
"the *church*."—See before, vol. i. p. 148, 149, 1ft edit.—p. 140, 2d edit.

On the other hand, the *church of Rome*, and more efpecially after the time of *Pope Innocent* III. converted the above *fcriptural* ideas of *lawful* marriage, into the damnable fin of *fornication* and *whoredom*; in this the *Proteftants* have followed them. But where is there fo much as a glimpfe of *fcriptural authority* for this ? Where can there be found a fingle *lawful marriage* throughout the whole *Bible*, if the formality of *facerdotal benediction*, or *paffing through*

CENT. XVI *through the forms of the church*, are necessary to constitute it? There is not the smallest trace of any such thing. Therefore, however this piece of *ecclesiastical knavery* may be part of the *craft by which some have gotten their wealth*—yet, as has been shewn at large, as it is subversive of the *order* of *Providence*—an insult on the truth of GOD—and big with *ruin* to the *weaker sex*, it may be deemed one of the most wicked, dangerous, and destructive impositions, that ever were invented, or forced on the credulity of mankind.

But there is something in the words of this *canon*, as of *others* to the same purpose, which are to be found in the course of the preceding evidence, which evince the nature and force of *truth* — it is like the *sun*; though clouds overwhelm its brightness, and conceal the full blaze of its splendor from our eyes, still it will be perceived sufficiently to make our day—thus will the *truth* of GOD, however darkened by error, shine sufficiently through it, to discover its power and influence on the human mind. Here it has forced the *Papists* into an acknowledgment of it, and such a one as contradicts their whole *system* on the subject of *marriage*. For if this be a mere *nullity* without the *forms* of the *church*, how can it raise an *affinity* between the parties? If it does, what is that *affinity* or *relationship*, but that which the

scripture

scripture hath holden forth to us under the idea of *marriage?* If it does *not*, how can there be any *affinity* reaching between defcendents to the *firſt* and *ſecond degree*, when there was *none* between the *parents* or *anceſtors?* The idea of a *nullity* deſtroys that of *affinity*—and that of *affinity* deſtroys that of *nullity*. Take the matter either way, it proves that the *truth* was too hard for them, and above their art to conceal *entirely*.

WHEATLY, on the Common Prayer, edit. 7th, p. 424, tells us, that " *baſtard* " *children*" (*i. e.* thoſe born *only* under the law of GOD and *nature)* " are no " more at liberty to marry within the " degrees of the *Levitical law*, than thoſe " that are *legitimate*" (*i. e.* born of parents joined by *prieſtly ceremony.)* But why not? If the *marriage* of the parents is a *nullity,* the ſuppoſed *conſanguinity* or *affinity* between the *deſcendents* muſt be a *nullity* alſo — for out of *nothing* can come *nothing*.

This ſtrange jumble between *truth* and *falſhood,* making the ſame *marriage* to be ſo *valid* as to fall within the reach of the *Levitical* law in reſpect of the iſſue, and yet ſuch a *nullity* with reſpect to the parties themſelves as to be no better than *whoredom* and *fornication,* is too palpable inconſiſtency and contradiction to agree even with *itſelf,* and can never be proved

CENT. XVI.

to harmonize with the uniform and confiftent fcheme in GOD's word.

Mr. WHEATLY, p. 219. concerning the place where the ceremony is to be performed, expreffes himfelf thus—" And fince GOD himfelf doth join thofe that are *lawfully* married; certainly the houfe of GOD is the fitteft place wherein to make this *religious covenant*. And therefore, by the antient *canons* of this church, the celebration of matrimony in taverns, and other unhallowed places, is exprefsly forbidden." Here he cites an old Popifh canon of *Winton*, made anno 1287, which was not long after *marriage* was made a *facrament*. " And the office is commanded to be performed in the *church*, not only to prevent all clandeftine marriages; but alfo that the facrednefs of the place may ftrike the greater reverence into the minds of the *married couple*, while they remember they make this *holy vow* in the place of GOD's peculiar prefence."

Thus we fee, what *reverence* is to be paid to the *marriage-ceremony*, of man's *invention*, while the *ordinance* of GOD's *inftitution* (GEN. ii. 24.) if without the *former*, is difhonoured with the opprobrious ftigma of *whoredom* and *fornication*.—Surely nothing but the *impudence* of *Popery* could ever have dared to have fet *fuch* an example of *contempt*.

A Jewifh

A Jewish *priest*, under the *law*, who had taken upon himself to introduce an *uncommanded ceremony* into the *temple-worship*, and had so spoken of it, as to endeavour to persuade the people that it was *ordained* of GOD—and that some other *ordinance*, which was of GOD, was not to be regarded but as *criminal* without it—would probably have been stoned to death for *sacrilege* and *blasphemy*, by the sentence of the *judges* of *Israel*.

For my own part, I can find just as much *scripture authority* for changing a *civil contract* into the *form* of a *sacrament*, to be administered, as *such*, by the hands of a *Popish priest*, as for turning it into a *religious ceremony*, to be administered by a *Protestant minister* at the *communion table* in a *church*. And I do believe, that we may venture to suppose, if the *former* had never been *invented*, the *latter* had never been *thought of*.

One thing is very certain, that, they almost *equally* contribute to hide from the eyes of men, the real *nature*, the true *essence*, the certain *obligation*, the antient *simplicity*, and the appointed *efficacy* of the *primary institution*, and thus assist to carry on that scheme of *female ruin*, which evidently results from vacating every *contract* but what arises from their own *authority*.

" 5. It doth take away all hope of *dis-*
" *pensation*, for *matrimony* wittingly con-
" tracted

CENT. XVI.

"tracted in degrees prohibited; and to
"those who have ignorantly contracted,
"without the *solemnities*, in case of proba-
"ble ignorance, a *dispensation—gratis*.

"But to contract in degrees prohibited,
"a *dispensation* shall *never* be granted, or
"*seldom* only, for a just cause, *without*
"*cost*; nor in the *second* degree among
"*princes*, except for a *public cause*.

"6. *Matrimony* shall not be contracted
"with a woman *stolen* away, so long as
"she is in the power of him that did *steal*
"her; and doth declare those *raptors*,
"and those who do assist them with coun-
"sel, aid, or favour, *excommunicated*, in-
"famous, incapable of all dignity; and
"the *raptor*, whether he marry the wo-
"man or not, shall be bound to give
"her a *dowry*, at the pleasure of the
"*judge*.

"7. It ordains that *vagabonds* shall not
"marry, without a diligent inquisition
"first made, and *licence* of the *ordinary*,
"exhorting the *secular* magistrates to pu-
"nish them severely.

"8. It doth ordain against *concubinaries*,
"that being admonished *thrice* by the *or-*
"*dinary*, in case they separate not them-
"selves, they shall be *excommunicated*, and
"persevering one year after the censure,
"the *ordinary* shall proceed severely a-
"gainst them; and the *concubines*, after
"*three* admonitions, shall be *punished*,
"and,

"and, if the *bishop* shall think fit, chased
"out of the territory, by assistance of
"the *secular power*.

"9. It commandeth every temporal
"*lord* and *magistrate*, upon pain of *excom-*
"*munication*, not to compel their subjects,
"or any others, to *marry*, directly or in-
"directly.

"10. It doth restrain the antient pro-
"hibitions of *nuptial solemnities*, from *Ad-*
"*vent* to the *Epiphany*, and from *Ash-*
"*Wednesday* to the *octaves* of EASTER."

The *Papists* borrowed many things from the *heathens*, and, among others, the prohibiting *marriage* at certain *religious sea-sons* of their own *creating:* thus the *Romans* would not permit those days that were dedicated by them to acts of *religion*, to be hindered or *violated* by *nuptial* ceremonies. See WHEATLY on *Com. Prayer*, edit. 7. p. 427.

The *heathens* also were so severe on children's marrying without *consent* of *parents* or *guardians*, as to declare the marriage to be *null*, and the *children* to be *bastards*. The antient *canon* law of the *Greek* church, accounts all *children* who marry without consent of parents, while under their power, to be no better than *fornicators*, The church of *England*, before the *marriage-act*, did not proceed to such extremities, though she took all imaginable
care

care before-hand to prevent such marriages. See WHEATLY, 427.

After the evidence which has been produced in this *chapter*, of the insolent and daring attacks upon the *divine œconomy*, respecting *marriage*, which were made and carried on for above 1500 years together, to the utter demolition of that *plan* which was ordained by the *Creator*, and by *His command* recorded in the *Hebrew scriptures*, it is to be hoped we shall hear no more of *church-authority* for the truth of any thing which is to be believed upon the subject.

We have been told, " that the *primary
" command* of GOD ALMIGHTY, in which
" He *ordained* and *blessed* the *increase of
" mankind*, is antiquated and passed away—
" that it does not relate to *Christians*—
" that the *intercourse* of the *sexes* is *evil* in
" itself—that marriage was the conse-
" quence of *sin*—that *celibacy* makes men
" like *angels*, and, that in comparison
" thereof, *marriage* is *sinful*—that all *se-
" cond* marriages are no better than *forni-
" cation*—that those who do not *marry*
" according to the *laws* of the *church*,
" live in *whoredom*, if they cohabit toge-
" ther—that a new ordinance of *marriage*
" was ordained by JESUS CHRIST, appro-
" priated to *Christians*, and that the *divine
" œconomy* respecting the *commerce of the
" sexes*, as revealed by *Moses*, is totally
" vacated

"vacated and destroyed by the *law of the* "*gospel*—that when the race of mankind "was to be increased, before the coming "of the *Messiah*, marriage was to be sought "after, and even *polygamy* allowed; but now "it is forbidden—that *celibacy* and *virginity* "ought to be looked upon as the highest de- "grees of perfection—that, next to this, is "the total *abstinence* of persons who are "*married* from each other."—These most notorious and horribly-destructive *lyes*, with as many more as would fill a *Winchester* bushel, may be picked out of the preceding evidence, and may serve to shew us how the *credulity* of one part of the world can be imposed on by the *knavery* of the other—and, consequently, how careful we should be, of adverting to any other authority for what we believe, *than* GOD's WRITTEN WORD.

In short, the *Christian* fathers, &c. seem to have endeavoured to contrive a *religion* of their *own*, as unlike that of the *Bible* as they possibly could; insomuch that JEHOVAH might well complain of them as of revolted *Ephraim* (Hos. viii. 12.) and say—*I have written to them* THE GREAT THINGS OF MY LAW, *but they were accounted a strange thing*.

The TWO GREAT COMMANDMENTS, on which hang all *the* LAW *and the* PROPHETS, contained nothing favourable to *clerical* ambition, pride, and covetousness,
and

Cent. XVI.

and those more *particular* precepts, which were derived from them, were too inconsistent with the views of the *clergy*, to maintain their weight and consequence among them—therefore neither *root* nor *branch* were spared, but destroyed by a series of *traditional* imposition on the minds of men, till the *laws* of the *church*, and not the *laws* of Jehovah, became the measure and rule of right and wrong. *Christianity* was not looked upon as the unfolding and completion of the mind and will of Jehovah, as revealed and promised in the *Hebrew* scripture, directing us to make His *laws* our *rule*, His *word* our *guide*; but as a *system* independent of every thing but *itself*, which was to be fashioned and formed into as many shapes as the imaginations of *churchmen* could give it, and as best suited to promote their total ascendency over the human *understanding*, their entire dominion over the *conscience*, and their uncontroulable disposal of the *persons* and *properties* of mankind.

The antient and perfect *law* of Jehovah, which He, in His infinite *wisdom*, ordained for the moral government of His reasonable creatures, was too inimical to the designs of *ecclesiastical* fraud, deceit, and violence, to gain an admission into the *plan*, either on the subject of *marriage*, or any thing else.—" Thus saith the
" *church*,"

"*church*," was the warrant for men's belief; and those who opposed this, were certain to suffer every pain and penalty, which the meanest and most wanton cruelty could suggest:—while wilful *murder, adultery, sodomy,* crimes made *capital* by the law of GOD, were absolved on a few years *penance*.

Such was the state of our *national Christianity*, at the beginning of the *reformation*—the *reformers* once more brought the scriptures into view, with what success, as to the matters which are the subjects of these *volumes,* will be considered in the following *chapter*.

CHAP.

CHAP. XIII.

Observations on the foregoing—applied to the Subjects of this Treatise.

HAVING now, by a long induction of particulars, shewn how the simple *ordinance of marriage*, and the CREATOR's whole plan for regulating the *commerce of the sexes*, have been taken out of *His hands*, into the *hands of men*, who have dared to throw aside those *laws* which the MOST HIGH established for the *propagation, continuance,* and *preservation* of the *human species*—and more especially for the protection of *female chastity*, from the ravages of ungoverned and intemperate *lust*—by vacating all obligation between the *sexes*, but what arises from *human contrivance*—it may not be improper, in this place, to make such remarks upon the evidence, as will demonstrably shew, that *our* whole plan is founded in error, and originates in the usurped power of *Popish churchmen* over the commandments and ordinances of JEHOVAH, as by him delivered in his MOST HOLY WORD.

It will then follow, that those miseries of the *female sex*, which have been so largely spoken of in the preceding *volumes*, and which it is the *author*'s grand *end* and *aim* to *prevent*, or *remedy*, on the *basis* of the *divine law*,

law, are the natural and inevitable confequences of *Popish usurpation* over the underftandings and confciences of mankind, and of the abolition of that *holy system* of fecurity and protection to the *weaker sex*, which is afforded them by the folemn and unalterable ftatutes of *Heaven*.

As in what concerns the reft of the *universe* in general, fo with refpect to the *human species*, the *laws* of *Heaven* are *simple*, unmixed with dark and hard *speeches*, conceived in words clear, plain, and eafy to be underftood: there are no *sophistical* diftinctions about what *is* or *is not* a *marriage contract*, thus leaving fo important a concern vague and indeterminate, as to the matter or effence of it in God's fight; there is nothing, in this refpect, faid about *priests, surplices, altars, churches, bells, mass-books, banns, licences, dispensations*, outward religious *rites* and *ceremonies*, or of any one requifite to marriage but the Creator's own *appointment*.

Therefore, whether thefe things were invented by *Popes, Councils, Synods*, or other human power in the *church of Rome*—or adopted by *John Doe* and *Richard Roe*, as requifites in the *Reformed churches*—they are equally out of the queftion, and can no more affect the validity and obligation of God's *ordinance*, than they can controul the courfe of the *sun*.

The general command, when God bleffed the *male* and *female*, and faid—" *Increase* " *and multiply*"—was evidently to be done in

a way

a way which the CREATOR himself was to appoint; no device whatsoever of the *creature* could any more interfere in this, than in the disposal and government of the *universe*.

That which was to be the *efficient cause* of *propagation*, was to be also the *matter* of indissoluble union between the *male and female*, so as to make them *one flesh*, and to create an *affinity* or *relationship* between them, even above and beyond that of parents and children.—Gen. ii. 24.

Thus the matter *stood* on the *original institution*—but as the human race increased, it seemed good to *infinite wisdom*, to make such regulations as should obviate the sad consequences of men's forgetting the strictness of the *matrimonial union*, and taking upon themselves to *dissolve* its *obligation*. The seduction of *virgins*, and then forsaking them for others, must be attended with consequences of the most fatal kind to *themselves*, as well as to *society*, in the confusion that would be occasioned, not only with regard to the property of the women, but also as to their issue—it was therefore ordained, that wherever the *marriage-union* had passed, it * must continue; the man could not forsake the woman, nor the woman give herself to *another*, during the first man's life—whether the man, taking the *virgin*, was before in possession of *another* or not, it made no differ-

* The *author* must be supposed to except such cases as are excepted by THE LAW. See, for instance, LEV. xviii. 6—18.

ence in thefe refpects, he having become *one flesh* with her, made her his unalienable property from that moment, and it was not only forbidden him to *put her away*, but fhe was to be *put to death* if fhe went to *another*; and any man who took a woman that had become another man's property, was alfo to fuffer *death*. Thus were *adultery* and *whoredom, feduction* and *proftitution*, provided againft IN THE MOST EFFECTUAL MANNER.

Thus alfo was a line drawn, which none could pafs with impunity; and, that it might be thoroughly underftood, it was delivered to *Mofes* by JEHOVAH, and afterwards committed to writing, for all future generations, in that facred and indelible fyftem of *divine jurifprudence*, which bore the moft SOLEMN COMMAND, that none fhould *add to it*, nor *diminifh from it*.

Such was the *law* of that *kingdom*, which GOD eftablifhed over *Ifrael*, when he delivered them out of *Ægypt*—bore them on *eagles wings, and brought them to himfelf*.—See Exod. xix. 4, 5; where the LORD fays—*Now therefore, if ye will obey my voice indeed, and keep my covenant, then ye fhall be a peculiar treafure unto me above all people: for all the earth is mine.*

What the *Jews* fuffered for not *obeying* GOD's *voice* in his *commandments*, their hiftory informs us, and our own daily obfervation, on their prefent fituation, evidently fhews us.

When it pleafed GOD, *in the fullnefs of time*, to take out of *the Gentiles a people for his name* (Acts xv. 14.) by *sending his own Son*, JESUS CHRIST, *to redeem them from all iniquity, and to purify to himself a peculiar people zealous of* * *good works*—one capital and gracious promise of the *covenant* ran thus—" *I will put* MY LAWS *into their minds, and in their hearts will I write them. I will be their* GOD—*and they shall be my people.* See Jer. xxxi. 33.—As in another place he says —*I will call them my people that were not my people*—Hof. ii. 23. Rom. ix. 25, 26.—HIS LAWS then, *put into their minds*, and written in *their hearts*, were to be the statutes of *that kingdom within them*—see Luke xvii. 21.—of which the LORD HIMSELF was to be SOVEREIGN.—No other *laws* do we ever hear mentioned, as the *rule* of their *obedience*, but the ROYAL LAW (see James ii. 8.) which had once been delivered by JEHOVAH, in all the awful majesty of GODHEAD at *Mount Sinai*.

JESUS, the great *prophet* like unto *Moses*— (see Deut. xviii. 15. Acts iii. 22.)—preached these *laws*—declared that *not a jot or tittle should pass from them—that he who broke the least of them, and taught men to do so, should be called least in the kingdom of heaven*.

Notwithstanding all this, as the *Jews* had made void these *laws* by *their traditions*, the *Christians*, as we have seen, soon began to tread in their steps, and to set up a *kingdom of this world*, which they called the *church*, over which *man*, not GOD, was to govern; and in which, not GOD's *laws*, but man's *devices*,

* See Tit. ii. 14.

were

were to be the rule of obedience. The consequences of this may be seen in the foregoing pages of this *volume*, and the dreadful effects are felt, severely felt, by thousands to this hour.

There arose men, who, under notions of *piety* and *purity*, found fault with every thing God had done, with respect to peopling the world; and plainly give us to understand, that if *they* had been to contrive the matter, they would either have done it by some other method, or have put an end to the human race. God had said—" *Increase and multiply*"—this they were for confining to the times of the *Jewish* dispensation, and exhorted *Christians* to live in *celibacy*, assuring them that this was " as far above *marriage* as the " *heavens were higher than the earth.*"

" Some there were of the most eminent
" *bishops*, and most zealous *Christians*, who,
" having imbibed the *philosophers* opinions
" and prejudices against *marriage*, as an estate
" in itself *unclean*, and so troublesome, that
" it was utterly inconsistent with an *holy* and
" *speculative* life, did ever retain such an an-
" tipathy against it, especially in the *clergy*,
" that they were inveighing against them
" that were *married*, insomuch that they
" brought it into general dislike."—See *Du Pin*, Cent. vii. p. 9. n. " The council of
" *Eliberis, anno* 305, can. 33, actually de-
" creed against *priests* marriage. Ib.

However, with regard to the *laity*, in order to sanctify the *unclean* as well as they could,

could, they invented *priestly benediction*, where people *married* but *once*; as for marrying a *second* time, it was called—" only a more spe-"cious and decorous kind of *adultery*"— and *priests* were forbidden so much as to be present at *second* marriages—which, by the way, proves that *marriages* were yet looked upon as *valid*, without a *priest*, only they were deemed *unholy*, as wanting the *benediction*.

In process of time, this *benediction* of a *priest* paved the way for other religious *forms of words*, and farther *ceremonies*. The reader may easily acquaint himself with their progress, by reviewing the state of the preceding evidence —Chap. xii.

At length, the *laws* of JEHOVAH, which held forth the primary *institution*, in its whole *nature* and *essence*, as making the *male* and *female one flesh*, and as conveying an exclusive property to the man in the *woman*, by the *simple ordinance* set down Gen. ii. 24. were so far laid out of the question, as not only to establish *no obligation* whatsoever, simply on the footing of the CREATOR'S OWN FIAT; but *This*, without the *ceremonies* which the *church* had invented and imposed, was stamped with *infamy*, called *fornication* and *whoredom*, and as such is looked upon in the *Christian* church to this hour!

That this was not effected, but by slow degrees, is very apparent from what passed in the *fourth century*; when *Constantine*, who was a great favourer of the *views* of the *clergy*, as well as a great promoter of their

power,

power, enacted a law to discourage *concubinage*, and to promote *matrimony*, as they * called it; which law provided for the legitimacy of *ante-nuptial* children, i. e. such as were born of parents who had lived together simply on the footing of God's *own institution*, and whose children began to be deemed *bastards*. —" The *church*," it is said, " meddled not " with these distinctions of the *civil* laws, " but, regarding only the law of nature, *ap-* " *proved* every conjunction of one man with " a woman, if it was with one woman, and " perpetual; and the more so, because the " holy scriptures employ the name of *wife* " and of *concubine* indifferently." See before, vol. i. p. 31, n. 1st edit.—p. 32. 2d edit.

By what has been said, it appears, that the notion of the unlawfulness of *second* marriages had taken deep root, and that *polygamy*, of course, was indiscriminately banished from the *Christian* plan of marriage—but, that *priestly benediction*, and religious ceremony, were by no means then established, as of the *essence* of the *lawful* conjunction of the *man and woman*.

As *churchmen* increased in *power* and *wealth*, the love of *both* increased, in every age; and, as we have already seen, by the most pregnant testimonies, *marriage* was entirely taken, as it were, out of God's hands, into the hands of *churchmen*; the *Hebrew* scriptures, relative to the *commerce of the sexes*,

---

* The word *matrimonium* was borrowed from the *Heathen*.—See Ainsworth—*sub* voc.

for certain very *cogent* reasons, laid out of the case; and what the *Popes, councils, synods,* and *human laws* determined to be *marriage,* was *marriage;* what they determined to be *whoredom* and *fornication,* was so; what they determined to be *bastardy,* was *bastardy;* but what GOD had determined to be, or not to be, any of *these,* signified no more than if He had never determined any thing about the matter.

The great affair of all was the invention of *Peter Lombard,* when he found out *marriage* to be a *sacrament*—this was the means of throwing it entirely into the hands of the *priests,* and making it an object of the jurisdiction of *ecclesiastical* judges. It gave the *churchmen* a power of *celebrating* it with what *rites* and *ceremonies* they thought proper, and to declare, that, on no *other* terms than what they had invented, could the parties be *man* and *wife* in the sight of GOD—so that all this may be deemed *pure, true,* and *genuine* POPERY —which, by leaving men and women under no obligation to each other, but on the footing of what was afterwards finally determined and settled at the *council of Trent,* has opened that door to *female ruin,* which, in all its increasing horrors, is so peculiarly the *disgrace* of all *Christian* countries in general, and of this in particular, as to call aloud for the restoration of the *divine law,* which is the only means of putting a stop to it.

As for the *reformed* church of *England,* it owns but *two sacraments,* and of course does not

not call *marriage* by that *name*; but when we consider, that our " *form of solemnization of* " *matrimony*" was compiled in the days of *Edward* VI. by men who had been educated in the *church* of *Rome*, and who must have had their minds prejudiced and deeply tinctured with the *Popish* ceremonies, we are not to be surprized that our *ritual* and that of the *Romish* church should bear so strong a resemblance.

It is to be administered by *a priest*—in a *surplice (superpellicio indutus*, says the *Popish* rubric)—in the *church*—at the *communion-table*—" the *man* and *woman* are to *kneel down* " before the LORD's *table*" at a certain part of the *service*—" *Sacerdos jubeat eos invicem jun-* " *gere dextras, dicens—Ego conjungo vos in* " *matrimonium, in nomine Patris, & Filii, &* " *Spiritus Sancti. Amen."* Rom. Rite " Then " shall the *priest* join their right hands " together, and say—" Those whom GOD " hath joined together, let no man put asun- " der——I pronounce that they be *man* and " *wife* together, in the name of the *Father*, " and of the *Son*, and of the *Holy Ghost*. " AMEN." Ch. of Engl.

The reason which the council of *Trent* gave for the use of these words, was, that— " in a short time it might become an *article* " *of faith*, that *those words*, pronounced by " the *parish-priest*, were the *form* of the *sa-* " *crament."*

Now, if an honest *Quaker* was to say to me—" Friend, thou dost not allow *marriage* " to "to be a *facrament*, that is, thou doft not call it by that name; but, how doft thou diftinguifh thy proceedings from thofe of the *church of Rome?* how doft thou, as to the *thing itfelf*, call it by what *name* thou wilt, make more or lefs of it in reality, than hath been made by the *council of Trent?*"—I do confefs, that I know not how I fhould get rid of my *plain friend*, unlefs he would be fatisfied with a *quibble*, inftead of an *anfwer*, or with a *diftinction*, without *difference* enough fairly and fubftantially to warrant it.

Were he to prefs me farther upon the fubject of *banns, difpenfations*, and *licences*, or to afk me to produce an authority from GOD's word for our *ritual*, or almoft any thing belonging to it, I muft turn him over to *popes, councils, fathers*, &c. and get out of his way as faft as I could, or elfe endeavour to filence him, by telling him, "that the aforefaid *ritual* is part of the *law of the land*, eftablifhed by *act* of *parliament*, and is alfo guarded by a *canon*, loaded with excommunication *ipfo facto* againft all impugners of it."—To this he might reply, that "in the days of *Henry the king*—it was made *felony* for our *priefts* to *marry*—to deny *tranfubftantiation* was *burning alive*, with forfeiture, as in cafes of high treafon; but thefe were ungodly laws, and therefore were repealed, and fo ought all other *laws*, which, like them, oppofe the truth of the fcriptures, or lead people into *error and*

" *superstition*, by hiding from them the true
" *nature* and *obligation* of God's *institu-*
" *tions.*"

The *Romish* ritual is in *Latin*; which, rendered into *English*, begins thus—" The *parish*
" *priest—parochus—*who is about to celebrate
" matrimony (publication of *banns* having been
" made on *three festival days* as before said)
" if no lawful *impediment* hinder, shall come
" into the *church*, cloathed in a *surplice (su-*
" *perpellicio)* and *white robe (albâ stolâ)* tak-
" ing with him at least *one clerk*, who may
" bring the *book*, and a vessel of *holy water*
" with a *sprinkler*, before three, or two, wit-
" nesses, shall ask the man and the woman
" (who for decency should be attended by
" their relations or neighbours) concerning
" their consent, severally, in this manner, in
" the vulgar tongue.

" *N.* wilt thou take *N.* here present, for
" thy lawful wife, according to the rite of
" *holy mother church?* The *man* shall an-
" swer—*I will*, &c. &c.

" Then the *priest* is to *sprinkle* the parties
" with *holy water*; then he is to *bless* the *ring*,
" and *sprinkle* it with *holy water* in the form
" of a *cross*; and the bridegroom, receiving
" the ring from the *priest*, is to put it upon
" the *fourth* finger of the woman's *left*
" hand" *(Digito annulari—*a phrase borrowed
from the *Heathens*, as the *custom* itself * was)

* See *Thelyph.* vol. ii. 203, n. 2d edit.—p. 222—3, n. 1st edit.

" the

" the prieſt ſaying—In the name of the *Fa-
" ther*, and of the *Son*, and of the *Holy
" Ghoſt*."

The nuptial ceremony among the *Hottentots* is as follows—" The men ſquat them-
" ſelves on the ground in a circle, all but
" the *bridegroom*, who ſquats in the center.
" The women, at ſome diſtance, ſquat them-
" ſelves likewiſe in a circle about the *bride*,
" who likewiſe ſquats. Then the *prieſt*, or
" maſter of the *religious* ceremonies, who is
" always that of the *kraal* where lives the
" *bride*," (and ſo may be ſtyled *parochus*)
" enters the circle of the men, and, coming
" up to the *bridegroom*, *waters* upon him a
" little—the *bridegroom* receives the *ſtream*
" with much eagerneſs, rubbing it briſkly
" all over his body, and making with his
" long nails ſeveral deep ſcratches in his
" ſkin, that the *urine* may penetrate and
" ſoak the farther. The *prieſt* then goes to
" the circle of the women, and coming up
" to the *bride*, *waters* a little upon her; ſhe
" receives and rubs the *urine* upon her body,
" with as much eagerneſs as the bridegroom.
" Then goes the *prieſt* again to the *bride-
" groom*, and having *watered* a little more
" upon him, away he goes again to the
" *bride*, and again *waters* upon her. And ſo
" he goes from one to the other, 'till he has
" exhauſted upon them his whole ſtock of
" *urine*, uttering from time to time to each
" of them, one of the following good
" wiſhes,

"wishes, till he has pronounced the whole
"upon them both.—*" May you live long and
"happily together.—May you have a son be-
"fore the end of the year.—May this son live
"to be a comfort to you in your old age.—
"May this son prove a man of courage, and a
"good huntsman."——This is the whole of
"the nuptial ceremony; after which the
"whole company rise, and prepare for a
"feast." See *Kolben*, Cape hist. vol. i.
p. 153.

Now, I do not suppose that the reader can peruse this account of so filthy, so ridiculous, so absurd a *ceremony*, without laughing, and feeling in his mind a most sovereign contempt for a people seemingly so lost to the possession of common *reason*. But this is not the case; there are doubtless as wise and understanding men among the natives of the *Cape of Good Hope*, as among the *Europeans* (why should there not?—" God hath
"made of one blood all nations for to dwell on
"all the face of the earth.")—Their fondness and respect for so beastly and absurd a *ceremony*, does not therefore proceed from a want of *natural reason*, but, from a prostitution of their rational faculties, to a certain thing called *superstition*; which, under the auspices of another certain thing called *priestcraft*, puts *Christians* and *Hottentots* upon a level, as to a blind submission of their understandings and consciences to those who have been artful enough to gain an entire ascendency

dency over them. *Lord Peter's holy water* has no more to do with GOD's ordinance of *marriage*, than the *Savage's urine* has; but neither the *Hottentot* nor the *Papist* will acknowledge that they are mistaken; and I should suppose, that a man would stand as bad a chance for his *life* in a *Kraal* at the *Cape*, as in the *Holy Inquisition at Rome*, were he to say, in either place, what I have said upon the subject.

The *Hottentot andersmaken*, it must be confessed, is not quite so cleanly as the *Popish ritual*; but it has this advantage over the latter, that it is not *lying in the name of the* LORD;—it is not a professed *imposition* upon the *minds of men*, in the very face of GOD's revelation—it is not an unauthorized use of that *venerable* and *holy* *name* of the LORD OUR GOD, in order to make men believe, that *marriage* is, what GOD has never made it—" a *sacrament*, ordained by *Christ*—appro-
" priated to *Christians*."

Perhaps my *Quaker-friend* might here remind me—" thou shouldst not throw *stones*,
" for *thine house* is also made of glass."

In short, wherever the *simple ordinance* of GOD is obscured, so that men are kept in the dark as to its nature and obligation—wherever those wise and holy *laws*, which GOD hath made for the preservation of his creatures from *mischief* and *ruin*, are suspended, on some terms and conditions of human invention, so that they cannot operate, or answer

fwer the ends for which they were revealed—wherever an *human ceremony* is impofed upon the underftandings of mankind, as that, without which, the pofitive inftitution of GOD ALMIGHTY is *null and void to all intents and purpofes whatfoever*—it makes little difference, by what *name* the obftacle be called, or by *whom* invented; it is an infolent attack upon the *divine fovereignty*—a daring invafion of the *divine prerogative* of *legiflation*—a downright and open *rebellion* againft the *majefty* of GOD—and, whether this be done by *Chriftians*, on this, or on the other fide the *Tyber*—

Tros, Tyriufve, mihi nullo difcrimine agetur. Virg.

We have feen, in the long detail of the foregoing evidence, fome dreadful *mifchiefs*, which have attended the unnatural oppofition, raifed againft the *primary decree* of Heaven, relative to the *propagation* of the *human fpecies*.—The *celibacy* of the *clergy*, being contrary to *nature* itfelf, as well as to fcripture, produced *evils* of the moft *horrible* and *deftructive* kind — this may be concluded, from the many *canons* we find againft *fodomy*, *child-murder*, either by caufing *abortion* or *otherwife* — likewife, the frequent mention of the crimes of *adultery*, *whoredom*, and *fornication*, particularly charged *on the clergy*, as alfo of *baftards* being excluded from holy orders, and the like.

Thefe are ftanding proofs of the * mifchiefs which

* The *Wickliffites* or *Lollards* as they were called, endeavoured to get their doctrine approved by *parliament*, and

which enfued from men's inventing *schemes* of *holiness* and *purity*, in order to maintain which, the *word of* GOD was thrown afide, and the *wisdom* of man exalted in its place. The *union of the sexes*, though ordained of GOD, as that *inftitution* by which the world fhould be peopled, was ftamped with a degree of *infamy*, as *impure* in itfelf, and caufing a defilement in thofe who engaged in it, unlefs *prieftly benediction* and religious ceremony interpofed: and even here, it was ftill too *impure* to be engaged in by thofe who miniftered in holy things; and therefore forbidden to the *laity*, without the purification of *holy water*, &c. and forbidden to the *clergy* entirely.

Impediments to marriage, which are mentioned in GOD's law, were difpenfed with—others were invented, which GOD's law never mentions, and made the grounds and caufes of diffolving *marriage*—fuch as between *god-*

and in 1395 prefented a remonftrance to the Houfe of Commons, containing many articles, one of which was—
" that the *celibacy* of the clergy occafioned many fcan-
" dalous irregularities in the church"—another was—
" that the vow of *fingle life*, undertaken by women, was
" the occafion of numberlefs diforders, and of the *mur-*
" *der* of multitudes of *children* unbaptized, and even un-
" born." Rapin, vol. i. 481.——Qu? Where is there any thing in the fcripture which authorizes bringing women under fuch a ftate of bondage to *fear* and *fhame*, as to induce them to *murder* their *children*, in order to conceal their *pregnancy* or *delivery?* No fuch thing was ever known or heard of in the *church* of GOD, 'till lyes and fictions took place of the *divine law*; when *celibacy* was preferred to *marriage*—and *marriage* itfelf only allowed under fuch *terms* as men invented, and impofed on their fellow-creatures.

fathers

fathers and *god-mothers* at *baptism* or *confirmation*—relatives to the *seventh degree*—and even as far as any *relationship* could be traced—a man's having *another wife* living, though she was under circumstances, by which every end of marriage was prevented—the apostle's rule was inverted, it was no longer *better marry than burn*, but better *burn* than *marry*—thus were the *Christians* laid under a *yoke* to which the *Jews* were utter strangers, and were taught to believe, that, whatever *marriage* was by the *Mosaic law*, it was now totally altered; it was " a *sacrament*, instituted " by *Christ*, and appropriated to *Christians*"—a *law of the gospel*, was to supersede the *law* of JEHOVAH as delivered at *mount Sinai*, and, in short, *marriage* was to be what *churchmen*, from time to time, were pleased to make it; for which, after some faint attempts to justify their proceedings, by, what they *styled*, " the *new evangelical law*," they fairly and honestly avowed the power of the *church*, i. e. of the *Pope*, and his coadjutors, the *cardinals*, *archbishops*, and *bishops* in *council* assembled, to be paramount to all other power whatsoever; they trampled *all laws, divine* and *human*, under foot; and not what GOD had said in his WORD, but what the *church* had said in its *canons* and *decrees*, was the rule of *faith* and *manners*.

There is a passage in the *Turkish Spy*, on the innovations which human imagination, and church power, introduced in the place of GOD's laws, which I shall make no apology for

for quoting on this occasion, as its subject-matter, and the reflections with which it concludes, are much to our purpose, and well worthy our observation.

"By the very same rule, they introduced
"the use of *images* and *pictures* in their
"*churches:* and the vestments of their *priests,*
"the ornaments of the *altar,* the *tapers,*
"*lamps, incense, flower-pots,* and other religi-
"ous gaieties, were fashioned according to
"the *patterns* they received from the *priests*
"of *Jupiter, Apollo, Diana,* and the rest of
"the *heathen deities.* Hence, the festivals of
"the *gods* and *goddesses* were turned to holy-
"days of *saints;* and temples, before conse-
"crated to the *sun, moon* and *stars,* were afresh
"dedicated to the *apostles* and *martyrs.*

"Thus the very *Pantheon* itself in *Rome,*
"or *temple of all the gods,* in process of time,
"by an *ecclesiastic* dexterity, was converted to
"the *church* of *all saints.*—In a word, *Chris-*
"*tianity* in all things seemed no other than
"*Gentilism* in disguise. And it must be thought
"a *pious fraud,* thus to wheedle so many
"millions of *sinners* into the bosom of the
"*church,* whether they would or no.

"Oh *father William!* dost thou not blush
"at these trivial excuses, for the manifest
"violation of the laws of GOD? Can man be
"wiser than the *Omnipotent?* Or will he pre-
"sume to correct the ways of HIM that is
"PERFECT IN KNOWLEDGE? Is the true
"*religion* to be propagated by imitating the
"idolatrous *rites* of *infidels?* Or by prosti-
"tuting

" tuting the sacred injunctions of Heaven
" to the caprices of human policy? Did any
" wise *law-giver* condescend to alter and new-
" model his laws, to humour a peevish cap-
" tious subject? Would he *add,* or *diminish*
" any thing for the sake of gaining a faction
" or party? and can we think, that God
" ever designed, to have His *divine laws*
" garbled and mixed with profane *indul-*
" *gences, dispensations,* and amendments of
" *mortals?* As if He had been *ignorant* what
" he did, when He divulged his *statutes,* and
" wanted the *counsel* of his *creatures* to help
" him out at a *dead lift*.

" Was that tenderness only to be shewn to
" the *Jews* for a time? And were they, for
" ever afterwards, to be scandalized? In vain
" does the *church* daily pray for the conver-
" sion of that people, whilst by her *doctrines,*
" and daily *practices,* she hardens them more
" in their *infidelity*." *Turkish Spy,* vol. vii.
p. 304, 305.

Though it be evident from the scriptures (comp. Isaiah vi. 9, 10. with Acts xxviii. 25, 26, 27.) that the rebellious obstinacy of the *Jews* provoked God to leave them under a *judicial blindness,* yet one *mean* of fastening it upon them is, the *doctrine* and *practice* of *Christians.* What must a thinking *Jew* conclude, from an *auto de fé,* where he sees, not only the disciples of *Moses,* but those also who are the professing disciples of *Jesus,* bound in one *chain,* tied to one *stake,* and tormented in the same *flame?*—what, when he reads of the *massacres* of *Paris* and of *Ireland?*—what, when he is told, that, above a *million* and an *half* of reasonable and innocent creatures, including all *ages, conditions,* and SEXES, have drenched the earth with their *blood,* and all this, because they refused to worship a piece of *wafer* or a log of *wood*—or to acknowledge the traditions and doctrines of men, as above the testimony of the scriptures?

How should the *Jews* ever give credit to a *system,* which contradicts their antient scriptures? which lays the *holy laws* of their *Pentateuch* in the dust, and treads under foot the *awful majesty,* the supreme and unrivalled *sovereignty* and *authority* of JEHOVAH? which tells them, they must renounce their LAWGIVER, LORD, and KING, (see Isaiah xxxiii. 22.) and listen only to *men* who have overturned the whole fabric of their œconomy, with respect to *marriage,* and destroyed those *bulwarks* which the GOD of *Israel* raised, for the security of their *wives* and *daughters* from *seduction and prostitution?*—that the protection of *female chastity,* which their forefathers experienced, is no longer the object of divine legislation; but, that every man is now at liberty, to ravage, as he can, upon the *weaker sex,* no *responsibility* left, no obligation created, no justice exacted?

How can they endure to hear the taunts of *Christians,* on their antient *statutes?*—or bear with *patience* to hear the *Christians* speak of their honoured and venerable *ancestors,* as *adulterers, whoremongers,* and *debauchees?*—licentiates

tiates in *sin*—*tolerated* in *forbidden lewdness* by their GOD—worthy the stroke of vengeance, and only spared from it by *divine connivance?* All this, and more, they must be content to hear, and to submit to, or they must keep out of the reach of *Christian* churchmen, or shut their ears and hearts against them.

So that while *Popish canons*, and *human laws*, are to lay down principles on which the regulation of the *commerce of the sexes* is to depend, we can entertain no great hopes of *men*, who, from the giving of the law at *mount Sinai* to this hour, have known no other *system* than that delivered by *Moses*, and acknowledge no appeal from their antient *scriptures*, to the more *modern inventions* of the *Christians*.

Another *article*, established on the foregoing evidence, is the indiscriminate prohibition of *polygamy*—this appears in several of the *canons* which have been cited, and at last, by the *council* of *Trent*, cent. 16. finally laid under a *judicial curse*. So that, no *necessity* of *circumstances*, no *situation* into which a man already married can be brought—his *wife's* insanity—distemper of body or mind, or other *unavoidable* deprivation of her *society*—can turn the point-blank of this dreadful *canon* from the unhappy objects of its vengeance.—The *Protestants* have added to the terror of this piece of *artillery* a *penal statute*, by which *polygamy*, under what circumstances of *necessity* soever, is prohibited on pain of *death*.—The *debauchery* of the *wives* of *others*, the seduction and ruin of *virgins*, the incentives to procuring *abortion*, the *murder* of *new-born infants*, though notorious confequences of *prieftly celibacy*, cannot prevail on their fellow-creatures to fuffer them to *marry*; and all thefe, though confequences equally of that *factitious celibacy*, which arifes from an *indifcriminate* prohibition of *polygamy*, cannot prevail for the repeal of that *law*, which makes it a *capital felony* for a man to do, what God not only *allows*, but in many cafes *commands*, (fee Exod. xxii. 16. Deut. xxii. 28, 29.) Add to all this, the driving men into *fornication* with *harlots*, or into other namelefs and numberlefs *inconveniences*, which *drown them in deftruction and perdition*. This is a *tyranny* over the confciences of men, well worthy the *Popifh* inventors of it. It was altogether unknown to the *antient people* of God, who lived under the immediate government of the Divine Law.

But here methinks I hear a *Jew* fay—
" *Our law* has an efpecial care of *population*,
" and provides againft the *extinction* of fami-
" lies by *barrennefs*.—Our father *Abraham*
" married *Sarah*, but finding fhe was *barren*,
" he took *another wife*, that he might have
" *children* by her, and this by the perfuafion
" of *Sarah* herfelf.—Our father *Jacob* alfo
" did the fame at the perfuafion of his wives
" *Leah* and *Rachel*."— See Gen. xvi. 2. xxx. 3. 9. " All this is very true, anfwer I; but
" if *Abraham* had lived among *Chriftians*, one
" *fect* of them would have *curfed and excom-*
" *municated him*, another would have *hanged*
" *him*,

"*him*, and sent him to the *devil* into the bargain; and so they would have served his grandson *Jacob*, and, for aught I know, *half* his *generation*."

Another observation is also to be made, as resulting from the foregoing *evidence*, and that is, on the subject of *concubinage*. When *Bucer* says—"*legitimæ etiam erant uxores*"— "They were also *lawful wives*"—I firmly believe him, because the HEBREW SCRIPTURES mention them as *such*.—As for the NEW TESTAMENT, I do not find any thing said about them. The word παλλακη, which the LXX use for the Hebrew פילגש, and which we render *concubine*, does not once occur—therefore this matter must be confessed to stand *singly* and *merely* on the scriptures of the Old Testament.

The *church*, in the days of *Constantine*, clearly held, that "the scriptures used the word *wife* and *concubine* indifferently," and therefore they would not enter into the distinction which that *Emperor* was making, between *marriage* and *concubinage*—the council of *Toledo*, anno 400, were of the same opinion—and *St. Augustine* also, who is styled the *father of the Latin church*, did not differ from them.—See before vol. i. 32, n.

As the church grew more *corrupt*, and *churchmen* more insolent, and more ambitious of increasing their dominion over the minds of men, they confounded all scripture definitions and ideas of things; and suffered the people only to *think* as they *would have them*, and as might beſt ſerve for the advancement of *prieſtly* power. The poor *clergy*, who were forbidden to *marry*, endeavoured to find a refuge in *concubinage*, or living with women which they took as *wives*, but without the *forms* which had been arbitrarily introduced into the *church*—however they were driven out of this, the practice itſelf *condemned*, by ſeveral *canons*, and, by little and little, *concubinage* was looked upon as infamous, and at length deemed no better than *whoredom* and *fornication*.

That *polygamy* and *concubinage* were both *diſpenſations* of GOD, both *modes* of *lawful* and *honourable marriage*, is a propoſition as clear as the *Hebrew ſcriptures* can make it—That *polygamous* and *concubinary* contracts are deemed by the *Chriſtians null and void*, and ſtamped with the infamy of *adultery* and *whoredom*, is as certain as that the *canons* and *decrees* of the *church of Rome* * made them to be ſo.—The

---

* Our having learned from the *Papiſts*, to call *polygamy*, *adultery*, and *concubinage*, *whoredom* and *fornication*—reminds one of the *wiſdom* of that ſapient and worthy *Town-clerk*, in SHAKESPEARE's *Much ado about Nothing*, in the examination of *Conrade* and *Borachio*—

1ſt. WATCH. This man ſaid, Sir, that *Don John*, the *Prince's* brother, was a *villain*.

TO. CLERK. Write down, *Prince John a villain*—why, this is flat PERJURY, to call a *prince's* brother *villain*.

SEXTON. What heard you him ſay elſe?

2d. WATCH. Marry, that he had received a thouſand ducats of *Don John*, for accuſing the Lady *Hero* wrongfully.

TO. CLERK. Flat BURGLARY as ever was committed.

DOGB. Yea, by the maſs, that it is.

conſequences

consequences of the *former*, were, the preservation of *female chastity*, and the prevention of *female ruin*—The consequences of the *latter*, have been, and still are, the *destruction* of *thousands* of *both sexes* (but more especially * of the *female)* in this *world* and in the *next.*

Leigh, Crit. Sacr. sub voc. פלגש—says—
" *Concubina-uxor.* Gen. xxii. 24. and xxv. 6.
" The Hebrew *Pilgesh* (whereof the Greek
" παλλακη and Latin *Pellex* are borrowed,
" which we call a *concubine)* signifieth *an half-*
" *wife,* or a *divided* and *secondary wife;* which
" was a wife for the *bed* (and thereby differ-
" ing from an *whore)* but not for honour, and
" government of the family, neither had
" their children ordinarily any right of in-
" heritance, but had gifts of their father,
" (see Gen. xxv. 6.)" On the *margin, Leigh*
cites *Grotius* on *Judges* xix. 1. " *Quidam vo-*
" *cem compositam volunt ex* פלג *divisit,* &
" אשה *uxor,* quasi *uxor divisa. Nomen He-*
" *bræum honestius est quam Græcum* παλλακη,
" & *Latinum* PELLEX, *quæ tamen inde vene-*

* After all the rout that has been made about *polygamy* and *concubinage* in the *Christian* church—the only real and substantial difference between the *antient Jews* and the *Christians* is this—The *former* took a plurality of women, whom they maintained, protected, and provided for, agreeably to GOD's word — the *latter* take a plurality of women, and turn them out to ruin and destruction, not only against GOD's word, but against every principle of justice and humanity.—Or, in other words if the *Jew* took as many as he could *maintain,* the *Christian* ruins as many as he can *debauch.*

" runt-

" *runt.* PELLEX *est* uxorem habentis—CON-
" CUBINA *potest esse* cælibis: *neque talis con-
" junctio contra legem & bonos mores erat illis
" temporibus."

" Some will have this to be a compound
" word—of פלג *he divided,* and אשה *a wife*
" — a *divided wife* as it were. The *Hebrew*
" name is of more *honest* import than the
" Greek παλλακη, and the Latin *Pellex,*
" which are however both derived from it.
" *Pellex* is understood in Latin to signify the
" woman who lives with a *man that has a
" wife*—*Concubina* may signify her who lives
" with a *single man.*" — (These distinctions,
made by different words, do not occur in the
Hebrew) " nor was such a conjunction con-
" trary, in those times, to *law* or to *good*
" *manners.*"

The *concubines* seem to have been usually of an inferior rank, as maid-servants, and the like, and to have been taken without the formality of *dowry,* or any other *outward* circumstance whatsoever—but still they were certainly esteemed as the *property* of the man, as clearly appears from what *Jacob* said, Gen. xlix. 4. and a *concubine* was frequently styled אשה—*a wife.* Comp. Gen. xvi. 3. with Gen. xxv. 6. See also Gen. xxx. 4. with Gen xxxv. 22 xxxvii. 2.

I have before observed, that *concubines* are not *once* mentioned in the New Testament; so that *concubinage* stands entirely on the authority of the *Hebrew scriptures.* These, indeed,

seem

seem to have been entirely laid aside, and *concubinage*, after the *fourth century*, gradually became the *sinful* and *abominable* thing which we are taught to believe it. There is now no *medium* between *whoredom* and *formal marriage*—the same *Popish* dexterity, which converted a piece of *wafer* into an *human body*, and *marriage* into a *sacrament*, turned a *concubine* into a *whore*, and *concubinage* into a *damnable sin*. See before p. 30. and n.

In short, *concubinage* brought no *grist* to the *mill*; no *licences, dispensations*, asking of *banns*, &c. enriched either the *Pope*'s coffers, or the priest's *pocket*; therefore it was found *better*, that a *poor seduced girl*, and the *man*, who to humour his own pride, or that of his *family*, did not chuse the *sacrament* of *marriage*, should be separated, and *she* turned adrift, by " being banished the territory;" *he* at liberty to *ruin* as many more as he could, without any incumbrance or expence, and all *these* to become vagabonds on the face of the earth, rather than *holy church* should lose her *prerogative* of *supremacy* over the *consciences* of her *votaries*; or those darling emoluments, of *power* and *wealth*, be *lessened*, or *interrupted*, in their increase.

This has been improved into an *article of faith*, and has been the destruction of as any *women*, as would out-number the *stars of heaven*, and, in its consequences, of as many *unborn* and *new-born* infants, as would make the *infanticides* at *Bethlehem*, or the
priests

priests of *Moloch*, comparatively *innocent*, if the *numbers destroyed* are to be standards of guilt.

> *Sure these themselves from primitive*
> *And heathen priesthood do derive,*
> *When butchers were the only clerks,*
> *Elders and presbyters of kirks:*
> *Whose directory was to kill,*
> *And some believe it is so still.*
> *The only difference is, that then*
> *They slaughter'd only* beasts, *now* men:
> *For then to sacrifice a bullock,*
> *Or now and then a child to* MOLOCH,
> *They count a vile abomination,*
> *But not to slaughter a whole nation.*
>
> HUD.

It has been before observed, vol. i. 58, n. how apt all arbitrary and living languages are to gain new meanings by length of time, some instances of which are there given, and many more might be given. Mr. *Warton*, in his *Essay* on SPENCER's *Faery Queen*, has observed, that—" words, by an impercep- " tible progression, from one kindred sense " to another, at length obtain a meaning " entirely foreign to their original *etymolo-* " gy."—And indeed they frequently change from a *good* sense to a *bad* one. Who would think the word *imp* was anciently a title of royal dignity? *Lord Cromwell*, in his last letter to HENRY VIII. prays for the *imp* his son. So HENRY V. is hailed, as " *Royal imp* of *fame.*" Now it is only used in contempt or abhorrence, as signifying an *evil spirit*—a *dæmon.* See *Steevens* and *John-*
son's

son's Shakef. vol. ii. 391, n. and vol. v. 607, n. and *Phillips*'s Dict. fub voc.

Thus has it fared with the words *concubinage* and *concubine*:—the *ideas* which have been annexed to thefe words by the *Papifts*, and after them by the *Proteftants*, are as foreign from the *fcripture ideas* of them, as it is almoft poffible for one thing to be from another.—*Concubinage*, as reprefented in the *Hebrew fcripture*, was evidently one *mode* of innocent and lawful *marriage*, and *concubines* were, of courfe, innocent and lawful *wives*—*legitimæ erant uxores*, faith *Bucer*. So late as the fourth century, the terms *wife* and *concubine* were ufed indifferently. So in the year 400, the council of *Toledo* decreed, that—" it was neceffary for " every member of the *church* to fatisfy " himfelf either with *one wife* or *one concu-* " *bine*—that he ought not to be excommu- " nicated who has only a *concubine*."—As *prieftly* benedictions, and other ecclefiaftical forms and ceremonies of *marriage*, increafed by the inventions of men, *concubinage* was not only laid afide, but was looked upon as *fynonymous* with *whoredom* and *fornication*, and a *concubine* was treated as a *whore*:—they certainly had as much authority for this from the fcripture, as to have *burnt* her for a *witch*.

Still the *thing itfelf*, as in GOD's fight, remains juft as it did, neither better nor worfe; for no *change* can poffibly be wrought either in the *divine mind*, or in the *facred language*

language in which it is expressed.—This mode of *marriage* being allowed of GOD, must be concluded to have been for the *wisest reasons*, not the least of which seems to have been, to preserve the *lower* order of *females* from *desertion* and *prostitution* (a thing not known among the antient *Jews*) but to which they have been consigned by the *Christians*, without *mercy* or *remedy*.

I dismiss this part of the subject, with referring the *reader* to *Martin Bucer*'s sound and scriptural thoughts upon it, in the *Appendix* to chap. ii. of *this work*, at the end of vol. i.

Another observation, which arises from the foregoing evidence, is with regard to those dangerous engines of *priestcraft*, and *church-tyranny*, called, in the *Popish canons*, *ecclesiastical courts*; which, together with all their *officials*, *commissaries*, and other *officers* thereunto belonging, were the *improvements* made by the *church of Rome*, on the power granted to *bishops* and *councils* for the *internal* administration of the *church*, by the Emperor *Constantine*. In short, when he and his successors became *Christians*, they thought it highly for the honour of *Christianity*, that the *clergy* should be invested with outward dignities, preheminences, and authorities, suitable to that *kingdom of this world* which then began to be erected—or, as I may say, when the *princes* of the empire became *Christians*, the *Christian churchmen* became *princes*, and this begot the *ecclesiastical courts*; from them came

came the courts of *inquisition*, and every other mode of oppressing mankind, under colour of law, by *ecclesiastical judges*. These *courts*, under the jurisdiction of the *bishops*, were erected in every *diocese*, and, together with *Popery*, transplanted into this country. They were the infernal *tribunals*, which harrassed, persecuted, distressed, tortured, and burnt *Protestants* alive, and might do so still, but for the 29 Car. II. c. 9. which takes away the writ *de heretico comburendo*, yet reserves all other punishments but *death*, in as ample a manner as before the making of the *act*, for " *heresy*, *schism*, and all other dam-" nable *doctrines* and *opinions*." But what these are, who can define? They are vague descriptions of *offences*, concerning which, mankind are not agreed to this hour, and yet punishable by these *courts*, by any *ecclesiastical censures* short of *death*, even to *excommunication* itself.

Outlawry in *treason* or *felony* is a *civil death*, but *excommunication* may be called a *death* both *civil* and *ecclesiastical*; and, when duly considered for *what* it may be inflicted, and by *whom*, and what its *consequences* are, can, in all reason and sense, only be looked upon as one of the most barbarous, oppressive, and iniquitous engines of *church-power*, that the *Pope* left behind him, when his immediate *supremacy* in this country was destroyed.

As for *what* it may be inflicted, it rests

very much in the breasts of the *ecclesiastical judges*, according to the construction they may be pleased to put on the words—" *he-resy, schism,* and *other damnable doctrines and opinions.*"—In some instances, indeed, there are determinate causes assigned of *excommunication ipso facto,* as the reader may see by turning to the " *Constitutions and Canons Ecclesiastical,* treated upon by " the *convocation* 1603," and affirmed afterward under the *great seal* of England, by that *pious, wise,* and *patriotic* prince, King *James* I.

In the *twelve* first *canons,* the reader will find no less than *eleven* causes of *excommunication*—nine *ipso facto,* not one of which have the least to do with the *Bible,* or were offences existing 'till the inventions of *men* gave them birth. There are also other causes of *excommunication,* in others of these said *canons,* which have as little to do with the *Bible,* as those have which are before mentioned. The last *three canons* also denounce *excommunication* for causes unknown to the *scriptures.*

The *person* by *whom,* either the *sentence* of *excommunication,* or the *excommunication ipso facto,* may be awarded, is the *ecclesiastical judge,* who is usually a *layman*; and, if prejudiced against the party, or a man of a severe and bad temper, may find out interpretative causes of *excommunication,* so many and so various, as to leave no man safe:—no *jury* interferes

interferes in the trial of the cause, no determinate definition of "*heresy, schism*, and "*other damnable doctrines and opinions*," to direct or confine the *judgment*—but it stands on the breath of a *single mortal*, to determine on whom this horrid engine of *excommunication* shall be played off.—Add to this, as all the proceedings are in *writing*, a man may be accused by a person he never knew, and convicted of the crime laid to his charge, without ever seeing the face of one of the *witnesses* against him.

As to the consequences of these *excommunications*, I can hardly suppose, that, as to any *spiritual* damage to a *man's soul*, any person of common sense would trouble his head about them, or give a *brass farthing* for his *absolution*; I am sure, if he did, he would give more, by all the money, than it is *worth*.—But as to the *temporal* inconveniences accruing from these *engines* of *ecclesiastical* despotism, they are certainly very terrible, so much so, as to render them very serious objects of our consideration, as a *free* and *Protestant* people.

There are two sorts of *excommunication*, called the *lesser* and the *greater*: the *lesser* is the depriving the offender of the *use of the sacraments*, and *divine worship*; and this sentence is passed by *judges ecclesiastical*, on such persons as are guilty of *obstinacy* or *disobedience*, in not appearing upon a citation, or not submitting to *penance*, or other injunctions

tions of the court. The greater *excommunication*, is that, whereby men are deprived, not only of the *sacraments*, and the benefit of *divine offices*, but of the *society* and *conversation* of the *faithful*—i. e. of all persons *not* excommunicated.

If a person be *excommunicated* generally; as if the *judge* say—" *I excommunicate such a* " *person*"—this shall be understood of the greater excommunication. Lindw. 78. Lindwood says, that *excommunication ipso facto* is—*nullo hominis ministerio interveniente*—which is about as equitable as hanging a man without a trial.

By art. 33, of the church of *England*, " that person, which, by open denunciation " of the church, is rightly cut off from the " unity of the church, and *excommunicated*, " ought to be taken of the whole multitude " of the faithful as an *heathen and publican*, " until he be openly reconciled by *penance*, " and received into the *church* by a *judge* " that hath authority thereunto."

By can. 85, " the *churchwardens* or *quest-* " *men* especially shall see, that all persons " *excommunicated*, and so denounced, be kept " out of the *church*." See Burn Eccl. Law, tit. *Excommunication*.

The consequences of all this are, that a man is deprived of the participation of the *means of grace*—inhibited the commerce and communion of the *faithful*—and moreover, after forty days, the *spiritual* court signifying this to the court of *Chancery*, by *significavit*, there issues a writ *de excommunicato capiendo*, which is all but as bad as the *heretico comburendo*, for it causes the man to be apprehended by the *civil power*, and thrown into *gaol*, where he may lie 'till he *rots*, if he has not money enough to purchase his letters of absolution, as in cases of *excommunication* for non-payment of * *costs*, and the like.

Moreover, it is to be observed, that the *excommunicate* person is so far put out of the protection of the *laws* of his country, as that he cannot sue an action *real* or *personal*.

He cannot make a last *will* and *testament*.

He cannot be an *advocate*—or a *witness*—nor a *juror*, if the record of the judgment be produced.

He cannot act as an *executor*, or prosecute any action for the testator's goods; and they which converse with an *excommunicate* person are *excommunicate* † also.

And

---

* One of the *twenty-eight grievances* complained of to the House of *Commons*, anno 1640, was—" the general " abuse of *excommunication*, which was inflicted for *tri-* " *vial* matters, and the *absolution* whereof could not be " obtained without money." Another—" the great " abuse of *ecclesiastical* courts."—See *Rapin*, vol. ii. 361.

† Let it be observed, that all these mischiefs may befal a man, who is neither guilty of a breach of any revealed *law* of God—nor of the known *law of the land*—no part of *this* can the *canons* be reckoned, as the highest sanction which they ever obtained, was that of the *great seal*.—How then is imprisonment of an *English* subject,

And that they may *be-devil* a man to the uttermoſt, it is ordered, by can. 68, that a *miniſter* is to be ſuſpended for *three months*, who affords *Chriſtian burial* to a perſon, againſt whom the *court-chriſtian* (for ſo the *eccleſiaſtical court* is ſometimes called, as the court of *inquiſition* is called the *houſe of mercy*—as *lucus* a non *lucendo*—) hath pronounced the * *greater excommunication*, which may be done by the ſingle voice of the *judge*, only ſaying—" *I excommunicate ſuch a one*," and that, for offences which have no foundation, but in the uncertain conſtruction of vague and indeterminate *human words*, or in the *canons* of the *church*, which are the pure inventions of an *eccleſiaſtical ſynod*, and framed, as near as may be, to ſave appearances, to the *canons* of the *church of Rome*.

Surely ſuch powers as theſe are too great to be truſted in the hands of *any man*, and are

ſubject, under *excommunication* for offending againſt theſe *canons*, conſiſtent with that axiom in the *grand charter* of *Engliſh freedom*, c. 29.—" *Nullus liber homo* " *capiatur vel impriſonetur*, &c. *nec ſuper eum ibimus, nec* " *ſuper eum mittemus, niſi per legale judicium parium ſuo-* " *rum vel per legem terræ.*"—" No free man ſhall be " taken or impriſoned, &c. nor we will not paſs upon " him nor condemn him, but by *lawful judgment of his* " *peers*, or by the *law of the land?*

* The church of *Rome* is rather more charitable in this buſineſs, for it has a—" *Ritus abſolvendi excommu-* " *nicatum poſt mortem*"—" A *rite* of abſolving an ex- " communicate perſon after death,"—and if *buried*, they will dig him up again for this purpoſe, provided he ſhewed a ſign of *contrition* on his *departure*.—The ceremony of *verberation* and *abſolution*, together with all the reſt of the *farce*, is in the *Rituale Romanum*.

ſuch

such as are too inimical to public *liberty* and *safety*, to be suffered to exist any where, much less in a *free* and *Protestant country*. While the *Pope* was supreme head of the *church of England*, had set himself above *all law*, and could cause a learned, brave, and *great king (Henry* II.) to be *flogged* by a parcel of rascally *monks*, at *Thomas a Becket*'s tomb, like a *thief* at a *cart's tail*—could lay whole kingdoms under an *interdict*, and cause the kings of the earth to be *excommunicated*, and *deposed* and *murdered* by their *subjects*—one can account for the people of this infatuated country's submitting to the *ecclesiastical tyranny* of the *spiritual courts*—but surely, after above *two centuries* have passed since the banishment of the *Pope*, it is high time for us to reflect as to the situation we are in, with respect to these dreadful *tribunals*.

I have before, (vol. i. p. 67) spoken of these *courts*, and called their power " *very feeble*"—this must be understood in a comparative sense, to what it was before the abolition of the *high commission* court, by 16 Car. I. c. 11.—the taking away the writ *de hæretico comburendo*, by 29 Car. II. c. 9. —and the passing that truly *Christian* law, commonly called the *toleration* act, 1 W. and M. c. 18.—but there is still power enough left, to make the subjects of this kingdom tremble for what may happen, in less moderate times than those we live in.

What *offences* can possibly arise, which a *temporal judge*, and a jury of *twelve men*, cannot

cannot punish? What evils, which they cannot properly and duly † animadvert upon? Or what laws can be imagined, which they cannot execute, on the constitutional principles of a fair and open trial on *vivâ voce* evidence, and on the words of determinate and certain statutes? Why are * *wills* and *testaments, matrimonial causes*, and other matters of a *temporal* nature, to be consigned into the hands of *ecclesiastical judges?* — I can give no other reason, than that the *Pope* wrested them out of the hands of the *civil* powers, and placed them there; which, by the way, is no bad reason for their being restored to the *civil power* again.

Much has been said, and much more

---

† " As *St. Paul* thought that men might *lead quiet and peaceable lives, in all godliness and honesty*, under proper subjection to, and coercion of the civil magistrate, I do not see that I should be ashamed to think so too." *Confessional*, 3d edit. 231.

* " The probate of testaments did not originally belong to the *ecclesiastical* jurisdiction, but to the *county court*, or to the *court baron* of the respective *lord of the manor* where the *testator* died, as all other matters did." 2 *Bac.* Abr. 398.

" The truth is, there were *wills* before there was any *ecclesiastical* jurisdiction, and consequently the cognizance thereof pertained then *solely* to the *civil* magistrate." See *Burn*, Eccl. Law. tit. *Wills*.

The truth of all is, that *papal* usurpation stopped at nothing, which could encrease the wealth, or gratify the ambition of *churchmen*. When the *Pope* sent his *superstition* into this country, by *Austin* the *monk*, his *power* followed hard after it, and laid its hands on what it pleased, none daring to resist. This is the true original of throwing *matrimonial* and *testamentary* causes into the hands of *ecclesiastical judges*. See *Thelyph*. vol. ii. p. 141, 2d edit.

might

might be said on the subject; but how we can call ourselves *Protestants*, or boast of our being a *free* people, while we are under this *imperium in imperio*, I cannot conceive—therefore, as the *parliament* of *England* abolished the *high commission* court, by 16 Car. I. c. 11, it would be an *act* becoming an age of still greater *Protestant* liberty, to *annihilate* every power of *churchmen* to do *mischief*, and leave them no other, than that of doing *good*.

Another *observation* which may be made on the foregoing *evidence*, relates more immediately to the subjects of these *volumes*; I mean, the contrivances of the *Popish* canon-law, to blind people from the real and true nature of *marriage*; to make them believe that it consists in an *outward ceremony*, which *man* has invented, and not in that *personal union* which GOD ordained *at the beginning*; and, of course, to throw *nullity*, and even *infamy*, on the *latter*; thus to strip it of all *obligation* and *validity*, and by these means, leaving the seduction and dereliction of *virgins* wholly in the power of their *betrayers*. To this the *church*, the *priest*, and the other religious formalities, have so greatly contributed, that neither *Papist* nor *Protestant* have the least doubt upon the subject.— The *Papist* calls *his priest*'s LEGERDEMAIN the *form* of the *sacrament*, but the *sacrament* itself is the *union* created by the *Ego jungo vos*, &c. The *Protestant* will tell us, that an *outward ceremony* is the *form* of the *marriage*, but that the *marriage* itself consists in the *union* arising from *certain words* spoken in *English* instead of *Latin*. —Without this there is no *marriage*, as both will confess; therefore both equally make *marriage* to consist in something, which, so far from being of the *essence* of it, is not so much as *mentioned*, or even hinted at, throughout the whole *word of* GOD, no, not even as the most distant circumstance attending upon it.

We are encouraging the revival and improvement of the liberal arts; *painting, sculpture, music*, and other ornaments of civil society, meet with their patrons and promoters; *schools* and *academies* are erected, and busily employed, in the more noble and useful researches of *navigation, astronomy*, and their concomitant *sciences*; how is it then, that we are, with regard to the important subjects of these volumes, contented to remain where the *dawning* of the *Reformation* left us, partly *delivered*, partly *retained* in the hands of that *superstition*, so much of which our first *reformers* shook off?—how is it, that the *miseries* of *ruined females* have little other effect upon us, than to provoke our *contempt*, or sometimes, perhaps, excite our *pity?*—Will —" *be ye warmed*"—relieve them from the winter's cold?—or—" *be ye clothed*"—cover their *nakedness?*—Why not search into the *records of everlasting truth*, to see whether there is not a solid provision made against their distresses— some mighty bulwark raised for their

their *security* and *protection* — some remedy provided against the crying, ruinous, and destructive evil of public *prostitution?* If there be such things—let them be brought forth into open daylight, let them be *proclaimed on the house-tops*—had we *Virgil*'s

Linguæ centum—oraque centum——

let them be all employed upon the glorious, salutary subject—let *Protestant* legislation destroy *Popish* encroachment; let it adopt the *laws of Heaven* for its guide—rendering unto *Cæsar the things that are Cæsar's, and unto* GOD *the things which are* GOD's.—Thus making *marriage* what GOD has made it—in its *nature, end,* and *obligation*; and confirming *all these*, by such *laws of the state*, as may insure, by OUTWARD RECOGNITION, what has been commanded and established by HEAVENLY and DIVINE INSTITUTION.

From the foregoing long series of evidence it likewise appears, whence has been derived the whole art and mystery of *sin-making*, and *unmaking* it again, by human contrivance—also *saint-making*—*cross-making*—*creed-making*—the consecration of *days* and *seasons*—framing *calendars*, which, like the *Fasti* of Heathen *Rome*, are filled with observances of superstitious veneration in honour of dead *men* and *women*.—The *Heathen* had their *Dii majorum gentium*, and their *Dii minorum*—their *Gods, Demigods,* and *Heroes*—*Christian churchmen* registered their *Lady* * the *Virgin Mary*—

---

* *Annunciation* of OUR LADY. See *Eng. Kal.* of *proper lessons.*

angels—

angels—apostles—saints—martyrs—confessors—and each of these had his day on which he was to be worshipped.

We likewise find the true origin of those uncommanded and humanly-invented *rites* and *ceremonies,* which corrupted the simplicity of the *divine ordinances,* obscured the true nature of *divine institutions,* and fixed the eyes of *Christians,* not on what GOD had *ordained,* but on what *men* had *invented.*

These were guarded, in the most tremendous manner, by the *ecclesiastical* powers, against all contradiction and innovation.—Many instances of this we have already met with—but let us hear the *Council* of *Trent,* Sess. 7. Can. 13.

" Si quis dixerit, receptos & approbatos ec-
" clesiæ Catholicæ ritus in solemni sacramen-
" torum administratione adhiberi consuetos,
" aut contemni, aut sine peccato a ministris
" pro libitu omitti, aut in novos alios per
" quemcumque ecclesiarum pastorem mutari
" posse—*anathema sit.*"

" If any one shall say that the received
" and approved *rites* of the *Catholic church,*
" which are wont to be used in the solemn
" administration of the *sacraments,* are to
" be contemned, or, without sin, can be
" omitted at the will of the minister, or can
" be changed for other new ones by any
" pastor of the churches—LET HIM BE AC-
" CURSED."

Now let us hear the *Protestant* church of *England,* CAN. 4.

" Whosoever shall hereafter affirm, that
" the

"the form of GOD's worship in the church
"of *England,* established by *law,* and con-
"tained in the book of the *Common Prayer,*
"and administration of *sacraments,* is a cor-
"rupt, superstitious, or unlawful worship of
"GOD, or containeth *any thing in it* that is
"repugnant to the scriptures, let him be
"EXCOMMUNICATED *ipso facto,* and not re-
"stored, but by the *bishop* of the place, or
"*archbishop,* after his repentance, and public
"revocation of such his *wicked errors.*"

Can. 6. Exhibits a like sentence against—
"Impugners of the *rites* and *ceremonies* esta-
"blished in the church of *England*"—Ex-
COMMUNICATION *ipso facto.*

So we see, that, as the *Papists* CURSE the *Protestants,* the *Protestants* CURSE *one another*—and all this, for matters entirely of *human invention.*—Surely this is a likely way to reconcile our *dissenting Protestant brethren* to the *church* as by law *established!* and to convince *infidels,* that when they laugh at us all for a parcel of *fools,* they are *very much* in the *wrong!*

As to *marriage,* the *Romish* ritual says—

"Parochus—Noverit ex probatis auctori-
"bus, quæ sint canonica impedimenta ma-
"trimonii contrahendi, & quæ contractum
"dirimant: & qui sint gradus consanguini-
"tatis & affinitatis, & item cognationis spi-
"ritualis ex baptismi vel confirmationis sa-
"cramento contractæ:

"Habeat imprimis ipse bene cognita præ-
"cepta illa omnia, quæ in matrimoniis rite
"conficiendis

" conficiendis fervari oportere, facri canones,
" et præcipue fancta fynodus Tridentina
" juffit, dabitque operam, ut illa in parochia
" fua accurate exacteque ferventur."

" Let the *parifh prieft* know, from *ap-
" proved authors*, what are the *canonical* im-
" pediments of contracting matrimony, and
" what things may deftroy the contract: and
" what are the degrees of affinity and con-
" fanguinity, alfo of fpiritual relationfhip,
" contracted by the facrament of baptifm or
" confirmation.

" Let him, above all things, be well ac-
" quainted with all thofe precepts which
" ought to be kept, in rightly and duly per-
" forming marriages, according to the *facred
" canons*, and efpecially according to what
" the holy *fynod* of *Trent* commanded. And
" he fhall do his endeavour, that thefe fhall
" be accurately and exactly kept within his
" parifh."

We find here *particularly*, as before in *general*, from whence we derive our notions of
fending people to *canons, learned authors*, and
acts of parliament, to be taught what are or
are not *impediments* to marriage; as likewife
how totally the *antient laws* of JEHOVAH, relative to what does or does not make a valid
marriage in His fight, are cafhiered and laid
out of the *queftion*—and how the ordinances
of men are fubftituted in the place of the in-
ftitutions of GOD.

There is another claufe in the *Romifh ritual*,
which, compared with the preceding evidence,

dence, shews how *second marriages* of all sorts have, through a long succession of *ages*, met with the disapprobation of the *church*.

"Caveat etiam *parochus* ne quando con-
"juges in primis nuptiis benedictionem ac-
"ceperint, eos in secundis benedicat, sive
"mulier, sive etiam vir ad secundas nuptias
"transeat: sed ubi ea viget consuetudo, ut
"si mulier nemini unquam nupserit, etiam-
"si vir aliam uxorem habuerit, nuptiæ be-
"nedicantur, ea servanda est. Sed viduæ
"nuptias non benedicat, etiamsi ejus vir
"nunquam uxorem duxerit."

"Let the *priest* also beware, lest, when
"*married* persons have in *former* nuptials
"received the *benediction*, he confer it on
"them in *second* nuptials, whether a *woman*,
"or even a *man*, passes on to a *second* mar-
"riage. But where the custom prevails,
"that, if a woman has never been married
"before, though the man has had another
"wife, the nuptials shall be *blessed*, there
"that custom shall stand. But he shall not
"bless the nuptials of a *widow*, although
"the man she marries never had another
"wife."

If it be asked, by what authority is all this?—I answer, by as *good* authority as we refuse the *benediction* to a man who has a wife in a *mad-house*, and who marries another to keep himself out of a *brothel*. Or to one who was to do the same because he had detected his wife in *adultery*, and could not afford to pay the monstrous expence of an act

of

of parliament to divorce her. Or to others who are as juſtly and unavoidably ſeparated, as if their wives were *dead*.

In ſhort, it is needleſs to cite any more authorities to prove, that the *ideas* which the ſcriptures have given us of *marriage*, in all the *forms* in which it appeared under the immediate diſpenſation of God, have long been changed into a very different *ſyſtem*, and that our ſentiments of the matter are to be entirely regulated by the contrivances of mortals, and not by the unerring *rule* of God's law. But when we conſider the miſchiefs with which this is attended, in the deſolation and ruin of the *weaker ſex*, and that all the inventions of human wit and wiſdom are utterly diſproportionate to the taſk of finding out a remedy, we ought to confeſs—that " *we have committed two evils, in forſaking* " Jehovah, *the fountain of living waters,* " *and hewing out unto ourſelves ciſterns, broken* " *ciſterns, that can hold no water.*" Jer. ii. 13.

The *Papiſts*, as we have before ſeen, teach, that " marriage is a ſacrament of the New " Teſtament, ordained by Christ, and *appro-* " *priated* to *Chriſtians.*"—This we deny in words; but how diſtant *our ſyſtem* is from it, or how different in truth and in fact, or how eſſentially more conformable to the *Bible*, requires a much more diſtinguiſhing head than I can boaſt of to define.

My friend, the honeſt *Quaker*, ſays—that —" *a cat in a window is like a cat out of a* " *window.*"—What he means by this I leave to the reader to determine, as well as what he means by affirming—

"That, if two men were to sit down to write a *glossary*, in which the *English* words—*Marriage—Whoredom—Fornication—Polygamy—Concubinage—Divorce, &c.*—were to be explained;—were these writers to be shut up apart in different rooms, *one* with the *Popish system*, as set forth in the determinations and decrees of *Popes*, councils, synods, &c. of the church of *Rome*—the *other* with the *statutes* at large, the "*constitutions and canons ecclesiastical*," and other muniments of this *Protestant* country—and both these men honestly and fairly adhered to their several *patterns*;—they would, when they came forth, produce *works* so *like* one another, and so *unlike* the *scriptures*, as to make one suspect (as has been thought of *Ptolomy's seventy interpreters*) that though the writers appeared to have been separated, yet they must have had some communication together, though so secret as not to be discovered."

As *Rome* was not *built* in a day, so neither could it be *demolished* in a day.—The Protestant *Reformers* did *much* towards its demolition, but they could not do *all*.—The prejudices which they had to encounter, the opposition and persecution which they endured, the controversies they were engaged in, and many other things which were inseparable from their peculiar situation, ought

rather

rather to make us wonder that they got fo *far* as they did, rather than be furprized that they got no *farther*.

When *Henry* VIII. quarrelled with the *Pope*, he yet by no means quarrelled with *Popery*, as the *fix* bloody *articles*, which were the ground of that antichriftian and bloody law, 31 H. VIII. c. 14. intituled, "An act "for abolifhing of diverfity of opinions in "certain articles concerning *Chriftian reli-* "*gion*," fully fhew. — Other laws, which took the *fupreme* power in *ecclefiaftical* matters out of the hands of the *Pope*, threw it into the hands of the *King*; and good care was taken that the *hierarchy* under *Henry* VIII. fhould have all powers of co-operation with his *Majefty*, as they had before with his *Holinefs*.—The kingdom in the next reign (of *Edward* VI.) affumed the name of *Proteftant* with much more colour of title than in the preceding—Queen *Mary's* acceffion bid fair to undo all again;—but in the long reign of her fucceffor *Queen Elizabeth*, the *Proteftant* eftablifhment gained that ftrength and firmnefs, which it acquired by fundry laws made in its favour; and was ftill more eftablifhed at the glorious *Revolution*, when the State found it neceffary to guard, in the ftrongeft manner, againft the danger of the return of *Popery*, in the perfon of a Popifh *Pretender*.

Still *marriage*, and all things relative thereto, were dependent on thofe *opinions* of *men*, which had been the ground of antient *canons*,

and

and other laws concerning them.—In many great and important articles of religion, the reformers had acted upon the great *Protestant axiom*, that " the scriptures are the *only rule* " *of faith*."—As to the *rites* and *ceremonies* of the *church*, these remained, with a very strong mixture of the old ones, which had been established before the *Reformation*—therefore all similarity between them and those of the *church of Rome*, must be accounted for, partly from the early * prejudices of the compilers, partly from the influence, which a more considerable alteration must have had, on certain very lucrative emoluments arising to the *church*, from things remaining in their present form.—*Henry* VIII. saw how much it was for his own interest to keep *marriage* within the power of human

---

* That masterly writer, the author of the *Confessional*, furnishes me with words to express what I mean.

" On this state of the case, it appears that the matter " of complaint does not affect the *fathers* of the *Refor-* " *mation*, by far so much as their *sons* and *successors*. " Our first *Reformers* were beset with their own and " other men's prejudices, to a degree that rendered them, " in a great measure, incapable of conviction. It was " next to impossible to convince them, that their esta- " blished confessions of faith" [and so their notions, doubtless, on many other subjects] " were unchristian " impositions, for which there was no just authority, " when they had the early practice of the *Christian* " *church* to appeal to, long before the tyrannical spirit " of *Rome* prevailed. Their veneration for antiquity " prevented their seeing that these very precedents were " some of the steps by which the *Papal* power ascended " to its height, and arrived at the plenitude of its usur- " pation." *Confessional*, 3d edit. p. 27.

legiflation, and to model it as he liked, for his own convenience; and it is moſt probable, that the *clergy* would not have made it very eaſy for his *Proteſtant ſucceſſors,* had they been inclined to it, to have wreſted ſo † profitable a branch of *clerical* profit and importance out of their hands. Hence it is, that things " are as they are;" and there is no

great

---

† Mr. VINCENT ALSOP (the famous author of ANTI-SOZZO) in his *Melius Inquirendum,* p. 68. on that poſition, " *that no reformation can be made, but what* " *will notably diminiſh the revenues, grandeur, and credit* " *of the church*"—obſerves, " that whatever have been " the ſpecious pretences, this has been the *real* obſtruction " of *effectual reformation*; *Kings* and *Parliaments* have " always been inclinable towards a redreſs of exorbi- " tancies, but the covetouſneſs and pride of *churchmen* " have ever impeded their pious endeavours. *A Par-* " *liament* in Queen *Elizabeth*'s reign, as we read in " Dr. *Fuller*'s Church Hiſtory, was bringing in a bill " againſt *pluralities,* and archbiſhop *Whitgift* ſends a letter " to her majeſty, ſignifying, that they were all undone, " horſe and foot, if it paſſed. Obſerve how he deplores " the miſerable ſtate of the *church*—*The wofull and dif-* " *treſſed ſtate into which we are like to fall, forceth us,* " *with grief of heart, in moſt humble manner, to crave your* " *majeſty's moſt ſovereign protection.*——Why, what is the " matter?—were they making a law againſt *preaching?* " No.—Or againſt *common-prayer?* By no means!— " What ails then the diſtreſſed man? Why—*we, there-* " *fore,* not as *directors,* but as *humble remembrancers, be-* " *ſeech your highneſs's favourable beholding of our preſent* " *ſtate, and what it will be in time, if the* BILL *againſt* " PLURALITIES *ſhould take place.*—No queſtion it muſt " be utter extirpation of the *Chriſtian religion.*

" Thus, in another letter to the ſame *Queen,* he com- " plains, with lamentations that would ſoften an heart " of marble—that, they have brought in a *bill* giving " *liberty to* MARRY *at all times of the year without re-* " *ſtraint.*—Well, but if men be obnoxious to *the evil*

" at

great likelihood they should undergo the least alteration, till we are thoroughly awakened to a sight and sense of the deplorable consequences of our present *system* (where *adultery* goes without due punishment, and *seduction* remains without all obligation from the *seducer* to the *seduced*) and we seriously wish to reform the deplorable state of things, by the *pattern delivered in the Mount*; I mean, by those MOST RIGHTEOUS LAWS which the GOD of *Heaven* revealed, for the *moral* government of his reasonable creatures, in that most important of all things in *this world—the commerce of the sexes.*

" at *all times of the year*, why should they not use the
" *remedy* which GOD hath appointed *at all times of the*
" *year?* The *Apostle*, who tells us—*It is better to marry*
" *than burn*, did not except *any time of the year.* But
" why may not a *Parliament* make *a law*, as well as
" the *Ecclesiastical Court* give *a licence*, that it shall be
" lawful to *marry at any time of the year?* Ay—but
" the *Parliament* will make the *law* for *nothing*, whereas
" those other will have *money* for their *licences.* But
" he proceeds — *It is contrary to the old canons con-*
" *tinually observed by us.* Why, but is it not *con-*
" *trary to the old canons* to take money for a *licence?*
" Yes!—but—*it tendeth to the slander of the church, as*
" *having hitherto maintained an error.* And now you
" have the bottom of the bag: all *reformation* must
" touch the *clergy*, either in their *credits or profits*, and it
" were better never to put *an hand to that work*, than
" touch *either of those* with a little finger." p. 69.

INTRODUCTION TO CHAP. XIV.

MR. Locke, b. ii. c. 33, "Of the associ-
"ation of *ideas*," observes, that—"Some
" of our *ideas* have a natural correspondence
" and connexion one with another: it is the
" office and excellency of our reason to
" trace these, and hold them together in that
" union and correspondence which is found-
" ed in their peculiar beings.

" Besides this, there is another connexion
" of *ideas*, wholly owing to chance or cus-
" tom: *ideas*, that in themselves are not at
" all of kin, come to be so united in some
" men's minds, that 'tis very hard to separate
" them: they always keep company, and the
" one no sooner comes into the understand-
" ing, but its associate appears with it; and
" if they are more than two, the whole gang,
" always inseparable, shew themselves toge-
" ther.

" This connexion in our minds, of *ideas*
" in themselves loose, and independent of one
" another, is of so great force to set us awry
" in our actions, as well moral as natural,
" passions, reasonings, and notions them-
" selves, that perhaps there is not any one
" thing that deserves more to be looked af-
" ter. Thus the *ideas* of *goblins* and *sprights*
" have really no more to do with darkness
" than light; yet let but a foolish maid in-
" culcate these often on the mind of a child,
" and raise them there together, possibly he
" shall never be able to separate them again

" so

" so long as he lives, but darkness shall ever
" afterwards bring with it those frightful
" *ideas.*

" Some such wrong combinations of *ideas*
" will be found to establish the irreconcile-
" able opposition between different sects of
" philosophy and religion; for we cannot
" imagine every one of their followers to
" impose wilfully on himself, and knowingly
" refuse truth offered by plain reason. That
" therefore which captivates their reasons,
" and leads men of sincerity blindfold from
" common sense, will, when examined, be
" found to be what we are speaking of:
" some independent *ideas* are, by education,
" custom, and the constant din of their
" party, so coupled in their minds, that they
" always appear there together, and they can
" no more separate them in their thoughts,
" than if they were but one *idea*; and they
" operate as if they were so.

" This gives sense to jargon, demonstra-
" tion to absurdities, and consistency to non-
" sense, and is the foundation of the greatest,
" I had almost said of all the errors in the
" world: or, if it does not reach so far, is at
" least the most dangerous one, since, so far
" as it obtains, it hinders men from seeing
" and examining the confusion of two dif-
" ferent *ideas,* which a customary connexion
" of them in their minds hath to them in ef-
" fect made but one, and cannot but fill men's
" heads with false views, and their reason-
" ings with false consequences."

On the principles of this great man, many

things are to be accounted for, which otherwife are unaccountable. When one looks (for inftance) into the ordinance of the CREATOR, by which the human fpecies is to be propagated and preferved—when we confider the fimple ground of *union,* as reprefented Gen. ii. 24, and the confequence drawn from it by the great *interpreter* of the *law*—Matt. xix. 5, 6—we muft afcribe the independent *ideas,* which, by long cuftom and ufage, have united themfelves in the minds of men concerning *marriage,* to their having been inculcated from early infancy, by others, who themfelves have come by them in the fame way; and thus having been delivered over, fince their *coinage* in the *church* of *Rome,* from generation to generation, they ftand in the public opinion as fo many abfolute and demonftrable truths: whereas, not a fingle trace of them is to be found in the *Bible;* neither *religious perfons,* nor *religious outward ceremonies,* have any more to do with the effence or validity of the marriage-union in GOD's fight, than *darknefs* has to do with *fprights* and *goblins,* or the *fign* of the *crofs,* or *godfathers* and *godmothers,* have to do with the ordinance of *baptifm.*—The neceffity of an *outward* contract does not therefore arife from any command of GOD, fo as to make the union null and void, or finful, without it; but from caufes of the moft difgraceful nature, and which are owing to the dreadful departure of mankind from truth and juftice, and from that reverence and obedience to the

CREATOR's appointments, which it was once the honour and happiness, and must be for ever the duty, of man to pay them.

CHAP. XIV.

Of the ORIGIN *and* NECESSITY *of* MARRIAGE-CEREMONY.

THE invention of *marriage-ceremonies*, is as great a proof of the depravity and corruption of human nature, as the invention of written *bonds* and *obligations* under *hand and seal*; they alike prove, that they are the effects of that necessity, which mankind laboured under, to secure themselves against the villainy, treachery, and deceit of one another. Was the *world* what it *ought to be*, no *obligation*, beside that of *conscience*, would be necessary for the security of men, with regard to any kind of bargains which they could make with each other. The man who lent another a sum of money, though without any other witnesses to the transaction than the *parties* themselves, would be perfectly secure, perhaps more so than he is *now*, with a bond duly stamped, and sealed, and delivered by the hand of the obligor, in the presence of witnesses —If we ask whence arose those voluminous securities, known in our law by the names of *marriage-settlements, mortgage-deeds,* and *specialties* of various kinds? it may be answered, "From men's being "afraid to trust one another without them."

The

The very same principle first gave birth to outward *marriage-ceremony*; the simple *institution* of *Heaven* would have been as sufficient to have bound the parties to each other at this hour, as it was in the days of *innocence*, had not the corruption of human nature destroyed the influences of *justice*, *mercy*, and *truth* within the human soul. The adventitious circumstances of *human ceremony*, on this account, became necessary; and, as the world increased, and villainy of all kinds increased, the means of security against it has at all times exercised the invention of *legislature*, and employed the vigilance of the *executive power*, in order to obviate the mischievous effects of it.

But what a strange thing would it be to hear, that a *bond*, on paper, stamped with a stamp of such a value, and sealed and delivered in the presence of witnesses, and *not* the sum of money *lent*, raised the *duty* in the obligor's conscience to pay it? and what a conscience must that man have, who looks upon an outward security as the only reason for acknowledging a just debt? yet this is the language of mankind with respect to *marriage*; the debt of *justice*, arising from the command of GOD, is all easily set aside, and nothing is looked upon as obligatory but the outward bond. To say, that this is less a mere *civil contract* than the other, is saying what is not true, and is the great advantage which has been taken of men's understandings in the business of *marriage*, to the no small emolument of those that have taken it,

and

and to the diſtreſs and deſtruction of millions that have ſuffered by it.

Again, let us ſuppoſe the whole body of *attorneys, conveyancers,* &c. banding together to perſuade mankind, that the doctrine of conveyances by *leaſe* and *releaſe*, by way of *mortgage*, and this farther ſtrengthened by levying *fines* and ſuffering *recoveries*, in caſes of *intailed eſtates*, came from *heaven*; and that no man was obliged in conſcience to be anſwerable for a ſum of money which he had borrowed, unleſs he employed a *conveyancer*, and ſet his hand and ſeal to *ſixty* large ſkins of parchment; and that if he borrowed money without this, and dared to pay it, he would be *damned*—we ſhould here ſee a lively emblem of what *churchmen* have taught us upon the ſubject of *marriage-ceremony:* — as the *lawyers* would place the ſole obligation of payment in their *wax* and *parchment*, and in the chicane of their art, and not in the command of *Heaven* " *to render to all their* " *due;*" ſo *churchmen* have placed the whole *marriage-obligation* in an outward ceremony, and not in the *command of God*, " *they ſhall* " *be one fleſh*"—they have let looſe all obligation whatſoever ariſing from this *command*, inſomuch that it is under pain and peril of *damnation*, that a man dares perſiſt in it, unleſs the *prieſt* accounts him *rectus in curia*, and can bring him to *ſign* and *ſeal* by an *outward ceremony*; which, under certain circumſtances, is impoſſible, becauſe human laws have made it ſo.

Now, what a *bond*, or *mortgage*, is by way of security for money, that a *marriage-ceremony* is, by way of security with regard to *marriage:* and as a man who lends another a sum of money has a right to demand a proper security for the repayment of the debt, principal and interest; so has every woman a right to demand the security of such *ceremony* as the laws of her country have ordained, with respect to the man who has *seduced* her — GOD has in effect COMMANDED it, Exod. xxii. 16. and therefore the severest penalty ought to be inflicted on the man who refuses it. The woman who delivers her person into the possession of a man, without the *ceremony* first performed, does not act a * *cautious, proper,* or

---

* Some may perhaps think, that I have spoken here too *mildly* of such an act, and that I should have introduced the epithet *sinful* among the rest; but, as I see no transgression of any *law of* GOD in the matter, and am told that *where there is no law there is no transgression*, I dare not adopt so *pernicious a tenet*, as to call that *sinful*, which GOD commanded with a *blessing*. See Gen. i. 28, and again Gen. ii. 24. See before vol. i. chap. 2. paragr. 1 and 2.

If mortals have entirely changed the dispensations and ordinances of GOD, into *systems* of their own invention, this can have no sort of effect on the real and determinate nature of *good* and *evil* as defined in the *holy scriptures*. For my own part, I am most perfectly convinced, that the *fear* and *shame*, which the *pernicious tenet* above hinted at hath by custom brought on the *mother*, hath, in numberless instances, occasioned the *murder* of the *child*; and therefore it may well be termed *pernicious*, in the most emphatical sense of the word. See before, index to vol. ii. tit. CHILD-MURDER. See also the doctrines of the *Albigenses* and *Lollards*, before p. 243.

wife

wife part; any more than the man who lends a large fum of money without the due execution of the *bond* or *mortgage-deeds*; but he who can take an undue advantage, in either cafe, muſt be a villain in grain. In the money-affair, he would be thought fo, and treated as fuch—a *court* of juſtice would be open to the *injured*, and redrefs afforded; but in the other cafe, though a villainy attended with irreparable mifchief, the very *law itfelf*, as it *now* ſtands, bars all redrefs, configns the wretched female to deſtruction, and leaves the man, to ruin as many more women as he can deceive.

All this is owing to our following the *Popifh* plan, which has been fo much fet forth at large in the former part of this *volume*; owing to *this* it is, that we make *marriage-ceremony* what it is not, and do not make *marriage itfelf* what it really is.

Our *lawyers* can well diſtinguiſh between that which raifes the debt or obligation, and that which is the fecurity for the payment of the *one*, or for the performance of the *other*.

Our *cafuiſts* would find little difficulty in determining, that a man is equally bound in *confcience* to pay a fum of money which he has borrowed, whether the *lender* has taken a written *fecurity* for it, or whether he has not; or whether the money was lent before an *hundred* witneſſes, or only when the *lender* and *borrower* were alone in *private*.

Now, let what has been faid be taken all together, and let none charge the *author* with
depreciating

depreciating those *securities* which men take of one another for the payment of money; let none say he wants to diminish the public revenue by what he has said on the subject of *bonds*, and other *deeds*, which carry *stamps*; or that he means to lessen the obligation on people to pay their debts, because he contends that *in foro conscientiæ*, and as in the sight of the *Judge of all*, a man would be as much obliged to pay what he owes, *without* any *bond* or *mortgage* as *with* it: what he has said on this subject, tends to prove, that if *men* were what they ought to be, and what the *divine law* requires them to be, every man's *word* would be as *good as his bond*; but that, as things are, it must be allowed, that *most* men's *bonds* are better than their *words*.

Ultima Cælestum terras ASTRÆA *reliquit*——

Therefore, in *all* cases it is *prudential*, because in *most necessary*, that the *creditor* should have something more substantial to depend upon, than the bare word of the *debtor*; and the *lender* be secured against the *borrower* by something of more notoriety than can possibly arise from a private transaction, or verbal agreement merely between themselves.

What is here said, I mean to apply to *marriage-ceremony*, by whomsoever, or howsoever, or wheresoever administered. Like all other *securities*, it tends to the ascertaining of property; to the protection of the honest and undesigning, against the machinations of treachery and deceit; and answers too many
valuable

valuable purposes to *society* in general, not to be *inforced* by the *severest laws*.

But, as in all other *contracts*, different nations have different modes of making them, so it is with respect to *marriage-ceremony*. As we find no trace of such a thing in the scriptures, unless the payment of the מהר—or dowry of 50 *shekels* to the *father of the damsel*—may be so called, we cannot, on any *divine authority*, say, there was any fixed or determinate *form* whatsoever; and even this *payment of the dower* was omitted in the case of *concubines,* who are also *called wives*, but certainly appear to have been of an inferior rank, though as *lawful wives* as those who were *endowed*. This was the case in the *Christian church*, so late as the time of *Constantine:* see before vol. i. p. 32. n.—and this vol. p. 30.

Were we to search the whole history of the world, we should hardly find many inhabitants of it, without some *marriage-ceremony* or other, and this, because *nature* itself, as now circumstanced, seems to point out a *necessity* for some outward recognition of so important a contract; for, as the corruption of human nature is to be found in all the naturally-engendered offspring of fallen *Adam*, so the dire effects of it have made it necessary to guard against them by some means or other.

As to the *Jews*—" There were, according
" to the *Talmudists*, three ways of *betroth-*
" *ing*. 1. By a written contract. 2. By
" a verbal agreement, accompanied with a
"piece

" piece of money. 3. By the parties coming
" together, and living as *man* and *wife;*
" which laſt they could not properly call
" *betrothing*, for it was *marriage itſelf*."—See
Alex. Hiſt. of Wom. vol. ii. p. 193.

As for their *ceremonies* on the *eſpouſals* or *marriage* (the payment of the *dowry* excepted) they are entirely of *human* invention, and I do not imagine that they are pretended to be otherwiſe—nor do I ſuppoſe that a *Jew* would venture to talk of them as of higher authority.

The *Roman Chriſtians* learned, from their *Heathen* * predeceſſors, to impoſe on the *credulity* of mankind, and to make their *prieſts* the grand engines of that *impoſition*. *Numa Pompilius*, the ſecond *king* of the *Romans*, in order to divert his ſubjects from the purſuits of ambition and violence of arms, multiplied *ceremonies* in *religion*, and gained a reverence and ſanction to them, by giving out that he received them nightly from the goddeſs *Egeria;* by whoſe direction alſo he inſtituted *Flamines; (prieſts* or *arch-prieſts) veſtal virgins,* (a ſort of *nuns*) the *Salian* prieſts, and *Pontifex Maximus* (or heathen *Pope.*)—So the Roman *Chriſtians* invented, firſt *Chriſtian*

---

* " *Obſervavi ſingularem patrum prudentiam, qui pa-*
" *ganorum multa inſtituta ad pios uſus retulerunt. Ego*
" *non nego poſteriorum culpâ multa mala inde proveniſſe.*"
" I have obſerved the ſingular prudence of the [antient] *fathers*, who applied many inſtitutions of the *Pa-*
" *gans* to *pious uſes*. I do not deny, that many *evils* ac-
" crued from thence, through the fault of thoſe who
" came after." *Caſaubon*, Ep. 931. *Thuano*. edit. Alm.

prieſts,

priests, then a *Pontifex Maximus*, or *Pope*, who, with the affistance of his *Flamines* or *arch-priests*, invented *rites* and *ceremonies*, all which were pretended to be *jure divino*; among the rest, *marriage-ceremonies*; afterwards, these were turned into the *form* of a *sacrament*, and pretended to be *divinely* instituted by *Jesus Christ*; which is just as true, as that *Numa* had his *rites* and *ceremonies* from the goddess *Egeria*.

I have little occasion to dwell any longer on this part of the subject in this place, because the first contrivance, and subsequent progression and increase, of *sacerdotal* knavery and imposition, through a long succession of many ages, has been fully manifested, to the discerning and attentive reader's observation, in the former parts of these volumes, but especially in the *first chapter* of *this*.

In a series of letters written from *Constantinople*, by *M. de Guys*, of the academy of *Marseilles*, to *M. Bourlat de Montredon* at *Paris*—which were translated and published in London anno 1772 — there is a most curious account of some people, who are inhabitants of the island of *Mitylene*, which tends to shew, that there may be some respect for *marriage-ceremony*, where there is none for the sacred obligation of *marriage*.

The title of the book is —" *A Sentimental* " *Journey through* Greece"—and, in one of the *letters*, of which the narrative is composed, *M. de Guys* relates a very extraordinary *custom* among the *Mitylenians*—" Now
" let

"let me inform you," says he, "of a custom subsisting at this day in the same island. About three days journey from the capital, is a small town, where every *stranger*, when he arrives, is compelled to marry one of the *women*, even though his stay should be for one night only. They generally present a *maiden* to him, whom he must take for *his wife*; but if he should prove to be a man of any property or importance, he has the choice of several to select one. Travellers of an inferior rank have no choice, but must absolutely put up with the *lady* offered to them, who, in that case, is generally the *oldest* and *plainest* in the province. A *priest* then appears, who performs the *marriage-ceremonies* with great solemnity; a *nuptial-feast* is prepared, and the new-married couple pass the night together. The *husband* may depart, if he pleases, the next morning. If he has any money or valuable effects, and chuses to make his *ephemeral* wife any present, it is received, and indeed expected; but if he does not, he may proceed on his journey without molestation. The *lady* thinks herself sufficiently obliged to him for having delivered her from the *reproach* of *virginity*, which it is ignominious to retain, or to give to one of the *province*. It is necessary, for the preservation of the *lady's honour*, that her *first* marriage should be with a stranger. It is of no consequence whether he remains with her, or ever returns.

" turns. At the expiration of a year, she
" may contract a new marriage with any man
" that presents himself, and should the *former*
" husband appear, he would have no legal
" claim whatever upon her. The fact is,
" that a *lady* cannot marry to advantage,
" until she has lain with a *stranger*. This
" *custom* is said to be of the *most antient date*.
" The only alteration which the teachers of
" the *Christian* religion have been able to ef-
" fect among these people, in the above par-
" ticular, is, that the *cohabitation* shall be
" preceded by a *marriage* according to the
" *forms* of the *church* now established there.
" By this compromise, the *priest*, the *bride*,
" and *all parties* quiet the scruples of their
" conscience."

" This *custom* is no less *curious* than well
" attested."

When we meet with such an instance as the above—that of the *Troglodytes*, mentioned *Thelyph.* vol. i. 213. n.—and numberless others which might be mentioned—what a *chimæra* is that of the *philosophers*, who contend for a *religion of nature*, or principle of *morality* common to all mankind, *mores communes naturali rationi consentanei*, as *Grotius* speaks! *Cicero* observed very truly, that, " *there is nothing
" so strange, which has not been maintained by
" philosophers;*" and, among the rest, the κοιναι εννοιαι, or primary and innate principles, or notions, which are so accurately discussed and refuted in the first book of Mr. *Locke's* Essay on Human Understanding.

Some few *savage* nations, which we meet

with accounts of, seem, if we believe the relations which authors have given us, to have little, if any, notion of *marriage-ceremony*; among these may be reckoned the inhabitants of the island of *Otaheite*, who are said " to pursue incontinent gratifica-
" tions, wherever inclination leads them;
" but when a woman becomes *pregnant*, the
" *father* of her child *thereby* becomes her
" *husband*." Alex. Hist. of Wom. vol. ii. p. 187.

These *savages*, and *we Christians*, are much upon the same establishment, as to " *the*
" *pursuit of incontinent gratifications, wherever*
" *inclination leads them*"—but as to the consequences of this, with regard to the *women*, the *females* at *Otaheite* have vastly the advantage of *ours*; for the *Christian* women, on their becoming *pregnant*, if not secured *verbo sacerdotis*, are treated with a degree of barbarity and inhumanity, which we may suppose the *savages* would be ashamed of.

The only object among us, is to secure a *parish* from the expence of what we call a *bastard*—therefore, if a female be *pregnant* —which is frequently the consequence of men's " being at liberty to pursue inconti-
" nent gratifications wherever inclination
" leads them"—she is persuaded by certain *tyrants*, called *parish-officers*, by the gentle eloquence of being threatened with *bridewell* or *starving*, to go before a magistrate, and to *swear* the *child* she goes with, to the *father* of it; this being done, a warrant goes forth

to

to apprehend the said *father*, and if he is caught, he is to find security to indemnify the parish, to appear at the next quarter-sessions, or must go to gaol; but no part of his recognizance engages for any amends or security to the *woman*, or to have any thing to do with the *child*, farther than to save the *parish* harmless from any *burden* it may bring upon it. If the fellow runs away, which is a common case, the poor *female*, after a *month* from her lying-in, becomes an object of one of the most severe and brutal statutes that could well be penned, viz. 7. Jac. c. 4. § 7. "Every lewd woman which shall have any "*bastard*, which may be chargeable to the "parish, the justices of the peace shall com- "mit such lewd woman to the house of "correction, there to be punished and set on "work, during the term of one *whole year*." —The readings on this clause, as cited by *Burn* from *Dalton*, are worth attending to.—" *Shall commit such lewd woman*]—But "such punishment shall not be, until after "that the woman is delivered of her child; "neither are the justices to meddle with the "woman, until the child be born, and she "strong again."—i. e. till (as we say) her *month* is up.

"Also it seemeth, that such *bastard-child* "is not to be sent with the mother to the "*house of correction*, but rather that the child "should remain in the town where it was "born, (or settled with the mother) and "there to be relieved by the work of the " mother,

" *mother*, or by relief from the *reputed fa-*
" *ther:* and yet the common opinion and
" practice is otherwife, viz. to fend the
" *child* with the *mother* to the *houfe of correc-*
" *tion;* and this may alfo feem *reafonable,*
" where the child *fucketh* on the mother."
Dalt. c. 11.

" But it feemeth much the beft, to com-
" mit the *mother* only, and not the *child*, but
" leave it to her choice whether fhe will
" take it with her, and if fhe will not, then to
" fend it to its lawful place of fettlement."

I am clearly of Doctor *Burn's* opinion, that " it feemeth *much beft* (i. e. *moft politic*) to
" commit the *mother* only, and *not the child*"
—becaufe it relieves the *parifh* from its *burden* much *fooner,* than by fuffering it to go with its mother to the *houfe of correction,* from whence, being preferved by the breaft and attention of its poor mother, it may return again, and then it may be *chargeable* to the *parifh;* whereas, if it be torn from the mother's breaft at the tender age of one *month,* and be committed to the cuftody of a certain fpecies of *fhe-wolf,* called a *parifh-nurfe,* unlefs it fhould have the conftitution of *Romulus* and *Remus* put together, the parifh will foon be rid of its incumbrance. Thefe fage and pious *matrons* commonly fupply the place of the *mother's milk,* with as little nutriment as they can, with any tolerable hopes of fteering clear of a *coroner's inqueft,* or of not diminifhing their own fcanty ftipend too much, adminifter. Others of them are very *public-fpirited,*

rited, and have too much *care* for the welfare of the parish, to suffer an incumbrance upon it longer than needs must, and they usually adapt their *care* of the child accordingly.

But suppose the wretched mother, influenced by the natural feelings of maternal tenderness, takes with her her poor infant, to be a sharer in the cold and filth of a prison, and for a *whole year* is to endure the stripes of her *punishment*, inflicted by the unrelenting hand of a sour gaoler; suppose her set to some laborious work, and at the same time to nourish her child, and to have no recruit for her exhausted strength, but the scanty provision of the * *gaol-allowance* of bread and water; in what a condition must she be?—to what state of constitution may she be reduced?—but, which is still worse, what are the probable consequences of her being shut up, for a whole *twelvemonth* together, with *common whores* and *thieves*, but that all the remains of decency, modesty, and of the comparative innocence which she carried with her, should all be obliterated, and she should become, on her return to her parish, a common pest and nuisance, and fit for nothing but to be exterminated from the face of the earth?

I question not but the terror of this statute has occasioned many a CHILD-MURDER, and wonder not, that, fourteen years afterwards, the legislature should be compelled to pass a law in hopes of putting a stop to it—*viz.*

* This, I have been informed, amounts to *three halfpence* a day.

21 *Jac.*

21 *Jac.* I. c. 27. the preamble of which clearly confirms what I am now saying—" Whereas many lewd women that have been delivered of baftard-children, to AVOID THEIR SHAME, and to ESCAPE PUNISHMENT, do fecretly *bury*, or *conceal* the *death* of their children; and after, if the *child* be found *dead*, the faid women do alledge, that the faid *child* was *born dead*; whereas it falleth out fometimes (although hardly it is to be proved) that the faid *child* or *children* were *murdered* by the faid *women*, their lewd *mothers*, or by their affent or procurement—For the preventing therefore, &c."

Now, what would have become of fuch a woman under the DIVINE LAW?—She would have been deemed the man's *wife*, and as fuch he muft have maintained and cohabited with her—and fo it would be among the *Jews* to this day.—So it was *once* by the law of *France*—fo it is *now* by the laws of *Switzerland* (fee vol. ii. 355, 1ft edit.—297, 2d edit.) —and fo it is (to our fhame be it fpoken) among the *favages* of the *ifland* of OTAHEITE!

By the way, we muft not forget, that while the poor creature has fo much done by the *civil power* for the correction of her *body*, it is by no means improbable, but, on due *prefentment* by the *right trufty* and *well-beloved* the *churchwardens*, the *fpiritual court* may think it worth their while to do fomething *pro falute animæ*, " *for the good of her foul.*"—

See

See the case of *Ann Jenkinson*, Thelyph. vol. i. p. 67, n. If these two modes of punishment were steadily and uniformly applied, it might be of *prodigious service* to parishes, in easing them from the burden of *lewd women* and *bastard children*, as furnishing a very strong inducement to the *mothers* to *cut their infants throats*, rather than run the risque of so much shame and misery; the consequence of which would probably be, that the *hangman* would ease the parish of the burden of the *mother*.

Anno 1780 —At *Nottingham*, a poor girl of a neighbouring village was libelled, in the *spiritual court*, for *fornication*; the case was, that, some time before, she had had a child that was born a *bastard*; she was sentenced by the court to do *penance*—in order to this, she was to pay down a sum of money, which she had not; my *informant* saw her weeping bitterly under this piece of oppression; however, by the help of a friend's charity, she was at last enabled to pay the *exaction*, and so was delivered from the jaws of *excommunication*.

It should seem, from the conversation which I had with the gentleman who related the above to me, that the poor people in the *northern* distant counties are dreadfully scourged and harrassed with these oppressive exactions, it being the constant custom, in many parts, to punish the unhappy victims with these *spiritual* extortions of money, besides exposing the delinquents to the contempt and scorn of the whole parish, by setting them publicly in the church in a white sheet.—My *friend* asked some of those whom he was conversing with on the subject, if people did not complain of it as a great oppression and hardship? "O no," said one, "we like it much, for "we should have so many *bastards* to keep, "as to be quite over-run with them, if it "was not for this."—How far this observation might hold, I can't say; but I am afraid, that, from a certain concatenation between *cause* and *effect*, such proceedings are a means of lessening the charge of parishes with respect to *bastards*, more by increasing the number of *murders*, than by any thing else. See before vol. ii. 347, n. 1st edit.—p. 307, n. 2d edit. concerning this *relic of Popery*.

I am acquainted with a certain *magistrate*, who, in cases of this sort, makes the best enquiry he can of the *parish officers* concerning the character of the woman; and if, from what they say, and from other circumstances, he has reason to think, that her situation is owing to the seduction of the man, and that she has had no *concerns* with any other, he always perswades a public marriage; he even inforces his arguments from the scriptures which have been so often mentioned, and scruples not to declare, " that, as in God's sight, the woman " is already the man's *wife*," and therefore to conjure him, as he shall answer it at the day of judgment, to make her so according to the laws of his country. In several instances, conviction has been wrought, the parties have
been

been married, and the magiſtrate has, on enquiry after them, had the ſatisfaction to hear, in ſeveral inſtances, that they go on well, and ſeem perfectly contented. How much for the honour of GOD, and for the good of the kingdom in general, would it be, if *magiſtrates* (as in *Iſrael*) had a power, in all caſes, to *inforce* ſuch arguments on the *refractory*, by the coercive power of a wholeſome law made for the purpoſe!

One caſe I cannot help mentioning, as it tends to illuſtrate what has been ſaid on the evil tendency of the *marriage-act*.

A young fellow, who had been ſworn to as the father of a child, with which a young woman was then pregnant, and who was within a little of her time, being brought by a warrant before the ſaid *magiſtrate*, was interrogated concerning a point which the girl had mentioned during the time of her examination, which was, whether he had not *promiſed* her *marriage*? The man owned he had—the *magiſtrate* then inforced, by every argument he could think of, the duty and neceſſity which the man was under to fulfil his * promiſe. The man, after ſome

* Such a *promiſe*, accompanied by ſuch an *act*, would be deemed by the *eccleſiaſtical law* a marriage *de facto*, and the man might have been compelled to have ſolemnized it publicly in *facie eccleſiæ*—but *now* there's an end of that, and one of the moſt atrocious and miſchievous villainies that any man can be capable of committing, has the ſanction of an *act of parliament*, by the expreſs words of which, the perpetrator of it is ſet free from all matrimonial engagement whatſoever. See before, vol. i. 30, 31. and vol. ii. c. 7. throughout.

little hesitation, owned himself convinced, and consented to *marry* the girl as the *next morning*. The *magistrate* was not a little pleased, to hope, that here was another *female* likely to be saved from *ruin*, another poor *infant* from the infamy and disadvantages of † *bastardy*;—but a check was put to it all, for, as by the *marriage-act* three *Sundays* must intervene for the asking of *banns*, the man's good intent could not be carried into execution without *a licence*—now a *marriage* by *licence* comes to above *forty shillings*, including the *church fees*—the poor fellow, by keeping out of the way for a time, had thrown himself out of work, the poor girl had been turned out of her service, and had been living on the little pittance which had come to her for *wages*, and on the disposal of part of her *cloaths*, till she applied to the parish; so that, between them, they could not raise a *fifth* part of the money. The *magistrate* having, on like occasions, applied himself to the *parish officers* with success, recommended it to those then present to be at

† Many cases might be put, where children, as the law now stands, must *necessarily* be born *bastards*, however willing the *parents* may be to prevent it. As for example—suppose *one* or *both* the parties to be *under age*, their parents dead, and no guardians appointed—they can't be married by *licence*; they can't, through their *poverty*, apply to the court of *Chancery*; the delay of three *Sundays* for *banns* may outrun the time of the *woman's* pregnancy —but how much more, where, as in some poor parishes in *Wales*, and in some parts of *England*, there is no *service* above *once* in a *month*; here *three months* may be to elapse before the *marriage* can be had and solemnized.

the *expence* of the *wedding;* one of them seemed inclined to it, but his surly partner interrupted all compliance, by entering his protest against it—" *Noa—noa*—we'll do no "more *vor un,* an't please your worship, we "ha' been at expences *enow aready*—what "wi' hunting *ater* the mon, and coming "backwards and *vorwards* about *zwearing* "the child, and one thing or *wother*, it has "cost the parish as good as *ten shillings,* and "we'll do no more *vor un.*"—All remonstrance was in vain, the honest farmer's— "we'll do no more *vor un*," prevailed with his partner, and there ended all hope of the speedy marriage, which had been proposed and assented to. The *magistrate,* therefore, finding the young man without sureties to answer for his appearance, and the impossibility of persuading either of the officers to do that kindness, or " *any more vor un*"—and that he could as soon have repealed the *marriage-act,* or have reconciled it to scripture, common sense, or true policy — made use of his *discretion,* and *committed* the young man to *prison,* 'till the *three Sundays* should be passed, and the *banns* published; with an order to the *gaoler,* to deliver him, on the *Monday* following the last day of *publishing the banns,* to the custody of the *constable* of the parish to which the *parties* belonged, that the said *constable* should convey him to the parish church at the appointed hour, see them *married,* and then discharge his prisoner.

This

This obligation to send the young man, to live near three weeks among the inhabitants of a common prison, might have been attended with consequences of the worst kind to the prisoner; who could be looked upon as no other than a *victim* to a cruel and unnatural *law*, and whose only crime, for which he was confined, was, that he could neither contract *three weeks* into the space of *twenty-four hours*, nor produce between *forty* and *fifty shillings*, to *pay* for doing an act of *retributive* justice to his fellow-creature, in the most expeditious manner.

However, the parties were married, and there was an end—the young man turns out a good husband, and the woman a good wife; but there can be little doubt, that there are many cases of this sort, which do not *end* quite so *well*; for of all *experiments* which can be tried for the corruption of the common people, none have been found so thoroughly to *succeed*, as that of sending them into a *gaol*; and to be laid under a necessity of doing this, merely because a man's power of doing a *right* thing is to be suspended for a length of time, beyond his desire and intention to do it, is a sort of practical solecism, unjustifiable in itself, irreconcileable to common justice, inconsistent with sound policy, and a most painful task imposed on the humanity and feelings of the *magistrate*—add to this, one good reason, among others, for the repeal of a law, which may

may occasion these things to happen every day.

The more merciful *Romish ritual* says—" *Publicationibus factis tribus diebus festis;*" and our own ritual (which follows the *Romish* pretty closely) till superseded by the *marriage-act*, said—" *three Sundays or holy days*"—so that, by possibility, a *few* days might determine the matter:—but now the interval between the *marriage-ceremony* and the *contract* is so far protracted, and so far out of the reach of the *poorer* sort to shorten by the enormous expence of *licences,* as to form, in many cases, a very *inconvenient*, in not a few, a very *dangerous* delay—and is surely well worthy the very serious consideration of the *legislative* powers.

'Till an alteration be made, we certainly are far behind, in point of policy and humanity, as well as in conformity to the *divine law*, the savages of *Otaheite*, and perhaps many others—who, *not having the law, do by nature the things contained in the law*. Rom ii. 14.

Though the *Otaheiteans*, and we, differ in what has been before mentioned, yet we wonderfully agree in certain other particulars. Dr. Alex. Hist. Wom. vol. i. p. 286, says—" *As* POLYGAMY *is not allowed among them*" (there we agree) " *they have a society among them called* ARREOY, *in which, to satisfy the lust of variety, every woman is common to every man.*"—And have we no such societies? what are our *brothels*, what are our
public

public streets after dark? what, many assemblies of men and women, of more ostensible decency perhaps, but really and truly so many ARREOYS?——"*And when any of these women happens to have a child, it is smothered in the moment of its birth, that it may not interrupt the pleasures of its infamous mother;*"—Children are rarely *murdered* by their mothers, among us, merely from this principle; but if from *fear, shame,* or the *dread* of *severe punishment,* women are terrified into the *murder* of their children, it amounts much to the same, with respect to the *children;* and if we take into the account the numbers destroyed by *causing abortion,* an art which it does not appear that the *savages* have as yet acquired, and those which are destroyed either *in the birth,* or *after*—many of which *murders* are never discovered, perhaps more than are discovered—it is hardly to be doubted, but this *island equals* at least, if not *exceeds,* in numbers of *murdered* infants, the island of *Otaheite*. Their *Arreoy* seems to be confined within a much smaller compass than *ours;* for as to the liberty our men enjoy, to ruin as many women as they *can,* it is unconfined and unlimited throughout the kingdom.——
"*but in this juncture, should nature revolt at so horrid a deed, even then the mother is not allowed to save the child,*—This, I confess, goes beyond us; and yet, the taking a young *infant* from the *mother's breast,* and committing it to the *care* of a *parish-nurse,* on sending the *mother* to be *punished* in the *house of correction,*

correction, is not without some *affinity* to this practice.———" *unless she can find a man who will* " *patronize it as a father;*"—This brings the matter into somewhat like a parallel again, as many children among us have been *murdered* through the *desertion* of the *pregnant* woman by the *father* of the *child*.———" *in which case,* " *the man is considered as having appropriated* " *the woman to himself, and she is accordingly* " *extruded from this hopeful society.*"

This particular has already been sufficiently observed upon, and the advantage of the *Otaheitean* pregnant women, above that of the *European*, pointed out.

To attempt a recapitulation of all the *marriage-ceremonies* of the different nations of mankind, would be a work far exceeding the limits as well as the intention of this *volume*; but whatever they may be, as to *matter* or *manner*, they are doubtless of *human* contrivance, and therefore ought only to be looked upon as the several modes of establishing a *civil-contract*, not only between the *parties*, but with respect to the *society* where their lot may happen to be cast.

Dr. Alex. Hist. Wom. vol. ii. p. 207, observes as follows:—" In the prosecution of " our enquiry, we have scarcely discovered " among other primitive nations" (besides the *Jews*, which he had mentioned before, as having no religious marriage-ceremonial revealed to them) " we have scarcely discovered " any of them even pretending that *marri-* " *age* (i. e. marriage-ceremony) was the in-
" stitution

" ſtitution of their gods; but of their firſt le-
" giſlators, as *Menes* in *Egypt*, and *Cecrops* in
" *Greece*; nor have we found, even among the
" *Jews* themſelves, that either *prophet* or
" *prieſt* were concerned in the *celebration* of
" *marriage*, though they managed every thing
" that was conſidered as *ſacred*, or of *divine*
" inſtitution: the ſame was the caſe among
" other primitive nations; they had *prieſts*
" to whom the celebration of every holy rite
" was committed; but their *magiſtrates*, and
" the relations of the contracting parties,
" were the only people who concerned them-
" ſelves about *marriage*; a ſtrong preſump-
" tion, that it was not conſidered in any other
" light than as a *civil-contract*."

There is, however, with regard to the *Jews*, no reaſon to talk of " ſtrong preſumption," for the light itſelf is not more clear and evident, than that, throughout the whole law of *Moſes*, there is not the leaſt hint or trace of *nuptial ceremony* of a religious kind, or the interference of any *miniſter* of religion in the matter—therefore the throwing *marriage* into the hands of *Chriſtian churchmen* (and by what means and by what degrees that has been done clearly appears from the foregoing evidence) and pretending that a ceremonial to be adminiſtered by *prieſts*—*jure divino*, was neceſſary and eſſential to make *marriages* valid as in God's ſight—and that all who came together, and lived together, without it, lived in " a ſtate of whoredom and fornication"— is alſo more than a *ſtrong preſumption*, for it
              amounts

amounts to *demonstration*, that *Christian churchmen* have been the greatest, and most errant and complete set of KNAVES, that ever infested the earth. None but *such* could, for their own profit and interest, have misinterpreted, perplexed, and confounded, as they have done, the holy and simple ordinance of GOD with respect to *marriage*, and then throw the dust of *priestly rites* and *ceremonies* into the eyes of the laity, to prevent a discovery of their *imposture*.—How all this originated, how it has been carried on, and how it stands at this hour, has been fully declared.

One should hardly think, that *such* a *contempt* poured on the *Hebrew scriptures*, in which the whole *mind* and *will* of JEHOVAH stands written, as with a *sun-beam*, touching those wise and beneficent regulations, which HE was pleased to ordain with respect to the *commerce of the sexes*, could admit of *aggravation*; but this matter leaves no sort of doubt, when we find the *impostors* placing the great *reviver, interpreter*, and *defender* of the *law* of JEHOVAH, at the head of their *faction*, and representing HIM as instituting a *new ordinance* of *marriage*, appropriated to *Christians*— this upon the foundation of a *new law*; and thus rendering *null and void* the fixed and unalterable *decrees* of *Eternal Wisdom*—on the important and interesting subject of *marriage*.

Let those who think I carry this matter *too far*, first read their *Bible*, then let them take *Du Pin's* history of *Ecclesiastical Writers*, &c. or, if they do not care to read over so voluminous a work, let them consider well the
preceding

preceding extracts from it; let them then compare the whole of *our syſtem*, with what they find there upon the ſubject, and if, after all this, they do not agree with me, then let them take for their motto—*Non perſuadebis, etiamſi perſuaſeris.*

In the foregoing long detail of evidence, we have often met with the word *Church*, which is the *Engliſh* tranſlation of the *Greek* εκκλησια, and of the Latin *Eccleſia*; theſe ſeem derived from the Greek ἐκκαλειν to *call out*, and denote the *church* of GOD, or an *aſſembly* or *ſociety* of men, *called out of mankind* by the WORD of GOD; theſe are, *through ſanctification of the ſpirit, and belief of the truth*, (2 Theſſ. ii. 13.) united to God and to each other, by the THREEFOLD CORD of FAITH, HOPE, and LOVE. They have ONE LORD—ONE FAITH—ONE BAPTISM. See Eph. iv. 5. All the members of this *ſociety*, however *diſtreſſed, diſtinguiſhed*, or *diſſipated* over the face of the earth, form, in a collective ſenſe, the *holy Catholic church*; and where only *two or three of* them *meet together* in the name of their common LORD, HE *is in the midſt of them*. Matt. xviii. 20. Therefore there are as many *churches* on earth, as there are ſuch ſocieties thus *meeting together*—but theſe, as well as the *individuals* which compoſe them, though *many*, form but one *Body*, of which CHRIST is the HEAD. Eph. i. 22, 23.

For my own part, I doubt not but there are members of this *church* among all *ſects* and *parties* of profeſſing *Chriſtians*, and it dilates my heart with a tranſport of joy, to think

think how many *thousands*, now divided from each other from various causes of separation, as to place, situation, and other unavoidable circumstances incident to the present state of things—perhaps divided by the narrowness of a *party*, or the prejudices and bigotry of *sectarian** zeal, which, like impassable gulphs, stand between them—shall one day meet together, and join with one heart and one voice,

---

* In the year 1644, at the treaty of *Uxbridge*, the reverend *doctors* of the *king*'s party affirmed *Episcopacy* to be *jure divino*—the reverend *ministers* of the other party, affirmed *Presbytery* to be *jure divino*. These disputes were carried on with great warmth, and pretty equal success, for both parties ended just where they began, and full as wide from each other's sentiments.—The foundation of *all*, seems to have been, something very like that of a certain dispute, which is recorded *Mark* ix. 34. If *both* sides had attended as they ought to the *rebuke* given ver. 35, matters would have ended more amicably—however, a third *jure divino* started up under the notion of *Independency*, which, by the help of the *jure divino* of *Presbytery*, overturned the government both in *church* and *state*—cut the *king*'s head off—and then took all into their own hands—'till the intolerable tyranny they exercised upon one another, obliged them to restore the antient government again. After this, the *Episcopalian jure divino* took care to secure itself, and pay off old scores, by cruel and oppressive laws against *dissenters*, which erected a *tyranny* sorely felt by *these last*; 'till, after the *Revolution*, its *claws* were cut, and its *teeth* broken, by the truly *Protestant* and *Christian toleration-act*.—However, history informs us, that persecution and intolerancy are too congenial with human *pride* and love of *power*, to be chargeable only on the *church of Rome*. All *sects* and *parties* have, in their turns, been calling for *fire from heaven*, as it were, against one another, little thinking *what manner of spirit they are of*, or what must become of them, if the JUDGE OF ALL should deal with them as they would deal with each other

in the united praises of their glorious HEAD, and blush to think, that they have suffered any outward distinctions to influence or lessen that inward affection, which, with respect to each other, ought to have been a transcript of the *Redeemer's* love to them. See John xiii. 34.

Such is the *church-militant* on earth, which, with that *triumphant* in *Heaven*, makes but one *family* (Eph. iii. 5.) which consists of the *redeemed* out of *every nation, kindred, people, and tongue.* (Rev. vii. 9.) This, in a *comparative* view, is styled—*a little flock*, Luke xii. 32; but, when *all* shall be *gathered together*, will appear to be *a great multitude which no man can number*.

After all this, it must surely appear to the diligent reviser of the former part of this *volume*, that the word *Church* is to be understood very differently, in those extracts from the annals of *Popery*, which so long detained his patience in the perusal of them.

There, this ill-understood and much-abused word *Church*, denotes a set of people, described by the *apostle*, Acts xx. 30. *as grievous wolves, entering in and not sparing the flock—speaking perverse things to draw away disciples after them.*—We have seen how early this *mystery of iniquity* began to *work*—how, under the name of THE CHURCH, a *kingdom of this world* was erected, and its *throne* filled with the *man of sin, who opposeth and exalteth himself above all that is called* GOD, *or that is worshipped; so that he as* GOD *sitteth in the temple of* GOD, *shewing*

shewing himself that he is God. 2 Theff. ii. 4. We have seen, how, in consequence of this, and in order to support this same CHURCH, the minds of men should be filled with such ideas as were best suited to maintain its dominion, not only over the *people*, but even over the *kings* of the earth.—Hence false *traditions* took place of the *written scriptures—legends*, full of lying *miracles* and *wonders*, supplanted the *records* of *divine truth*—laws of *councils*, *synods*, and *Popes*, were substituted for the *laws of Heaven*—the love of *power* supplanted the humble spirit of the gospel—*ambition* and *pride* drave out *lowliness* and *meekness*—an iron *sceptre*, wielded by the hand of *tyranny*, succeeded to the mild and gentle reign of *Christian* liberty—adamantine chains of *ignorance* and *superstition* were forged for the reason and understanding of mankind—the *easy yoke* of CHRIST was laid aside, and the intolerable burden of *church*-power crushed all who refused to submit to it.

Such being the form and government of this *worldly kingdom*, its *ministers*, who were to carry it on, must be suitable to the nature of it. Hence arose, in the shape, and under the venerable names of *cardinals, archbishops, bishops, priests, deans, canons, prebendaries,* &c. &c. as many Lords over GOD's *heritage* as the wit of man could invent, or the power of the *Pope* create; *riches* * and *worldly* grandeur

---

* It was a fine check which was once given to a certain *Pope*, who was, with no small satisfaction, descanting

deur gave them pre-eminence, and every means to advance thefe were devifed and employed. Among the reft, the ordinance of *marriage* was framed anew; its antient and fimple difpenfation afforded no *revenue*, added no *importance* to *churchmen*; where it was *divinely forbidden*, no *difpenfation* from *man* could authorize it; where it was *divinely allowed*, no *licence* from man could add to its perfection and obligation:—this was found neceffary, therefore, to be changed; the *thing itfelf* muft be deftroyed, and framed anew; its *nature* and *effence* muft no longer remain upon the CREATOR's inftitution, but depend on certain *rites* and *ceremonies* of man's invention—thefe were to be fuppofed to be coëval with the difpenfation of the *gofpel*, and the laws of JEHOVAH, by which it had been regulated and fettled from the *beginning*, were deemed *antiquated* and laid afide. We have feen the degrees by which this was effected, from the firft introduction of clerical *benediction*, to the total invalidation, not only of the *divine law*, but of all *civil contract*, by the *council of Trent*—we have feen what mifchiefs have been produced to the world, more efpecially to the *female fex*, by thefe *papal* inventions; and happy would it be for *millions*, did we alfo fee, that nothing can obviate thefe mifchiefs, but returning to

canting on the great acceffion of *riches* to the *church*—" Now," faid he, " the church can no longer fay, as St. " Peter did—*Silver and gold have I none.*"—" No," anfwered one, " Neither can it fay, as he did—" *In the* " *name of* JESUS CHRIST *of Nazareth, rife up and walk.*" See Acts iii. 6.

that

that from whence we are fallen — the HOLY, WISE, BENEFICENT, and SALUTARY LAWS OF HEAVEN.

The way to do this, is to restore to the *civil power* that which has been evidently taken from it; to suffer no longer a *system* to remain, which hides from the eyes of mankind the real and true nature and obligation of the *divine ordinance*. The *civil magistrate* ought to have the *sole* jurisdiction over *civil contracts*, in *this* as well as in all other cases—and surely a way might easily be found, by which this might be brought to pass, so as to answer every good end that can possibly accrue from the present mode of marriage, and defeat those mischievous ends which are the infallible consequences of the present system; above all, that *anti-scriptural* and destructive notion, that men are under no obligation to that retributive justice which GOD has commanded, unless bound upon them by the word of a *priest*. On such occasions, the access to the *magistrate* should be facilitated as much as possible, and his power, like that of the magistrates in *Israel*, should instantly compel such an observance of it, as they would have done in the like case. See before vol. ii. p. 73. 1st. edit.—p. 67. 2d edit. This would rid the world of all the mischief which now accrues from the difficulties laid in the way of *marriage*, by *ecclesiastical* contrivance, and by the false policy of the *marriage-act*.

One would think, that in such a country as this, when we are driven to such a state of *depopulation*, as to make laws to invite *foreigners* to navigate our ships, and find ourselves obliged to allow our merchants *three fourths* of *foreign seamen*, in order to carry on our trade, (See 20 G. III. c. 20.) all the causes of *depopulation* should be well considered, and as many of them removed as possible; that *marriage*, so far from being clogged with difficulties and impediments which are solely the inventions of men, should be facilitated and encouraged, by being restored to its *antient* footing, as it appears to have been ordained, instituted, and regulated, by the GREAT LORD OF HEAVEN AND EARTH.

This would also, as has been already shewn at large, greatly destroy that *destroyer* of so many—*public prostitution.*—It would rescue multitudes of breeding women from that fatal obstacle to *population*, the *promiscuous* intercourse of the *sexes*—it would be a means of eradicating that dreadful *disease*, which is the baneful consequence of it, and which, in different ways, robs us of so many people.

By recommending a restitution of the *divine law*, I am recommending no *new invention*, no *Utopian* scheme, no *medicine* for our sad and mournful state of *constitution*, but what has been tried and found to succeed; there is not an *ingredient* in it, but what has been thoroughly *weighed and prepared by unerring wisdom.*—Let us only take a view of its effects on *Israel of old*, who were as *the sands on the sea shore, and as the stars of heaven for multitude.*—The *plan* which they pursued was of GOD—from whence the plan which we are pursuing is *derived*, or by *whom devised*,

I should

I should imagine the *reader* can be at no lofs to determine, after having attentively red, and confidered, the contents of this, and of the two preceding *volumes*.

From the foregoing *evidence* it alfo appears, from whence we derive our oppreffive and unjuftifiable notions of *divorce* a *vinculo matrimonii*—of permitting men to forfake women entirely, if not *married* to them with every given requifite of fome *human form*, though fuch *requifites*, or the reafons of annulling marriages, which are wholly grounded on thofe *requifites*, fo far from having *fcripture-warrant*, directly oppofe the *mind* of God as revealed in the *fcriptures* upon the *fubject*.

We may farther be inftructed, whence is derived the depriving men of that moft important privilege of *divorce* in cafe of the wife's *adultery*, and *forbidding* them to *marry* others during the *adulterefs's* life, unlefs fet free by *human authority*; this at fo enormous an expence as few can afford.—Thus is a man placed in a moft cruel fituation, either to fhare his wife with others, and be liable to the maintenance of other men's children; or, if he feparates himfelf from her, he is reduced to all the temptations and mifchiefs of a *celibacy* which is impofed on him by the fole tyranny of *human authority*, without any power whatfoever of flying to that redrefs, which is gracioufly and gratuitoufly afforded him by the God of *nature*. We have feen the dreadful confequences which attended the *celibacy* of the *clergy*—we are aftonifhed at the wickedness of those *canons* which enjoined it—we wonder, that, to this hour, it should be continued in the *Romish* church—we approve, and justly, in the highest terms, the banishment of it from among the *Protestants* —how is it that we do not see, that our continuing to follow the *Popish* canons relative to *divorce*, is productive of a sort of factitious *celibacy*, with respect to men who cannot *afford* divorces on the footing on which the *Pope* placed them, and on which we have in effect continued them, only with having increased the expence an *hundred fold*, and by this having placed them so much further out of the reach of the *injured*—how is it, I say, that we cannot see, that *this sort* of *celibacy* is attended with all the mischiefs of the *other*, and, without doubt, as great an incentive to *adultery* and *whoredom*, and, in consequence, to the *ruin* of *women* both *married* and *unmarried*? What difference can it possibly make to a man, whether he be left a wretched prey to his passions, because he has *taken orders*—or because his *wife* is become *no wife* to him, and he is forbidden to take *another*, but on impossible terms?

We have had also laid open before us, in the preceding long testimony, the insult put on the *ordinance* of *Heaven* by the several *canons* which were made for preventing *clandestine marriages*, and making them *null* and *void* —a matter which was so far from being unanimously agreed upon, even at the *Popish council of Trent*, that *Cardinal Varmiense* absented

sented himself the day on which the voices were to be collected for the *decree*; and no less than *fifty-three* others of the *council* gave their voices against it—" for, that, marriage " being a *divine*, not an *human* ordinance, " *could not be dissolved by any power of man*."— See before vol. ii. p. 39. 2d. edit. n.—p. 41. 1st. edit. n.

By what art of *logic* can it be made out, that this is not as good a reason against our " act for preventing *clandestine marriages*," as it was against the proceedings of the *council* of *Trent?* Or how can the *influence* of that *great man*, who brought in the *marriage-act*, and who, by dint of the weight of that *influence*, carried it through all its stages in *parliament*, create a more *scriptural* sanction of that law, than the *influence* of the *Pope* over the members of the *council* of *Trent*, could justify passing the *decree* for preventing, and making void, *clandestine* marriages?

We likewise may see the power assumed to vacate *marriages*, which are had and solemnized before a certain time of life, which is arbitrarily fixed to the age of 21 years in both parties, unless had by consent of *parents* and *guardians*. A Pope of *Rome* could fix the age of the *man* at 30, and of the *woman* at 25: we are more moderate—but where doth GOD make *such* marriages void?

The law, antecedently to the *marriage-act*, stood thus, viz.

" From the age of *seven* to the age of " *twelve* as to the woman, and of *fourteen* as
" to

" to the man, they cannot contract matri-
" mony *de præsenti*, but only *de futuro*.

" A *man*, so soon as he hath accomplished
" the age of *fourteen* years, and a *woman*, so
" soon as she shall have accomplished the
" age of *twelve* years, may contract true
" and lawful matrimony.

" But by *can*. 100 — no children, un-
" der the age of 21 years complete, shall
" contract themselves without the consent of
" their parents or guardians, and governors,
" if their parents be *deceased*."—It is to be
observed, that here is nothing said of vacating actual marriage. See *Burn*'s Eccl. Law,
tit. *Marriage*, § 2.

By 25 of Hen. VIII. c. 21, power is given
to the *archbishop* of *Canterbury*, to grant *faculties, dispensations*, and *licences*—as the POPE
had done before. This *Papal* power is reserved
by the *marriage-act* to the *archbishop*, who,
by virtue thereof, can *license* persons to *marry*
at any time or place; which *marriages*, without such licence, would be void to all *intents
and purposes* whatsoever! So that now, all
that glorious and beneficent plan, which was
ordained of GOD, for regulating the *commerce of the sexes*, and more especially for the
preservation and protection of the *female sex*,
is set aside, and we are to consider the validity of the *divine ordinance of marriage*, in
all cases, as dependent on the laws of men,
and in very many cases, as narrowed into the
compass of an *archbishop's* licence!—*Deo non
obstante*.

Thus

Thus have we been brought to a thorough acquaintance with the whole doctrine of *marriage*, as it is in *deed* and in *truth* the ordinance of GOD, and as it is now in *deed* and in *truth* a creature of the state, or rather a sort of creature of *Popish* extraction, yet of the *amphibious* kind, partaking partly of *ecclesiastical law*, partly of the *civil municipal law*, but hardly a trace remaining of its antient conformity to the LAW OF HEAVEN.

The effects and consequences of all this have been clearly pointed out, and laid before the *public*—ocular demonstration proves their truth, and every day's experience brings in its evidence for the necessity of REFORMATION.

Lastly, and upon the whole—It does appear, that *Christian churchmen* have imitated the *apostate Jews*. The cause *these* had to serve was the subversion of *Christianity*; therefore, when " they got the New Testament " into their hands, and saw the evidences it " was built upon, they turned *Masorites,* " *Rabbies*, Expounders, Scribes, &c. patched " up *Talmuds, Mishnas, Cabbalas,* &c. and at " last set up that outrageous impostor *Mahomet*; all to facilitate their main plot."— See Hutch. Abr. p. 205.

So when the *others* had framed a plan to establish a *worldly kingdom*, and to wield a *sceptre* of *despotism* over their subjects the *laity*—when they saw the evidences against their whole plan, which were contained in the *sacred writings*—they turned *Commentators,*

tors, Expositors, Traditionists, &c. patched up *Bulls, Decrees, Canons, Synodal Determinations,* &c. and set up that outrageous impostor the *Pope,* to facilitate their main plot against the liberties and properties, the understandings and consciences of mankind.

Whereas, in truth and in fact—

The whole of JEHOVAH's *institutions* was renewed to the *Israelites* at mount *Sinai,* minutely described and recorded in the *law* committed to their custody, and ordered to be preserved as a sacred *depositum* for the benefit of all nations—the long succession of *prophets* confirmed its stability and importance—and the whole of the New Testament refers us to no other foundation for the truth and obligation of all its precepts.

It follows then, that, as JEHOVAH created man upon the earth—*commanded* the increase and propagation of the human species—*ordained* the means of it—*circumscribed* those means, by positive statutes, as to His infinite wisdom seemed good — no *man* or *men,* of any *description* * or *character* whatsoever, hath or have any power or authority whatsoever, to add to, diminish, change, or alter, one single *statute* relative to *marriage,* as to who

---

* " As surely as God hath revealed true religion, so
" surely has he inhibited magistrates, and all others,
" from establishing any thing *contrary* to it, or *devi-*
" *ating* from it." *Confessional,* 3d edit. p. 258. — This appears to be so self-evident an *axiom,* as to admit of no controversy; and yet, as we have seen from the foregoing long detail of evidence, has been practically denied for many ages.

may

may or who may not intermarry—what does or does not conſtitute it as valid and obligatory in the ſight of God, either with reſpect to the parties themſelves, the lawfulneſs or unlawfulneſs of their iſſue, or any circumſtance whatſoever concerning the divine ordinance delivered in the *revelation* of God's *mind* and *will,* and *recorded* in the *book of the law.*

Much leſs, if poſſible, have they any power or authority to forbid *marriage* where God hath allowed it—to make that *criminal* which he hath made *lawful*—that *null and void* which he hath *eſtabliſhed*—that *infamous* which he hath made *honourable.*

What abundant reaſon then hath God to complain of the *Chriſtians,* as he did of the *Jews*—Ezek. v. 6.—*They have refuſed my judgments,* and *my ſtatutes, they have not walked in them?* And again—Amos ii. 4.—*They have deſpiſed the law of* Jehovah, *and have not kept his commandments, and their lyes cauſed them to err, after the which their fathers have walked.*

Many other remarks might be made from the foregoing long detail of inconteſtible evidence, which probably have not eſcaped the intelligent *reader's* obſervation; I do not at all wiſh they ſhould, as each of them muſt tend to diſcover the frauds and fallacies which have been made uſe of, to wean the minds of people from the *great* and *only ſtandard* of *all truth,* and to conciliate a reverence and eſteem for the traditions and inventions of

men;

men; thus to emancipate them from the *commandments* of GOD, and to bring them into that worse than *Ægyptian* bondage, a blind submission and subjugation of their understandings to the *sleight of men, and cunning craftiness whereby they lie in wait to deceive.* Eph. iv. 14.

The undeniable proofs of this, are too glaring to be denied, with the least pretence to fairness; and afford a very useful caution, against believing things to be true, because they make a part of a *popular system*, or of a *national religion*. We have seen how many *forgeries* and *lyes* have grown into credit and reverence, merely from their introduction by *men* in *power*, and their having acquired consequence by *length of time*. We have seen how the coercive terror of *capital* punishment has been made use of to inforce a veneration for *falshood*, and the terrors of *heresy* and *schism* brandished at the heads of those, who have dared to oppose *scripture* to *human tradition*. We have seen laws of GOD annihilated, and laws of men put in their place. We have seen *Christianity* made incompatible with the *statutes of Heaven*, and the *statutes of Heaven* repealed by *Popish* canons, and acts of *parliament*. All this, and much more, *ejusdem farinæ*, we *have seen*.—I leave it to the common sense and reason of every judicious and obfervant person to determine—what we *still see*.—And to HIM, who is alone the *supreme disposer of all events*—*whose ways are not our ways, and whose thoughts are not our*

our thoughts—do I most humbly, submissively, and unreservedly, leave whatever *shall be seen* hereafter: most assuredly believing, as most fully persuaded, let appearances be what they may to the eye of human wisdom, that a time will come, when *the kingdoms of this world*—however now divided by human policy—deceived by ecclesiastical contrivance—imposed on by priestcraft—misled by folly—or blinded by superstition—will *become the kingdoms of* JEHOVAH *and* HIS CHRIST—and that *the earth shall be filled with the knowledge of* JEHOVAH, *as the waters cover the sea.* See If. xi. 9.—Rev. xi. 15. Then will the *song of Moses the servant of* GOD, and *the song of the Lamb*, be found in exact harmony with each other—and the *burden* of *both* be—*Great and marvellous are thy works*, LORD GOD ALMIGHTY!—*just and true are thy ways*, THOU KING OF SAINTS! Rev. xv. 3.

CONCLUSION.

THE author having now finished his design, in laying before the *public* as complete a *system*, as he was able to collect and lay together, for the prevention of *adultery*, and of the *public prostitution* of women—which said system is founded solely on the basis of the *divine law*—he desires to conclude the whole, with some very essential parts of his *creed* relative to the subjects herein treated.

1. He does most solemnly *believe*—that the *moral laws* and *precepts* contained in the *Pentateuch*, or *five books* of *Moses*, were designed for the *moral government* of God's *people* in all *ages* of the *world*.

2. That all the *statutes* therein, relative to *marriage*, and all that concerns it, as to it's *nature* and *essence*, are the fixed and immutable determinations of *Infinite Wisdom*.

3. That no *power* on *earth* can lawfully *add* to, or *diminish* from them, a single *jot* or *tittle*.

4. That all variations, and departures from them, are so many *insults* against the *power, wisdom, holiness,* and *purity* of the Divine Lawgiver.

5. That all *human* contrivances to evade their force, and to destroy their influence and obligation—which were begun by *primitive Christians* and *fathers*—carried on and completed

completed by *Christian churchmen*, whether *Popish* or *Protestant*—are so many instances of human *corruption* and *depravity*, which cannot admit of much greater *aggravation*, than having appeared in the world under the specious garb of *piety* and *sanctity*, while they are ruining the bodies and souls of mankind—but more especially of the *female sex*—and setting the *laws*, made by the GOD of *nature*, for their security and protection, at open defiance.

6. That all these positions are proved in the foregoing *volumes*, and abundantly confirmed by every day's experience.

7. That, as far as the *divine law* is adopted into our *municipal system*, so far will the ruinous and destructive crimes of *adultery* and *prostitution of women* be checked—but by no other means which ever has, or can be, invented.

8. That we are all more the creatures of *custom* than we are aware of—that the human mind, having no *innate ideas* of *right* and *wrong*, because it has none of that *law* which constitutes them, takes up with the first that offer themselves to its observation; these grow up with it, and form themselves into those various modes of opinion, which divide one part of mankind from another in their sentiments and judgments of things; these are improved into habits by education and usage, and hence arise the opposition and difficulty which *truth* meets with, when it presents itself, on its own simple authority, to the

mind of man, and would supplant those *prejudices* which are found to have usurped its place and influence within the soul.

9. That the *Hebrew* tongue, in which the *divine law* is revealed and recorded, has one fixed and determinate meaning, with regard to the things therein contained; and, that not a single word, phrase, sentence, paragraph, verse, or chapter, has any other meaning *now*, than when first written by the sacred *pen-men* — that every part of the creation, whether animate or inanimate, is just what it is there described, and that all the *moral* actions of men are *good* or *evil*, only as they are conformable, or not, to the true intent and meaning of the unchangeable *laws* of the *Creator* there recorded.—Therefore,

10. To imagine that the *sun* which rules our *day*, and the *moon* which governs our *night*, are not the same identical *luminaries* of which we read in the *Hebrew scriptures*, is not more false, absurd, and unwarranted, than to say that *marriage*, under all the *forms* in which it existed under the dispensation of GOD, as revealed in the *Hebrew scriptures*, and there recorded, is not *now* one and the same in GOD's sight. And we are no more authorized to suppose, that it is in the power of *man* to create a new *sun* or *moon*, than we are, that *he* can make *marriage*, as in GOD's sight, any thing else than what GOD Himself hath made it in His most *holy law*.—To assert that there is ANY LAW, *holier*, *purer*, *wiser*, or *better* adapted to regulate the *commerce of*

the sexes, than that which JEHOVAH published at *Mount Sinai*, is *horrible blasphemy!*

11. The author doth most certainly believe, that as the sacraments of the *Lord's Supper* and *Baptism* have been corrupted by *antichristian* inventions—so the ordinance of *marriage*, as appointed by GOD, and regulated by *His laws*, hath shared the same fate—and that nothing can restore any of these to their primitive simplicity, but an unreserved submission of the minds of men to the pure and perfect WORD OF GOD.

12. He doth also believe, that if ever the increasing ruin and desolation of *the sex*, the *lower orders* thereof especially, should be deemed, as it ought, a serious object of *parliamentary* consideration, as a national *evil* of the most *desolating* and *destructive* kind, not only to *individuals*, but to the *public* in general—if ever the *legislature* should think, with *Baron Montesquieu*, that—" in a popular state, " *public incontinence* may be regarded as the " greatest of misfortunes" — if ever they wish to discourage and check *adultery*, *whoredom*, and *celibacy*, which are the causes of *depopulation*, and of other *numberless evils*; and to promote the interests of *chastity* and *marriage*, which are the approximate causes of *population*, and of other *numberless benefits*—no plan that ever can be devised or thought of will ever answer these most desirable ends, like that exhibited to us in the *divine law*; which has been considered and set forth in these *volumes*, and which, however antiquated

quated and laid afide by the craft and policy of *Popifh* contrivance, to anfwer the purpofes of *prieftly* importance, ambition and wealth, *is* yet, as it *was*, and ever *will be*, the only *rule of right*—millions have had caufe to *curfe* the day when it was *laid afide*—*millions* would have reafon to blefs the day when it fhall be reftored.

As for the experiments which have been try'd, to improve upon the *difpenfations* of the Most High, with refpect to the *moral* government of mankind, they certainly have precedents of a very early date. They began with our *firft parents*, and have been handed down to us in regular fucceffion for near fix thoufand years. The *Jewifh* church was very fertile in fuch *experiments*, as its *hiftory*, both in the *Old Teftament* and *New Teftament*, abundantly informs us. As for the *Chriftians*, they have not been behind hand; they have always had *projectors*, of very high and diftinguifhed abilities in *that way*—their *projects* and *experiments*, with refpect to God's *laws* which were to regulate the *commerce of the fexes*, have been fet forth without referve in thefe *volumes*, but more efpecially in the *firft chapter* of *this*—and what has been the confequence?—We have almoft loft fight of that *fimple*, *plain*, and *falutary* Plan, held forth to us in the *divine law*—and are now under a *complicated*, *dark*, and *deftructive* System, which, inftead of refembling the *plain* and evident *way* of *duty* pointed out to us in the *ftatutes* of *Heaven*, rather may remind

us

us of *Virgil's* account of the *Cretan labyrinth*, where the devouring monster *Minotaur* was kept—

Ut quondam Cretâ fertur labyrinthus in altâ,
Parietibus tectum cæcis iter, ancipitemque
Mille viis habuiſſe dolum; qua ſigna ſequendi
Falleret indeprenſus et irremeabilis error.
Æn. v. 588.

Like as the *Cretan* labyrinth of old,
With wandering wave, and many a winding fold,
Involv'd the weary feet without redreſs,
In a round error which deny'd receſs.
DRYDEN.

Fable tells us, that *Ariadne*, the daughter of King *Minos*, gave *Theſeus* a *clew*, by which he found his way out of the *labyrinth*, after having ſlain the *Minotaur*.

If theſe *volumes* ſhould be made inſtrumental to our deliverance, by unravelling the iniquitous *myſtery* of human ſyſtems reſpecting *marriage*, and by checking the devaſtations of thoſe *worſt* and moſt deſtructive of *monſters* * — *adultery* and *female proſtitution*—their *end* will be anſwered.

SOLI DEO GLORIA.

* See before vol. ii. p. 104. 1ſt. edit.—p. 98. 2d. edit.

ADDENDA.

Note, vol. i. p. 263. l. 1—4. 1st edit.——
p. 250. l. 7—10. 2d edit.

IN the *Quæst. et Responf. ad Orthodox*, usually printed with the works of *Justin Martyr*, the former part of the 132d *Question* runs in English thus:

"If, according to the *Mosaic* law, a man
"taking the wife of his brother, who was
"dead without issue, begat *issue* of her, which
"*issue* by *nature* were his, but by the *law*
"his *brother*'s — how could this be other-
"wise than wrong, in case the surviving
"brother had *another* wife, together with
"whom he also took the relict of his de-
"ceased brother?"

THE ANSWER.

Τȣ νομȣ μη κωλυσαντος τȣς Ισραηλιτας γυναικα λαβειν, ει ἐβȣλοιντο, ȣ μονον συγγενιδα, αλλα και αιχμαλωτιδα και παλλακιδα· ȣδεν αρα ατοπον, ȣδε βλαπτει εκ τȣ γυναικα επι γυναικι λαβειν αδελφȣ τȣ τελευτηκοτος, τȣ νομȣ μη καταλυομενȣ· πασα γαρ ατοπια επι τῃ παραβασει τȣ νομȣ καθιϛαται.

" Since

"Since the law did not prohibit the *Israelites*, if they chose, from taking a wife, not only of their own nation, but likewise a captive and a concubine, there could, therefore, be nothing wrong or injurious in a man's taking the *relict* of his *deceased brother* to a wife he had before; for the law was not hereby violated: *for all wrong consists in the violation of the law.*"

Vol. ii. 215, n. 1st edit.—2d edit. 197, n.

In the time of the *troubles* in the last *century*, by an ordinance of *August* 1653, 'twas enacted,

"That all persons intending to be *married*, shall come before some *justice* of the *peace*; and if there appear no reasonable cause to the contrary, the marriage shall proceed in this manner:—The *man* to be married, taking the *woman* by the hand, shall plainly and distinctly pronounce these words:—I *A. B.* do, in the presence of GOD, the searcher of all hearts, take thee *C. D.* for my wedded wife; and do also, in the presence of GOD, and before these witnesses, promise to be unto thee a loving and faithful husband.—The *woman* promises, in the same form, to be a *loving*, *faithful*, and *obedient wife.*—— And it is further enacted, That the *man* and *woman* having made sufficient proof of the con-

"sent

" sent of their parents and guardians (if un-
" der the age of twenty-one years) and ex-
" pressed their consent unto *marriage,* in the
" manner and by the words aforesaid, before
" such *justice,* in the presence of two or more
" credible witnesses, the said *justice* may and
" shall declare the said *man* and *woman* to be
" thenceforth *husband* and *wife*; and the mar-
" riage shall be good and effectual in law,"
&c.—The *reader* may find the whole at large in *Schobel*'s Collections, 2d part, p. 236.

This was called—" being married by the *Directory.*"—— The generality of the *Presbyterians* were then married in this manner, enjoined by the *Directory,* and not by the *Liturgy,* though there were some instances to the contrary; and among these, Mr. *Stephen Marshal* (who was a zealot, and had a chief hand in compiling the *Directory)* did marry his own daughter by the form prescribed in the *Liturgy,* being unwilling to have his daughter " returned to him as a
" *whore,* for want of legal marriage, the sta-
" tute establishing the *Liturgy* not being re-
" pealed:" and having so done, he paid down *five pounds* to the churchwardens of the parish, as the fine or forfeiture for using any other form of marriage than that in the *Directory.* See HEYLIN's *Examen Historicum,* p. 364.—GREY HUD. vol. ii. p. 177, n.

By this we may perceive, that they did not attempt the *invalidation* of *marriages,* because not solemnized according to a particular *form* or *ceremony.*

In the above, there was an effectual care taken of the *civil contract*; and, by placing it in the hands of the *civil magistrate*, it was restored to its *ancient* and proper jurisdiction.

Vol. iii. p. 271. l. 13, 14.

I mentioned vol. i. p. 79. 2d edit. n. this *third volume*, in which I said it would appear, that the "making *marriage* under the "New Testament different from what it was "under the Old Testament, is *true genuine* "*Popery.*"—I appeal to the above *sentiment*, or rather *dogma*, for the fulfilment of what the reader was to expect.

In this there are three *propositions*, every one of which is a downright *falshood*— 1. "That marriage is a *sacrament*" of the New Testament. 2. "That it was instituted by "CHRIST." 3. "That it is appropriated "to *Christians*;"—and, of course, the whole dispensation of *marriage*, as revealed in the Old Testament, is as much antiquated and laid aside, as the rites of *circumcision* and the *passover*.

Now, how does the matter really stand? It is surely evident, that the *specific ordinance* by which *the man and woman become one flesh*, is set down Gen. ii. 24; and that the *indissolubility* of the *union* arises from what is there said.

OUR SAVIOUR, so far from making the least alteration in this point, recites this *very passage*—Matt. xix. 5.—and infers from it
(v. 6.)

(v. 6.) the indiſſolubility of the contract, in order to ſhew the *Jews* the unlawfulneſs and inefficacy of their wanton and arbitrary *divorces*.

St. *Paul* ſtates the very ſame paſſage, as his authority for determining the abuſe of the *marriage-ordinance*, in the illicit commerce with an *harlot*. 1 Cor. vi. 15, 16.

The ſame *apoſtle* cites alſo the ſame paſſage of Gen. ii. 24. in order to prove what conſtitutes *marriage*, ſo as to render it an emblem of the *union* between CHRIST and his *church*.——See Eph. v. 31.

After all this plain, clear, unequivocal evidence, what ſhall we ſay to the poſition, that — " *marriage* under the New Teſtament " is different from what it was under the " Old Teſtament ?" — We may as well ſay, that *arithmetic* has changed its calculations; that among the *ancient Jews two* and *two* made only *four*, but now they make *fifty*.

Note, vol. iii. p. 275. l. 23—26.

Dr. GREY, in his edition of *Hudibras*, among many other curious and inſtructive anecdotes, which are well worthy the *reader's* peruſal, has the following : — *Part* iii. *Canto* i. l. 627, 628. n.

" The Emperor *Leo* (as my very worthy
" and learned friend Dr. *Dickins*, profeſſor of
" *civil law* in the *Univerſity* of *Cambridge*,
" informs me) allowed a *ſeparation* in the
" caſe of *incurable madneſs*.

" Per

"Per conjugium, inquiunt, in corpus co-
"ierunt, oportetque membrum alterum al-
"terius morbos perpeti: & divinum præcep-
"tum est *quos Deus junxerit, ne separentur.*
"Præclara quidem hæc & divina, utpote
"quæ a Deo pronuntiata sunt: verum non
"rectè neque secundum divinum propositum
"hic in medium adferuntur: si enim matri-
"monium talem statum conservaret, qualem
"ejus in principio *pronuba* exhibuisset, quis-
"quis separaret, improbus profecto esset, ne-
"que reprehensionem effugeret.
"Jam verò cum præ furore ne vocem
"quidam humanam a muliere audias, nedum
"aliud quidquam eorum quæ ad oblectamen-
"tum & hilaritatem matrimonium largitur
"ab illâ obtineat: quis adeo acerbum hor-
"rendumque matrimonium dirimere nolit?
"Ea propter sancimus, &c. ut si quando post
"initum matrimonium, mulier in furorem
"incidat, ad tres annos infortunium maritus
"ferat, mæstitiamque tolleret: & nisi inter
"ea temporis ab isto malo illa liberetur, ne-
"que ad mentem redeat; tunc matrimonium
"divellatur, maritusque ab intolerabili illa
"calamitate exoneretur. *Imp. Leonis No-
"vella* CXI.

"*Per Novellam Sequentem:* Si maritus per
"matrimonii tempus in furorem incidat in-
"tra quinquennium matrimonium solvi ne-
"queat: eo autem elapso, si furor eum ad-
"huc occupet, solvi possit.

"By marriage, they say, there is a bodily
"union, and it behoveth the one member to
"bear

"bear the diseases of the other: and it is a
"divine precept—*those whom God hath joined
"together, let them not be put asunder.* A
"most excellent and divine saying, as pro-
"nounced by GOD; but here it is not
"brought into the question (of divorce)
"rightly, nor according to the divine pur-
"pose: if the matrimony remained as at the
"beginning, maintaining the same state as
"when the woman was first a *bride*, who-
"ever should *separate*, would indeed be
"wicked; nor would they escape reprehen-
"sion. But when, through *madness*, you can-
"not hear from the woman even a human
"voice, nor can the husband obtain any of
"those things which matrimony bestows for
"delight and comfort, who would not de-
"stroy so bitter and horrible a marriage?
"Wherefore we ordain, &c. that if, at any
"time after the marriage, the wife falls into
"madness, the husband shall bear his mis-
"fortune and grief for *three years*—and, un-
"less she shall be delivered, and return to
"her right mind in that time, then the mar-
"riage shall be dissolved, and the husband
"released from so intolerable a calamity.

"If the husband falls into *madness* during
"the coverture, the marriage cannot be dis-
"solved within *five years*; but, that time
"being elapsed, if the *madness* still possesses
"him, it may be dissolved."

The *Emperor* seems to have carried his notions and allowance of absolute *divorce* farther than the scriptures warrant; yet on reasonable proof of the above facts, a *separaration*, but so as that the man shall still maintain and provide for the woman as his *wife*, might surely be allowed; as also, that he might marry another, not only on account of *madness*, but where through other *diseases*, or unavoidable causes of *separation*, the man ceases in fact to have any one end of marriage.

The allowance of absolute *divorce* on the *madness* of the *husband*, or other cause of unavoidable *separation* from him, is a very *different question*, and does not appear to have any warrant whatsoever from GOD's *word*. See Rom. vii. 3. 1 Cor. vii. 11.

Here I would add another remarkable matter, which occurs among the *canons* of Gregory II. and should have had a place before, p. 84. but was omitted by mistake, though it is mentioned in *Du Pin*.

"*Si mulier infirmitate correpta non valuerit*
"*debitum viro reddere, quid ejus faciat jugalis?*
"— *bonum esset si sic permaneret: Sed quia*
"*hoc magnorum est, ille qui se non poterit con-*
"*tinere, nubat magis:* — *non tamen subsidii*
"*opem subtrahat ab illâ quam infirmitas præ-*
"*pedit, non detestabilis culpa excludit.*"

" If a wife be seized with some infirmity,
" so that she be not capable of rendering *the*
" *debt* to the husband, what should he do?
" — It would be good if he remain as he is.
" But because this is very difficult, he who
" cannot *contain*, had better *marry*. Not
                                           " that

"that he is to withdraw the affiftance of "his fupport (and maintenance) from her "whom infirmity hinders (*i. e.* as aforefaid) "even fome deteftable crime does not ex- "clude this."

Though this be the language of *a Pope* of *Rome,* it is yet fo agreeable to *nature, reafon,* and *fcripture*—to the moft apparent dictates of *common fenfe,* and *underftanding*—to every principle of *juftice* and *equity*—and is fo calculated to prevent numberlefs *evil confequences,* which muft flow from a conftrained, involuntary, and unnatural *celibacy*— it is as much to be *lamented,* that the *church* could ever alter or abrogate this *canon,* as it is to be *wondered* at, that there fhould be found a *Chriftian* legiflature which has not adopted it. Well—perhaps—*non ut male nunc, & olim fic erit.*

To RICHARD HILL, Esq.

My dear Sir,

I AM entirely of opinion with *you*, that *religion*, instead of lessening our *ideas* of *friendship*, tends to exalt them; for which reason, it gives me a concern which I cannot express, to be forced into a *remonstrance* against any *conduct* of *your's*, with whom it has been my honour and happiness, for *many, many years*, to live on a footing of the most disinterested, tender, and affectionate friendship. I hope I shall not forget this in any thing which I may say on the present occasion.

It is not my purpose to write a regular answer to your late book, intitled, the " *Blessings of Polygamy*, &c." In the first place, *that*, in general, appears to me so completely done to my hands already, in the *publication* which you attack, that there is little reason for me to repeat the trouble; and, if you will read the *books* which you censure, with more attention than you seem to have done, I am not without hopes, that your *candour* may lead you to be of that opinion.

However, you must give me leave to ask you, in the first place, how far it is reconcileable to those notions of *urbanity* and *politeness*, which I have so often observed to be remarkably conspicuous in Mr. Hill, to put any man's *name* to a work, where the *au-*

thor has not done it himfelf?—but, more efpecially, where there is little other intention, than holding forth the *man* and his *work* in the light in which you have been pleafed to exhibit your old and *faithful friend*—that is to fay, in as *injurious* a point of view as he could well be placed, fo far as relates to the *publication* which you cenfure.

In the next place, I would obferve, that I cannot think it very confiftent with that warmth and delicacy of *friendfhip*, which has fo long fubfifted between us, to fay nothing to your old *friend* of your intention to produce fuch an attack upon him in the face of the *public*, before you fent it to the prefs:— Would it not have been more *friendly*, not to fay more like *yourfelf* as a *gentleman*, to have fhewn him the *manufcript*, heard and weighed maturely his objections, and to have corrected the *language* or *fentiment*, where you might have been convinced that your *pen*, in fome places, had *haftily* overleaped the bounds of that *refpect* and *regard* which you profefs for the *Author* in other parts of your performance? As far as I know myfelf, and can judge from my prefent feelings, I could not, on any account, have publifhed *fuch a book* againft *you*, without firft fhewing it to you, and liftening, moft attentively, to whatever might tend to correct any *afperity* of exprefſion, or any *perfonal reflection*, which might *hurt* you in your own mind, or injure your *character* in the fight of the world.

It is not an enemy that has done me this difhonour,

diſhonour, &c.—As to your *animadverſions* on *Thelyphthora*, I could wiſh for your *own ſake*, as well as *mine*, that you had taken *more time* to conſider them before they were publiſhed, and to have reflected how far they agreed with the ſubjects of them in point of *accuracy*. For inſtance—you certainly attempt to charge the *author* " with recom-
" mending an *indiſcriminate* and unlimited
" practice of *polygamy*, and wanting a *law*
" to eſtabliſh it."—This, though not the very words, is yet the undoubted *ſubſtance* of your accuſation on the point, as it may be fairly deduced from your book.—How is this conſiſtent with the following paſſage, *viz.*

" As to *Polygamy*—which is certainly one
" *link* in the *chain* of God's diſpenſations,
" as ſo abſolutely neceſſary to prevent, in
" many caſes, the deſertion and proſtitution
" of women, as well as to preſerve men from
" vice and profligacy, under various circum-
" ſtances of unavoidable difficulties and
" temptations, which *neceſſary ſeparation*
" may render them liable to (ſee before,
" vol. i. p. 181—2) the cauſes of which
" may fall ſhort of being grounds for *utter*
" *divorce*—it is, conſidered in *itſelf*, one of
" the *laſt* things which a man ſhould think
" of, who wiſhes and aims at the happineſs
" of a domeſtic life. The weight and bur-
" den of a double family, the diſtractions
" which moſt probably muſt be the effect of
" jealouſy between the women, each envying
" the other her ſhare in the huſband's af-
" fections,

"fections, must be productive of disputes,
"quarrels, and perpetual disquiet. We see
"this to have been the case even among the
"best of people, who were *polygamists.*—
"What were *Abraham*'s trials, which arose
"from his connections with *Hagar?*—What
"those of *Jacob,* from the jealousy and
"discontent of *Leah* and *Rachel?* So *Elka-*
"*nah* suffered not a little, at the treatment
"which his favourite *Hannah* received from
"her rival *Peninnah*—and, indeed, it is so
"much in the nature of things, that matters
"should fall out alike in all times, where there
"are the same *causes* to produce the same
"*effects,* that one should imagine most men,
"who consulted the peace, quiet, and com-
"fort of themselves and families, would sub-
"scribe to *Horace's*

"*Felices ter & amplius*
"*Quos irrupta tenet copula; nec malis*
"*Divulsus querimoniis,*
"*Suprema citius solvet amor die.*

"*Thrice happy they, in pure delights,*
"*Whom love with mutual bonds unites;*
"*Unbroken by complaints or strife,*
"*Ev'n to the latest hours of life.*
"FRANCIS.

"It is most readily to be allowed, that
"such people can have nothing to do with
"the subject of *polygamy.*" ["Except it be
"to abhor and execrate the very thought of
"it." 2d edit.] See *Thelyph.* vol. ii. 187—191.

I might also refer you to p. 378, n.

which stands thus:—" Doubtless in this,
" as in all things else, which, however *law-*
" *ful* or *innocent* in themselves, may become
" *sinful* by *abuse* or *excess*, we may say with
" Horace—

> " *Est modus in rebus—sunt certi denique fines,*
> " *Quos ultra citraque nequit consistere rectum.*

> " Some certain *mean* in all things may be found,
> " To mark our *virtues*, and our *vices* bound.
> " Francis.

" That *polygamy* is *lawful in itself*, and in
" many cases *expedient* (See before 192—3, n.)
" in some *duty* (See vol. i. p. 297—8.)
" none can deny, who will yield to the tes-
" timony of the scriptures and plain matter
" of fact. But where it is entered upon
" with no other view than to *pamper the ap-*
" *petite,* and to indulge a *love of variety*, it
" degenerates into *evil*; and seems to be
" to *marriage,* what *gluttony* and *drunkenness,*
" and excess of *apparel,* are to *food* and *rai-*
" *ment*—a *sinful*, because a forbidden, *abuse*
" of *lawful* and necessary things."

I am much concerned, Sir, that I am constrained to remind *you* of these passages; more so, that they did not prevent the *severity* of some of your *censures* on the *author*, as a maintainer and recommender of *indiscriminate* and *unlimited polygamy*—an *idea* as much abhorred by him as by *yourself*.

Again—you seem to argue, as if the author meant to disparage *marriage-ceremony*, or to *dispute* the *necessity* of it; though afterwards, indeed, you do allow, that he contends for it.

it.—My dear Sir, you say (p. 124) that you will not dispute with me, whether "the mere in-"tercourse of a man with a virgin constitute "a marriage in the sight of God"—but as to the necessity of "some solemn act of recognition," (p. 125.) can you yourself say more than is said in the following words?

"Now to apply what has been said to the "subject of this *chapter*, it will be neces-"sary for us to keep the ideas of *marriage*, "as it is a *divine ordinance* with respect to "God, and as it is a *civil contract* with respect "to the *public*, distinct in our minds. It is the "*first* only which constitutes the indissolu-"ble union in God's sight, but it is the *se-*"*cond* which recognizes and ratifies that "union in the sight of the world; and this "is a sort of security which (as so much de-"pends upon it with respect to *society*) the "world has a right to require, consequently "to exact; and those who wilfully refuse to "give it, deserve to lose every privilege "and benefit which are annexed to it. "Were the *consciences* of men what they "*ought to be*, the *fear* and *love* of God "would reign within them, and a strict ob-"servance of his commandments be the "measure and rule of all their dealings to-"wards God and each other. But in this "corrupt state of things, this is not the "case, therefore human laws are necessary "to enforce the *divine law*, in no instance, "perhaps, *more necessary* than in the case "before us. If no *contract* of a *public nature* "was insisted upon, but all left to the pri-
"vate

" vate agreements and determinations be-
" tween the parties, men might take women,
" and women men, and keep or put one
" another away as humour or fancy suited;
" the woman who was the wife of A. to-
" day, might become the wife of B. to-
" morrow; in short, it is impossible to
" *conceive*, much more so to *express*, the con-
" fusion which must ensue on such a plan.
" Therefore, when human laws are made to
" exact a public contract between the par-
" ties in the face of the world, which con-
" tract cannot be broken nor dissolved but
" for the *one cause* which GOD's word al-
" lows, such laws are in affirmance of the
" law of GOD, and therefore are righteous
" laws; and, as such, ought to be obeyed;
" nor have any persons a right to that respect,
" and to those privileges, which are due to
" married persons, who despise such an or-
" dinance of man as creates a *civil contract*
" in the sight of the world, by way of *re-*
" *cognition* of that *private contract* which
" they have entered into between themselves
" in the sight of GOD. Those who wilfully
" live together, as *man* and *wife*, without
" this, are deservedly reckoned infamous,
" and as deservedly cut off from the benefits
" of marriage, so far as *civil society* is con-
" cerned: therefore to discourage, and even
" to *punish*, such a conduct, is certainly with-
" in the authority of all *civil government*,
" nor would any government be justified in
" not doing it, for without this, men and
" women

" women would be living like the beasts of
" the field. No fault is therefore to be
" found with our laws for enforcing the
" public recognition of GOD's *ordinance*,
" but for not enforcing it *in all cases*, and for
" making it *null* and *void* in *any*, where GOD's
" law hath not made it so. Instead of shut-
" ting up the *ecclesiastical* courts against the
" complaints of deserted females, or pre-
" venting their enforcement of *that redress*
" which GOD's law commands, every court
" in *Westminster Hall*, and every *magistrate*'s
" house in the kingdom, should be open to
" them, and on pain of death, or at least of
" perpetual imprisonment till compliance,
" every man who had seduced a woman, whe-
" ther with or without a promise of *marriage*,
" should be obliged to wed * her publicly.
" Under what *rite* or *ceremony* this is done,
" is of very little consequence, so that it be
" effectual for the notoriety of the contract,
" and the prevention of causeless divorce.
" That which makes the *marriage* before GOD
" is the same every where, that which re-
" cognizes it in the sight of men, is, and
" may be different, but all tending to one
" point, that of affording to the state, as
" well as to the parties themselves, such a se-
" curity for their cohabitation, as is neces-
" sary for the peace, good order, and wel-
" fare of the whole. Something like what
" *Q. Curtius* reports *Alexander* to have said,
" when he cut the famous *Gordian* knot, I

* See *Thelyph.* vol. i. p. 290, 2d edit. and n.

" would

" would fay on the *tying* the *nuptial knot,* as
" far as public ceremony is concerned—" So
" it *be* done, no matter *how.*"—*Thelyph.*
vol. ii. 70—73.

After an attentive revifal of the above, I
hope you will be very forry that you fo far
forgot *yourfelf,* and injured *your friend,* as to
tell the *whole world,* under your *own hand*—
p. 125—that " he *explodes* * every thing of
" *this fort,*" (i. e. external *marriage-ceremony)* " as fuperftitious prieftcraft."

Something akin to this may be found
p. 140, where you quote the following paffage from the advertifement to *Thelyphthora,*
1ft edition.—" In the eye of our municipal
" laws, women are of lefs confequence than
" the beafts of the field—for it is *lefs penal*
" to feduce, defile, and abandon to profti-
" tution and ruin a thoufand women, *mar-
" ried* or *unmarried,* than to fteal, kill, or
" even malicioufly to maim or wound an ox
" or a fheep. See 22 and 23 Car. II. c. 7.
" 9 Geo. I. c. 22."

On this you comment thus:—" I had
" like to have faid, that there is a moft pal-
" pable *falfity* in this affertion, but I will re-
" call the word, and inftead of *falfity* we will
" read *fallacy.*"—i. e. here is not a *lye,* but
only an *equivocation.*

In order to make out this *charge,* which
you muft permit me to call rather of the *il-*

---

* From this, and from *other ftrokes* of Mr. H's very
hafty pen, I am perfectly convinced, that *my friend* has
fcarcely one *real idea* of the book which he writes
againft.

liberal kind, far more fo than I could have thought *you* capable of towards any body, much lefs towards *me*—you afterwards cite only the firft fentence—" In the eye of our " municipal laws women are of lefs confe- " quence than the beafts of the field."—This, as it ftands by itfelf, as an unlimited and univerfal propofition, you have my free leave to call a downright *lye,* and a very *nonfenfical* one into the bargain—but why did you omit what follows, which fhows that the *author* means this *reftrictively,* in a *certain refpect,* which is mentioned, and in which *refpect* the propofition is certainly true? —it is *more penal,* malicioufly to *hamftring* an *ox,* than to " feduce, defile, and abandon to " proftitution and ruin a thoufand women, " either married or unmarried," for the of- fender in the *firft cafe* would be hanged; and if you can prove that this would be the fate of the *feducer,* &c. then I will grant that the law is not *lefs penal* towards him than towards the other.

But, my dear Sir, why would you pafs over in filence that farther explanation of the *au- thor's* meaning, which muft have met you, vol. ii. p. 58, and fo entirely elucidates his fentiments on the fubject, as furely to leave no reafonable ground for fo *heavy* a *charge* as you have brought againft his *fince- rity?*—the whole paffage alluded to runs thus:—

" The more we examine the *law of* God, " the more fhall we be apprized of its har-
" mony

" mony and confiftency with itfelf, as well
" as with the peace, good order, and welfare
" of human fociety; more efpecially with
" regard to its care and watchfulnefs over
" thofe who ftand moft in need of its pro-
" tection, the *weaker fex*; which, as matters
" are now ordered, feems of lefs value than
" the beafts of the field. If a man goes into
" his neighbour's field, and wilfully *maims*
" or *wounds* his *cattle*, it is *felony without be-*
" *nefit of clergy*; but to *feduce*, and *debauch*
" his *daughter*, and then to look upon him-
" felf as free from all legal obligation to
" *marry her*, is the grand privilege which
" he finds annexed to our repeal of the *laws*
" *of Heaven*. As for the fufferer, if fhe be
" *poor*, fo that her maintenance depends upon
" her *character*, this being gone, fhe muft
" ftarve for want of employment, or plunge
" herfelf into the depths of proftitution to
" get food and raiment." I cannot perceive
any *falfity* or *fallacy* in alledging, that, in
this refpect, the law takes more care of a
man's *ox* than of his *daughter*, or that it is
lefs penal to debauch and abandon her to
proftitution, than to *maim* or *wound his cattle*.

What occafion was there for your talking
of *rapes, attempts to commit them*, &c. and
ftealing, killing, or *malicioufly* wounding a wife
or a virgin? though, by the way, a man
might *malicioufly wound* either of *thefe*, and
not be liable to *death*, as he would in the
cafe of the *cattle*—and as for the *action* for
damages by a *father*, againft a man who *vio-*
lated

lated the chastity of his daughter *of marriageable age*, I believe, if it came out in *proof*, that the " man had intercourse with her by " her *freest consent*,"—as you speak—he would get little more by his *action*, than a very large *bill* from his *attorney*, for which he might be *arrested*, and sent to *gaol*. Besides, Sir, the *poorer sort* of people could hardly venture on the risque and expence of such an action at all. I therefore still *venture to believe*, that the *Jewish laws*—Exod. xxii. 16. and Deut. xxii. 28, 29—had by far more *wisdom* and *justice* in them, than there is to be found in any *other plan*, which mortals ever *have* contrived or *can* devise.

You say, p. 11—" I would not be un-
" derstood to insinuate, that polygamy was
" ever a part of the law of GOD. On the
" contrary, there is no *command whatever*
" which injoins it, or even leans towards it."
—What think you of the *Levirate*, or law of *marrying the brother's wife?*—See *Bp. Burnet's* opinion, *Thelyph.* vol. i. p. 313.—Again, what say you to Exod. xxii. 16. and Deut. xxii. 28. 29? Hear your friend *M. Luther*—
" Nota sunt jura *Mosaica*, de fratris defuncti
" uxore, & de filia correpta invito patre, quæ
" *cogunt plurium esse uxorum virum*. And
" again, in *Comment* in *Gen. in propos*, &
" in libro *de bigamia episcoporum*. We find that
" LUTHER asserted—*Polygynæciam* non esse
" contra *legem naturæ*; aut *moralem*, aut ipsam
" *scripturam sacram.*" See *Pol. Tri.* THESIS, xc.
—I should recommend it to you, not to be over
fond

fond of calling either *Luther* or *Zuinglius* (See *Thelyph*. vol. i. 406, n.) as *witnesses* for your *sentiments*, or honest *M. Bucerus*, or indeed any of the chief *Reformers*.

P. 13.—Prov. v. 16. relates to the *children*, so no occasion for the *Kennicottian* NOT: The omission of which is certainly not *exactly of the same kind* as " the printer, whom " *Laud* fined," was guilty of; since in Prov. *all* the *printed editions* which I have seen, and among them the *Complutensian*, want the Hebrew word for *not*.

P. 16, 17.—Incestuous marriages would still have been lawful, *if not expresly forbidden by God*—prove that *polygamy* has been so forbidden. (But why must the marriages immediately after *Noah*'s flood be *incestuous*—might not all his grand-children marry their *first cousins?*)

P. 18.—A comparison of Numb. xv. 32, 33, &c. with Exod. xxxv. 2. xvi. 23. shews the reason of the severity against the *stick-gatherer*.—The law against *lighting a fire* on the *sabbath* seems only *temporary*, while they were fed miraculously with the *Manna*.

P. 29.—What authority has Mr. *H.* to substitute, in Exod. xxi. 8. *humbled her*, for *dealt deceitfully with her*.—A knowledge and proper regard to the *Hebrew* Bible would here have been of use to him.—The *textual* reading of verse 8, in all the printed *Bibles* which I have seen (especially the *Complutensian*) is " who hath *not* betrothed her;" and the words at the end of ver. 8. should have been rendered—*in dealing*, or *to deal deceitfully with her*. These *remarks* give a different view of the passage.—Ver. 9. "If he have betrothed her *(his female slave)* to his son," is a very different case from "a man's *enticing a virgin and lying with her*." In the *former* instance, the *man* treats the *maid* as his property, as she truly was (for he had *bought* her, ver. 7;) but even here GOD provided a *remedy*, that the *master's son*, to whom she had been *betrothed*, should not treat her otherwise than any other *wife*. If he would not be a *husband to her*, she should not be a *wife to him*. Such is the *equitable* and *benign* spirit of GOD's law by *Moses!*

P. 30.—What think you of our LORD's superseding the *judicial* law of *retaliation*, to be executed by the *magistrate*, by that more *benign* and *evangelical system* which enjoins us (in our *private* capacity) to return good for evil? I believe the *law* of retaliation, in *all* cases of *corporal injury*, *(an eye for an eye,* &c.) as well as in *murder*, would, in the event, be a most benign and merciful law.

P. 32, note—directly contradicts *Josephus*, who, in this case, is an unexceptionable witness.

P. 37. "*Suppose*, &c. to *all his days?*"— What? *without evidence*, either positive or circumstantial, upon the *mere say-so* of the woman or women? Do our laws hang men for *rapes* in the like *nonsensical* manner?

P. 40.—"The *tyrannical* authority of *Sarah*

over

over *Hagar*."—Her *treatment* of her was expresly approved by GOD *himself*, Gen. xxi. 12. though perhaps it might not be so by a *Bolingbroke* or a *Voltaire*.—Mr. H. in his zeal against *polygamy*, forgets that *Hagar*'s son *mocked Isaac*, with whom GOD had established his covenant; and that *St. Paul* calls this *mocking* a *persecution*, Gal. iv. 29. If Mr. H. alludes to *Hagar*'s first flight from the *resentment* of her mistress, let him advert to the foundation of that *resentment*, as mentioned *Gen*. xvi. 4, 5. and it will be found a *just* one.—Her contempt of *Sarai*, no doubt, produced a very improper conduct towards her, as appears by *Sarai*'s complaint to *Abram*, ver. 5.

P. 87. Mr. H. mistakes the case of *Jael*, when she slew *Sisera*, by saying she acted *under the immediate direction of God*, of which there is no proof.—She acted as a voluntary and faithful subject of the *Israelitish* state. See Bate's note on Jud. iv. 17, who is the only *commentator* I know that has explained this.

These cursory remarks on particular parts of your book, I submit to your *revisal*. Your taking the *marginal* reading of Lev. xviii. 18. as the true sense of the passage— and your controverting the interpretation of Mal. ii. 15. after your acknowledgment that you are *no Hebræan*—when the right understanding of those texts must depend on the original words—might, perhaps, as well have been omitted.—You remember the old *proverb*—*Ne sutor*, &c.

Your free *declamation*, and very extraordinary

nary cafes *imagined* on this occafion, prove nothing but the livelinefs of *my friend*, and that it fometimes hurries him into *reflections*, which may poffibly fall where I am fure he does not mean they fhould. The fyftem defended in *Thelyphthora* is that of the *Divine law*. I can meet with no fuch cafes as that of " *Lady A.* and Sir *Thomas A.*"—nor as that of " The humble petition of *Mary*, the wife " of *John Williams*"—nor of " *women* of the " *St. Giles's* breed, crying *murders** about the " ftreets," as the confequences of the *Jewifh fyftem*; thefe are fallies of your *vivacity*— which might have been as well fpared, where the queftion before you was not merely concerning human judgment, but concerning a matter *allowed* by the "*permiffion*' at leaft (as you confefs) of God *himfelf*, for many ages together.

I could wifh you to reflect on a paffage in *Thelyphthora*, which, on this occafion, you will give me leave to remind you of.

" To argue againft any thing, from the
" *abufe* of it, is the moft unfair of all me-
" thods of refutation. There are no abfur-
" dities, and, indeed, no lengths of *impiety*
" and *blafphemy*, into which, by fuch means,
" we may not be carried.

" We may even difpute the *wifdom* and

---

* Alluding to the difmal ftory of that *Patient Grizzel*, who is fuppofed " to cut the throats of her *hufband* and " his new *wife*, and then her *own*." P. 49.—I would advife *my friend* Mr. H. to leave off Tea, efpecially in an *evening*; it is very apt, in fome conftitutions, to create *difordered fleep* and *frightful dreams*; thefe leave impreffions on the *fancy*, which are not *eafily* got rid of.

" holinefs

" *holiness* of the CREATOR in making the
" *human species* of different SEXES—in or-
" daining the means of *increasing and multi-*
" *plying* the human race, by the union of
" the *male* and *female*—in implanting, for
" this purpose, a desire towards each other
" —for if all this had never been, *adultery,*
" *fornication,* and *whoredom,* could not have
" existed:—Nay, we may carry the argu-
" ment so far, as to conclude against the
" *Divine wisdom* and *holiness* in the *creation* it-
" self; for, if this had never been, no *evil,*
" either *moral* or *natural,* could have ever
" been known. See vol. i. pref. p. xxiii.

" Let us go a little farther, and we shall
" get into *scepticism*—and from thence into
" *atheism*—like those

" ———who tread the high *priori* road,
" And argue downward till they doubt of GOD.
                                " POPE.

" In 1536, *Archbishop Cranmer,* who was
" projecting the most effectual means for a
" reformation of doctrine, moved in *convo-*
" *cation,* that they should petition the *King*
" for leave to make a translation of the *Bible.*
" But *Gardiner,* and all his party, opposed
" it, both in *convocation,* and in secret with
" the *King.* It was said, that all the *heresies,*
" and extravagant *opinions,* which were then
" in *Germany,* and from thence coming over
" to England, sprang from the *free use* of
" the *Scripture:* And whereas in the *May*
" last year, nineteen *Hollanders* were accused
                                " of

" of some heretical opinions, for which opi-
" nions *fourteen* of them were *burnt* in *pairs*,
" in several places; it was complained,
" that all those drew their *damnable errors*
" from the indiscreet use of the *Scripture*.
" And to offer the *Bible* to the whole nation,
" would prove the greatest *snare* that could
" be. See *Burnet* Hist. Ref. vol. i. p. 195,
" second edit.

" Whoever reads with attention this ex-
" cellent and entertaining *history*, will see
" what reliance the *Popish* party had on this
" *mode of argumentation* against the *Reformers*,
" their *writings*, and indeed the *Reformation*
" *itself*. The great *Sir Thomas More*, in his
" writings, exercised all his dexterity in ex-
" posing the *ill consequences* that could follow
" on the *doctrine* of the *reformers*. Ibid. 356.'

" Assuming certain prejudices as true,
" and thence drawing *conclusions*, which rest
" singly on such prejudices, is not only *un-*
" *fair*, but is one of the meanest and most
" despicable *sophisms* that error can have re-
" course to; it is that sort of deceit and
" imposition, which " imports the misre-
" presentation of the qualities of things and
" actions to the common apprehensions of
" men, abusing their minds with false no-
" tions; and so, by this artifice, making
" *evil* pass for *good*, and *good* for *evil*, in all
" the great concerns of life. South's *Ser-*
" *mons*."—*Thelyph*. vol. ii. p. 324, n.

And indeed, my dear *friend*, after all you
have said—though your *haste* has made you
forget

forget your resolution, p. 8, of making "use of no other sword *than that of the Spirit, which is the word of* God"—you yourself seem to be a little suspicious, that you may have gone rather *too far* in your *censures*, with respect to the *Old Testament* at least.—Thus you express yourself.

"But after all, suppose I cannot reconcile this difficulty to my own apprehension; suppose I am fearful of saying that *polygamy* was no sin under the *Old Testament*, and am also fearful of asserting that *Abraham, David,* and *others*, lived and died in *adultery*; still why cannot I content myself with what is plainly revealed, and leave it to God to clear up the justice and equity of His own dealings with the children of men? *Secret things belong unto Him.* Infinite wisdom has its own reasons for whatever it does, and will be accountable to none. Whatever be dark, this is certain, that God thought fit to *permit polygamy* under the law: but *permission* does not by any means imply approbation; nay, God often permits that which, from the very holiness of his nature, is his abhorrence."

Here I would just stop to ask you, how far from "*implying approbation*" it is, where an action is "*permitted*," not merely on some *special, particular* occasion, under some extraordinary circumstances, but uniformly allowed, regulated by *positive laws*, and openly practised by the people of God (even the *best* of them) through an uninterrupted succession of many ages, and no where *condemned*, but in some cases *absolutely commanded?*

"On the other hand, it is *equally certain*, that GOD has thought fit to prohibit *polygamy* under the *Gospel*—and therefore, though *permission* may well enough accord with disapprobation, yet prohibition and approbation are so far from agreeing, that they cannot stand together."

Here *my friend* ends the *controversy at once*, and has established his *point* with one *stroke of his pen*. In vain have so many great and learned men, such as *Wetstein, Barbeyrac, Bishop Burnet*, and others, given their suffrages on the other side of the question; my dear *friend* has *decided* it *tout d'un coup*. The excellent and learned *Dr. Doddridge*, whose very name is honoured so deservedly by all that remember him, and who, I believe, was never suspected of *licentiousness*, either in principle or practice, thus modestly expresses himself in his note on 1 Tim. iii. 2.

"*The husband of one wife.*] Mr. *Hallet* and Mr. *Whiston* both infer from hence, that *second* marriages are unlawful to the *clergy*; and the *Muscovites* suppose, that *one wife* is so necessary, that no man can become a *bishop* till he be *married*, nor continue to exercise *that office* longer than his *wife lives. Perry's Russia, p.* 230. But circumstances may be so adjusted, that there may be as much reason for a *second* marriage as for a *first*, and as little inconvenience may attend it. Upon the "whole,

" whole, therefore, it seems to me most rea-
" sonable to believe, that (as there is *no ex-*
" *press precept in the Bible*, requiring a man
" who had several *wives* at the time of his
" embracing Christianity, to *divorce* or dis-
" miss *all but one)* the divine wisdom might
" judge that it was a proper *medium* between
" encouraging *polygamy*, and too great a ri-
" gour in *condemning* it, to fix such a brand
" of infamy on this irregular practice, by
" prohibiting any man, let his character be
" ever so extraordinary, to undertake the *mi-*
" *nistry* while he had more than *one wife*,
" and to *discourage* it in those already con-
" verted, by such passages as Matt. xix. 9.
" and 1 Cor. vii. 2."

You find here, how *cautious* this learned and reverend man was in his *expressions.*—I will answer for it, that if he had seen *your book*, he would have been *grieved*, if not *shocked*, at the *peremptoriness* with which *you determine*, and the *levity*, I had almost said *profane ribaldry*, with which you treat a subject of such *serious importance*, and *vilify* a *practice* which you *yourself* acknowledge " GOD *thought fit to permit under the law*," p. 88. How far does it become you, Sir, to treat in so very *ludicrous* a style, any practice which the GOD that made you *thought fit to permit?* Even supposing what you take upon you to assert as " equally certain," be so—viz. that "GOD, who thought fit to *permit polygamy* " under the *law*, prohibited it under the *gospel*" —how far is it *decent* to treat the subject with so much *facetious raillery*, and to charge it with horrid confequences, which you cannot bring a fingle inftance of from the *Bible*, wherein you *muſt*, and indeed *do*, confefs the practice of it to be recorded, under the permiffion of GOD himfelf?

Did you ever read *Lord Bolingbroke's Letters* on the *Study and Uſe of Hiſtory?* Do you recollect what he fays upon the fubject of the *ark*, and on certain other parts of the *Jewiſh laws, worſhip*, and *œconomy?*—And do you think him at all the more *juſtifiable*, becaufe the *ceremonial law—is waxed old, and vaniſhed away?*—My *friend* would be one of the laſt men upon earth to excufe the *ſneers* of Mr. *Voltaire* upon the *Jews* and their *law*, by faying that the contents of the *Dictionaire Philoſophique* relate chiefly to the times of the *Old Teſtament*.

I throw out thefe *hints*, which I hope will be taken as they are meant, in a *friendly view*—for I do apprehend, that whatever can, in the moſt diſtant manner, reflect on the *propriety* and wiſdom of *any* of GOD's *diſpenſations*, are very unbecoming a zealous *profeſſor*, much more, what I fincerely believe Mr. H. to be, a real *poſſeſſor* of *true religion*. For this reafon I think it would have been full as *decent* to have fpared the *ironical title* which you have been pleafed to place at the *head* of your *performance*, as well as the *ſarcaſm* of your *dedication*.

Now, my dear Sir, you have nothing to do, but to produce fome one plain mark or act of the "*disapprobation*" which you speak of.—You have the *Bible* open before you; you have the history of near four thousand years; you have numerous instances of *polygamous* contracts to refer to;—produce one instance of the divine *prohibition* or *disapprobation*, and you will have the *Old Testament* on your side.

Then turn to *Rom.* vii. and you will find the chapter begins thus—viz.

" 1. Know ye not, brethren (for I speak
" to them that know the law) how that the
" law hath dominion over a man as long as
" *it* liveth.

" 2. For the woman which hath an hus-
" band is bound by the law to her husband
" so long as he liveth; but if the husband
" be dead, she is loosed from the law of her
" husband.

" 3. So that if, while her husband liveth,
" she be married to another man, she shall
" be called an adulteress: but if her hus-
" band be dead, she is free from that law;
" so that she is no adulteress, though she be
" married to another man."

The *Apostle*, you observe, speaks to them *who knew the law*—and, on the footing of *that law*, plainly and openly delivers his sentiments on the *case* mentioned. Now, if you can find as *plain*, as *express*, as *unequivocal*, as *indisputable* an authority from the *law*, for the prohibition of *polygamy* on the *man's* side, as in this place of the New Testament, and throughout the whole Old Testament, there is on the *woman's*—I promife you, and I promife the *public*, to retract all I have faid on the fubject. Otherwife, I muft freely declare, that I cannot believe the fcriptures fhould be fo uniformly *explicit* on *one fide*, and fo dark and perplexed on the *other*, as to leave us to feek the meaning of the *lawgiver* out of his words (as *Bifhop Burnet* fays) " by " the fearch of *logic*," where a point of fuch infinite and eternal concern is at ftake, as whether any given *practice* or *action* is *finful* or *not*, and of courfe *damnable*.

The Scripture, 1 Pet. iii. 8. fays—be *pitiful*, be *courteous*, Φιλοφρονες—*friendly* or *friendly-minded—benign:*—I know none of my acquaintance, in whom I have had occafion to obferve more of *thefe tempers*, than in my beloved Mr. H.; and yet his *zeal* on the prefent occafion has hurried him into a *temporary oblivion*, at leaft, of thefe conftituent parts of his amiable character. He even goes fo far as to charge his friend with " *low chi-* " *canery*"—this he " *at firft felt himfelf* " *hurt at*"—" but I prefently recollected," fays Mr. H. " *that he had been bred to the* " *bar*—and therefore paffed it by with a " *fmile*."

Now, what is this *low chicanery?* Why, the Author of *Thelyphthora*, in full confiftence with the *one principle* which he lays down at the *beginning*, and continues throughout to the *end*, that the word *adultery* is never ufed, but where the defilement of a *married woman* is concerned—for which he has

the

the uniform and undoubted authority of the *whole Hebrew* scripture—construes the γυναικα, woman, Matt. v. 28. in this sense—and this is done, among other reasons, for the grand purpose of representing scripture as consistent in all its parts. However, my dear Sir, what will you say to *Wetstein* on the place?—He thus explains it—" *Per* γυναικα *autem intelli-* " *gitur uxor alterius.*"—" By the word γυ- " ναικα—*woman*—the wife of another is un- " derstood." See Thelyph. vol. i. p. 122, n. 2d edit. When your friend has such respectable authorities for his interpretation of the text, I think he might have escaped the charge of " *low chicanery,*" and a very *liberal, learned,* and *honourable profession,* have avoided a very severe and indiscriminate censure.

The mention of *Wetstein,* who was certainly the most learned, laborious, and accurate *editor* of the *Greek Testament* that ever lived, reminds me of another part of your *critique,* I mean that on the word αλλην—*another*—in Matt. xix. 9, which I say, p. 385, " *may* be " construed in the sense of αλλοτριαν γυναικα" —for this I appeal to that great man's comment on Matt. xix. 9. His words are— " Αλλην] i. e. Αλλοτριαν *ab alio itidem viro repu-* " *diatam*—*vel ab illo divertentem ut* HERODIAS " *& * SALOME."———" *Another*] that is, *ano-* " *ther man's wife,* who has been *repudiated* by " him, or who has *left* her husband; as did " HERODIAS and SALOME."—Had you attended to what follows in *Wetstein*'s note on Mark x. 11. p. 387, 391, 392, and carefully

and

and deliberately weighed the matter, perhaps you would have treated your *friend* with rather more *respect* than you have done on this occasion.—But if you was not of opinion with him on the interpretation of the word ἀλλην, how comes it that you pass over in silence his explanation of the μοιχαται? Is it quite fair, my dear Sir, to take one argument, condemn it, and so condemn the *author*, without noticing another most material support of his opinion? and, when *Wetstein*'s authority lay before your eyes, to charge the author as " taking the liberty to change the word αλλην " for αλλοτριαν?"

You tell us in your Postscript, that " the " treatise had been published *full half a year* " before you could *persuade yourself to read it.*" Your book is dated Jan. 15, 1781. Now the *treatise* was published the beginning of *June* (a few days before the *riots*) so that, "*full* " *half a year*" brings it to pretty near the *date* of your *book* — This accounts for the *haste* in which you wrote, and *this*, for many passages in your *book*, which I am sure you would have *expunged*, had you taken a longer time, either to consider the *treatise* you was opposing, the *friendship* of the *person* you was writing to, or that *inconsistency* with the *sweetness* and *benignity* of your own *disposition*, which occurs here and there throughout your " *affectionate address.*"

I cannot help also thinking, that, for that "*full half a year*," how hard your *prejudices* must be at work — they appeared pretty
clearly

clearly in your letter of *February* 2, 1780, before you had seen *a line* of the performance; and when you could "*perſuade your-ſelf to read it,*" did not your *prejudices* incline you to wiſh that they might rather be *juſtified* than *removed?*—Aſk *yourſelf* this *queſtion*— It may not be quite impoſſible (if I may judge from ſome parts of *your book)* that the *honeſty* of your *heart* will anſwer you very faithfully in the *affirmative.* — This is but *human nature.* On this principle I can account for your repreſentation of our LORD's intention, in his conduct towards the *woman taken in adultery.* (John viii. 1, &c.) " It appears clear to me," ſays my friend, " that, " under the *goſpel,* he, *indirectly* at leaſt, prohibited that either party, in ſuch caſe, " ſhould ſuffer death, either by ſtoning or " otherwiſe, as they were to do by the ſe-" verity of the *Jewiſh* law."

I think you may fairly be underſtood to mean by this, that CHRIST repealed the *judicial law* of GOD, ſo often repeated, againſt *adultery.* If ſo, how are we to conceive of *His coming not to deſtroy the law, but to fulfil it?* Matt. v. 17. How of His declaration—that *not a jot or tittle ſhould paſs from the law, till all be fulfilled*—Matt. v. 18?—I own I cannot help underſtanding theſe ſolemn aſſertions as totally inconſiſtent with an *indirect,* as with a *direct, repeal of the law.*

The *Phariſees,* no doubt, brought this *woman* to OUR LORD, with a moſt malicious

and

and wicked intent — *to tempt Him, that they might have to accuse Him.* ver. 6. *i. e.* either as an enemy to *Cæsar*, as taking upon Himself to exercise a *judicial* power independent of the authority of the *Roman* government, if He ordered the woman to be stoned to death; or, if He did not, to incense the people against Him as a favourer of sin, and as an enemy to the law of *Moses*.

The *manner* in which OUR LORD avoided the *snare*, and the *way* which He took to get rid of His malicious *enemies*, can never be sufficiently admired for their wisdom and prudence (see ver. 7—9.) any more than we can express, or even conceive, the tenderness and compassion with which He looked on the poor *sinner*, who calls Him LORD (ver. 11.) and receives her *pardon* from His gracious lips. Thus have we left us on record, my dear Sir, one instance, among many others, of that free and condescending grace, which is the only *hope* of guilty creatures like ourselves.

But what has this to do with a repeal of the *law* of GOD against *adultery?* If CHRIST could repeal or change *one judicial precept* of the *moral law,* He certainly could alter any other;—but as my dear *friend* has no inclination, I am very certain, to stir a single step towards *Socinus,* I will say no more on the subject.

You say, after mentioning (p. 135.) Matt. v. 28 — and xix. 9 — " In both these in-
" stances

" ftances you infift, that *a woman* muft mean
" a *married woman* only, becaufe otherwife
" *polygamy* cannot ftand."

Your afferting this as the author's reafon for his interpretation of the word *woman*, in the *texts* above alluded to, is another proof, either of the *hafte* in which you *wrote*, or of the *prejudice* with which you *red*; otherwife you muft have adverted to a reafon of a much more important nature, *viz.*—that of exempting CHRIST from declaring a *doctrine* in the face of the whole *Jewiſh nation*, and this as deduced from the law of *Moſes*, without any other foundation for what He faid, than ufing the word *adultery* in a fenfe in which it never once occurs throughout the whole *Hebrew ſcripture*. This I do acknowledge to be faid "*again*, and *again*, and *again*" in *Thelyphthora*; and yet this reafon is *overlooked*, and another *ſubſtituted*, which is of my friend's own *invention*.

My *friend* has fallen under a miftake, which I find has been the cafe with many; that is to fay, " that, on the principles of
" *Thelyphthora,* there is no fuch thing as
" *fornication* or *whoredom*; confequently, that
" fuch a character as an *whore* or an *harlot*
" cannot exift, but every *woman* who goes
" from one man to another is an *adultereſs,*
" always remaining the property of the *firſt*
" *man* that *humbled her."* p. 84.

In anfwer to which, I fay—what you own you " *will not diſpute with me"*—that the " in-
" tercourfe of a *virgin* with a *man* conftitutes a
" marriage

"marriage in the sight of GOD," because it is written, *they shall be one flesh*;—and our SAVIOUR, from this, concludes—that what GOD *hath joined together, no man shall put asunder*.

But I farther say, that if this *woman* departs from this *first* man to *another*, the *bond* with the *first* is totally vacated by her act of *adultery*; so that the *first* man is totally released from her. If afterwards she goes from man to man, and sells or gives her favours promiscuously to all alike, she is *everybody's* and *nobody's:* no man can lay any claim to her, or look upon her as his *property*, or be injured, as a *given, appropriated* husband might be, by her infidelity. She is, in short, *nullius inter bona*, and is an *whore, harlot*, or *prostitute*, in the true sense of those words.

I really feel *hurt* and *ashamed* at your strictures on the story of *Judah* and *Tamar*, p. 85. You had just written down the very words of Gen. xxxviii. 24, where "*they who told Judah* "*that she was with child by whoredom*" call her his *daughter-in-law*—how so?—why, she had been *married* to two of *Judah's* sons, *Er* and *Onan*, successively, under the *custom* of the *Levirate*; (which was afterwards enacted into a law, Deut. xxv. 5.) the *remarkable deaths* of *these*, must be too notorious not to be known among the *men of the place*—see ver. 21, 22— as also, that the widow of the *deceased* devolved on *Shelah*, the surviving brother, and, of course, that she was engaged to him (Comp. ver. 11, 14.) so that *Tamar* must, by what she did,

did, appear in the light of a *betrothed woman* who had gone astray, and liable to suffer as an *adulteress*; for, in consideration of law, she was a *man's wife*. (Comp. Deut. xxii. 23, 24.) How is it my *friend* could, with his *Bible* open before him, take no notice of *Tamar's* real situation, as engaged to *Shelah*—represent her on the footing of a *woman* that *had no husband*—and then call this "a fact standing on record, as full "proof" of what he advances on the subject of *single women?* It may be said of *my friend—Quod vult valde vult.*——N. B. Try what you can make of the *maid* that is *not betrothed*—Exod. xxii. 16.—and of the *damsel*—Deut. xxii. 28.—Are these stigmatized as *whores?*

You do me justice, when you say, that I only "defend *polygamy* in some *rare instances*."—But how can it be *defended* in those *rare instances*, if it be against the *law of* GOD? Therefore, the purpose of *Thelyphthora*, so far as it relates to the subject, is to prove its *lawfulness*, that, in those *rare instances*, it may be sought to, as a remedy against the manifest *evils* which accrue from an *indiscriminate* and *total* prohibition of it; which I deny to be warranted from GOD's *word*, and is no better than the effect of men's taking the whole œconomy, relative to the *commerce of the sexes*, out of GOD's hands into their own, and of that *false policy*, so deservedly and ably censured by the *Marquis of Beccaria*, in his *chapter* on *false notions of utility.*—See *Thelyph.* vol. ii. 424, n.

The

The laſt ſheet of this *volume* was ſent me to reviſe, when I received your book: I ſtop the *preſs* for the inſertion of this Letter to you; which muſt account for my haſte in writing, and for my not being more methodical and accurate in following you through your publication.

My full determination is, to enter into no freſh *controverſy* with any body. I ſhall *read* what may be *written*, and thankfully adopt into any future edition of *Thelyphthora*, ſuch uſeful *hints* as either my *friends* or *enemies* may occaſionally throw out.

My dear Sir, I now take my leave, with aſſuring you, that I remain your affectionate and faithful (tho' I am ſorry I muſt add, on this occaſion, your highly-injured)

Friend and ſervant,

March 26,
1781.   *The Author.*

POSTSCRIPT.

YOU will pleaſe to obſerve, that the references and quotations from *Thelyphthora*, in this Letter, are from the firſt *edition*; as you do not appear to me to have ſeen the *ſecond*.

I ſhould

I should have noticed the *question*, which you have so often repeated — "Why write "*Thelyphthora? cui bono* * *scribere?*"— I answer —*pro bono publico* —To check the overflowings of *adultery* and *prostitution* —to establish the *means* of doing this on the *basis* of the *divine law* — to set forth *that law*, as revealed in the *Bible* — to contend for its *wisdom, holiness, purity*, and *justice* — to shew how the *responsibility* which that *law* establishes between the *seducer* and the *seduced*, would tend to curb the *licentiousness* of what is called *gallantry*, and, of course, to prevent the *ruin of women*, with all its fearful appendages— to assert that *unrivalled sovereignty*, and *uncontroulable supremacy* of JEHOVAH, which *mortals* have dared to dispute with Him for so many *ages*, by setting aside His *laws* relative to the *commerce of the sexes*, and substituting their own *inventions* — to point out, from *deductions* drawn from undeniable *facts*, and from the most incontestible *proofs*, the *mischiefs* of that *irresponsibility* of MEN to WOMEN, and of WOMEN to MEN, in *instances* of the most *important* concern to BOTH, but more especially to the *weaker sex* —to recommend it to the *legislature* to take these matters seriously under their confideration, and, being thus apprized of the *mischief* and its *remedy*, if *times, circumstances*, and the *situation* of *things* will not enable them to adopt the *whole* of the *plan* proposed, yet to adopt

* N. B. This is not my *Latin*.

as much of it as shall be found *practicable*.— That *something ought* to be *done*, none can DENY.— The *book* which you censure, has endeavoured to point out what *may* be done —and it must be left to the *wisdom, humanity*, and *discretion* of *the powers that are* in this *Christian* land, to determine what *shall* be done.

Though I am *at present* so circumstanced as not to be able to add any more, yet, *my friend*, you will probably find, that *forbearance is no acquittance*; and on *a future occasion*, your *explanation* of 1 Cor. vii. 1—10. or (as you express yourself) your—" *affront* put " on the clear and plain language of the " *apostle*, where every word carries with it " *perspicuity* and *conviction*" (which, by the way, is saying a good deal, on a passage of scripture which, from the different interpretations it has received from *commentators*, seems to be one of the most *dark* and *difficult* parts of St. *Paul*'s writings, especially as we are not possessed of the *letter* written to him by the *Corinthians*) may probably meet with *due observation*. The *confidence* with which you treat this *scripture*, as you do *others*, singly on your *own* authority, without calling in aid or quoting a single *commentator, historian*, or *other author*, to justify your *peremptory* determinations on the sense of words—wherein you contradict some of the *greatest, best*, and most *learned* men that ever lived—shews how far your *zeal* has outrun your *discretion*, and
the

the impetuosity of your *imagination,* the sober dictates of due *consideration* and *reflection.*

The light in which I shall find myself obliged, in justice to the *public* (to say nothing of *Thelyphthora*) to place *you*, as a *critic* and a *philologist*, will hardly be more disagreeable to yourself than to the *author*—but be it remembered, Sir, that, happen what may, you have nobody to thank for it but yourself.— I heartily wish, that the "*sense*" which you express (p. 148.) "*of the deficiency of your "own abilities"* (at least so far as a controversy which depends on the knowledge of the *original* scriptures is concerned) had been as REAL as you profess it to be—you would then have left it to *others* to attack your *own friend*, while you had been following the *apostle*'s advice (1 Thess. iv. 11.) *Study to be quiet.*

I think the CARICATURAS which you have imagined for the *fair sex*, in the *strange* stories which you have *invented*, and exhibited for the *entertainment* and *edification* of your *readers*, (the *wit* of every one of which contains a very strong *sarcasm* on the *Mosaic* law) represent the *ladies* in such a light of *vengeance* and *assassination*, and, in short, as such a set of FURIES, as to outdo, if possible, the *three* famed *daughters* of ACHERON and NOX:—these tormented *other people*, but *your's* even *hang* them*selves* into the bargain.—However, put some *snakes* on their *heads* in your next edition,

tion, and then they may pafs for the lineal defcendents of ALECTO, MEGÆRA, and TISI-PHONE. I marvel not that *my friend* has ftill to complain with *Horace,*

MARTIIS COELEBS QUID AGAM CALENDIS?

N. B. I did not receive your *book,* till FRIDAY, MARCH 23d.

F I N I S.

INDEX,

INDEX.

A

ATHENAGORAS, condemns second marriages, 11.
———— ATHANASIUS, 14.
AMBROSE, Bishop of *Milan*, extols *virginity* above *marriage*, 21.
ARLES, Council of, 24.
ANCYRA, ib.
AUSTIN, ST. 40.—asserts that *virgins* shall have a particular reward in Heaven, 43.
——————— holds the desire of the sexes to each other *sinful*, 44.
——————— recommends total *continence* in *married persons*, 45.
ANJOU, Council of, 54.
AGATHA, Council of, 66.
ARLES, ditto, 69, 168, 170.
ANTISIODORUM, Synod, of, 72.
AQUILEIA, Council of, 91.
ATTO, Bishop of *Verceil*, 104.
ALFRIC, Archbishop of *Canterbury*, 109.
ANSELM, ditto, 125.
———, a great opposer of *priests'* marriage, ib.
ARRAS, Council of, 130.
AENHAM, 136.
ABELARD, PETER, 149.
ALEXANDER III. *Pope*, ib.
AVRANCHES, Council of, 153.
ALBY, ditto, 170.
ALCALA, ditto, 180.
ALPHONSUS TOSTATUS, Bishop of *Avila*, 183.
ÆGIDIUS CARLERIUS, Dean of *Cambray*, ib.
ANGERS, Council of, 184.
AUGSBURG, Diet of, 207.
ADULTERY, no cause of dissolving marriage among *Christians*, 217.

ALBIGENSES,

INDEX.

ALBIGENSES, 173—75—their doctrine of marriage, 243.
ALSOP, quotation from, 304, n.
ABSOLUTION of the dead excommunicate, 290, n.
ARREOY, an horrid assembly so called, 331—2.

B

BASIL of *Cæsarea*, 15.
────── denies that the command Gen. i. 28. respects the times of the New Testament, 16.
────── lays a foundation for separating the New Testament from the Old Testament, 18.
BOURIGNON, *Madame*, a strange sentiment of her's reproved by Mr. *Leslie*, 35. n.
BENEDICT, ST. 60.
BARCELONA, Council of, 74.
BRAGA, ditto, 81.
BONIFACE, Archbishop of *Mentz*, 83.
BARKHAMSTEAD, Council of, 87.
BERENGER—his doctrine about the *Eucharist*, 112.
────── attacked by LEO X. ib.
────── persecuted by *Henry* I. of *France*, ib.
BENEVENTO, Council of, 121.
BOURGES, ditto, 130, 172, 188, 218.
BERNARD, ST. 147. Threatens and affrights the Duke of *Guiénne*, ib.
BOURDEAUX, Council of, 171.
BUDA, ditto, ib.
BENGAL—interpreters, 191.
BOLEYN, ANN, married to *Henry* VIII. 210.—Beheaded, 212.
BARRENNESS, one cause of *polygamy* among the *patriarchs*, 276.

C

CLEMENT, his two epistles, 5.
────── , a great favourer of celibacy, 6.
────── of *Alexandria*, blames *second* marriages, 10.
CYPRIAN held *virginity* to be nearest the state of *martyrdom*, and much more excellent than marriage, 12, 13.
CONSTANTINE encourages *celibacy*, 14.
CYRIL of *Jerusalem*, 15.
CARTHAGE, first Council of, 27.
────── other Councils of, 28, 29, 46.
CHRYSOSTOM, ST. 33.
────── his *lyes* and *blasphemy* with respect to *marriage*, 34, 35.
CÆLESTINE, ST. Bishop of *Rome*, 48.
CONCUBINES allowed in the Church, 30.

CHALCEDON,

INDEX.

CHALCEDON, Council of, 52.
CLERMONT, ditto, 70, 121.
COLUMBANUS, ST. 75.
CONSTANTINOPLE, Council of, 81.
CHRODEGAND, ST. 85.
CHARLEMAGNE, Emperor, 86.
COLOGNE, Council of, 96, 221.
COBLENTZ, ditto, 106.
COYACO, ditto, 139.
CASSEL, in *Ireland*, ditto, 153.
CHARITOPULA MANUEL, Patriarch, 165.
CHATEAU GONTHIER, Council of, 167.
COGNAC, ditto, 169, 170.
COMPEIGNE, ditto, 178.
COLEN, ditto, 179, 184.
CONCUBINAGE, abolished and persecuted, 189.
CONCUBINARIES condemned, 248.—allowed, 261.
CLEVES, *Ann* of, 213.
CROMWELL, disgraced, beheaded, 213.
CAJETAN, CARDINAL, 234.
CORNELIUS AGRIPPA, 235.
COCHLÆUS, JOHANNES, 238.
CONCUBINAGE, farther considered, 277—84. Probable reason of its abolition and condemnation, 281. Mischiefs arising therefrom, ib.
CONFESSIONAL quoted, 292, n. 303, n.
CEREMONY, marriage, compared to bonds and other securities, 309—315. Ought to be enforced by the severest laws, ib.
CHURCH, the *word* explained, 336. Ditto as relative to the *Church* of *Rome*, 338—9. *Marriage* changed by the *Church*, 340.
CANTERBURY, Archbishop of, his licence for marriages, 346.
CREED, the author's on the subjects in this treatise, 352—6.

D

DIONYSIUS the *Areopagite*, his works a forgery, 4.
DIDYMUS of *Alexandria*, 14.
DOWZY, second Council of, 95.
DUNSTAN, ST. 107.
——————— his insolence to an *Earl*, ib.
——————— takes the *Devil* by the nose, 108.
DAMIEN, PETER, Bishop of *Ostia*, 123.
DECRETAL, 146.
DOMINICAN and *Franciscan Fryars*, the first *Inquisitors*, 177.
DEFENDER *of the Faith*—original of that title, 200.

INDEX.

E

EUSEBIUS of *Cæsarea*, 14.
EPHRAIM, ST. of *Syria*, 15.
EPIPHANIUS, ST. 22.
ELIBERIS, Council of, 22.
——————— decrees against *priests'* marriage, 259.
ENNODIUS, Bishop of *Pavia*, 55.
EPAONE, Council of, 67.
ELIGIUS, ST. 76.
EGARA, Council of, 77.
EUGENIUS III. Pope, 148.
ERNULPHUS, Bishop of *Rochester*, 150.
ERROR, *Heresy*, and *Schism*, ecclesiastical *scare-crows*, 181.
ERASMUS—his *colloquies* censured, 223.
——————— an account of him, 226—32.
ECCLESIASTICAL COURTS, 284. Their power of *excommunication* dangerous, 285. Consequences thereof, 287, & seq.
EPISCOPACY, and *Presbytery*—disputes about, 337, n.
EXPERIMENTS made for the improvement of GOD's laws, 356.

F

FULGENTIUS, ST. 56.
FULCUS, Archbishop of *Rheims*, 110.
FULBERT, ST. Bishop of *Chartres*, 111.
FRANCE, Councils held in, 133.
FREDERIC II. Emperor, favours and protects the *Inquisition*, 177—8.
FABER, JOHN, maintains that a doctrine of the *Church* is not to be abolished by allegations out of the scriptures, 205.
FISHER, Bishop of *Rochester*, 235.
FRANCISCUS DE VICTORIA, 237.
FORNICATION, affinity by, considered, 244—5.

G

GREGORY, ST. NAZIANZEN, 19.
——————— writes a *poem* in praise of *celibacy*, 19.
GREGORY, ST. NYSSEN, speaks out on the subject of a *new law*, 19.
GELASIUS, Bishop of *Rome*, 52.
GREGORY, ST. surnamed THE GREAT, 62.
——————— sends *Austin* the Monk into *England*, 63.
——————— answers *Austin's* questions, 64.
GERUNDA, Council of, 66.
GODFATHERS and GODMOTHERS, *non-descripts*, 83, n.
GREGORY II. and III. 84.
GERMANY, Council of under *Carloman*, 87.

INDEX.

GUITMOND, Archbishop of *Averse*, writes against *Berenger*, 113.
GARTH, DR. quoted, 148.
GREGORY X. Pope, 165.
GILDAS, a writer of the 6th Century, 199.
——— his account of the *English* Bishops, ib.
GAUFRIDUS BOUSSARDUS, 233.

H

HILARY, 14.
HOLT, CH. J. his saying of an *Herald*, 47, n.
HILARY, ST. Bishop of *Arles*, 51.
——— Bishop of *Rome*, 52.
HORACE's story of *Prometheus* quoted and applied, 68.
HILDEBRAND, or GREGORY VII. 116.
HILDEBERT, Bishop of *Mans*, 149.
HUGH, Archbishop of *Roan*, 151.
HENRY VIII. takes away the *Pope's* power in *England*, 187, Pulls down monasteries, ib. Marries his brother's widow, 208. The *Pope's* dispensation thereon, ib. This marriage protested against, ib.
HOWARD, *Katherine*, 214. Beheaded, ib.
HILL, *Richard*, Esq; letter to, 366.

I

INNOCENT I. *Pope*, 36.
JEROME, ST. a great extoller of virginity, 38.
——— his character, 39, and n.
ISIDORE, ST. PELUSIOTA, 47.
——— his thoughts on the *polygamy* of the *Patriarchs*, ib.
JUSTINIAN, Emperor, 57.
JOHN, ST. surnamed CLIMACUS, 61.
ISIDORE, ST. 75.
JOHN, ST. *Damascene*, 85.
JOHN VIII. *Pope*, 101.
IVO, Bishop of *Chartres*, 140.
——— his directions about a *priest*, who had used other *ceremonies* and *words* than were prescribed in the form of marriage, 141.
——— his *idea* of *fornication*, 142.
INNOCENT III. Pope, 157.
——————— IV. Pope, 164.
INQUISITION, origin of, 175.
JULIUS II. grants a dispensation for the marriage of *Henry* VIII. with his brother's widow, 208.
IGNORANCE of the Original Scriptures defended, 224. By the *Papists*, and by the *Fanatics* of the last Century, 225.

JEROME,

INDEX.

JEROME, an horrid saying of his on the subject of *marriage*, 230.
JEWS, hardened in part by practices of *Christians*, 273—4. How these differ as to *polygamy* and *concubinage*, 279, n. Their ways of contracting marriage, 315.

K

KATHERINE's, ST. still a convent, 213, n.
KNAVES, *churchmen* have been the greatest of all others, and why, 335.

L

LAODICEA, Council of, 26.
LESLIE, Mr. his saying of Madame *Bourignon*, 35, n.
LEO, ST. Pope, 48,
—— denies *concubines* to be *wives*, and says they may be cast off, 49, 50.
LUCIUS CHARINUS, his horrible *blasphemy* against the GOD of the Old Testament, 65.
LERIDA, or ILERDA, Council of, 68.
LYONS, ditto, 73.
LEO, Emperor, his quarrel with *Nicholas* the Patriarch, 101.
LEO VII. Pope, 104.
LANFRANC, Archbishop of *Canterbury*, 115. A bitter enemy to *Berenger*, 112.
LATINS and *Greeks*, their foolish disputes, 122.
LIMOGES, Council of, 132.
LISIEUX, ditto, 134.
LONDON, ditto, 138, 153, 154, 168, 171, 180.
LATERAN, ditto, 147, 155, 156, 166.
LOMBARD, PETER, 151. Finds out *seven sacraments*, ib. 262.
L'ISLE, Council of, 168, 172.
LANGEIS, ditto, 171.
LAMBETH, ditto, 181.
LOLLARDS, 181. Their doctrine of marriage, 243.
LAW of *Moses*, different from the *laws* of *Christians*, 183, n.
LAILIER, severely persecuted, 185.
LUTHER rises in *Germany*, 187, 192.
LAWYERS, in Cent. XVI. their definition of marriage, 190.
LUTHER's three positions concerning matrimony, 193. Condemned by the *divines* at *Paris*, ib. Is abused by his adversaries, 194. Protected by the *Elector* of *Saxony*, and concealed in a castle, 196. Many ecclesiastics *marry* in consequence of *Luther's* teaching, 197. His opinion of *cathedral* and *collegiate* churches, 198. Marries *Catherine Bora*, 207.
LOUVAINE, *University*, its divines consulted, 217.

LATOMUS,

INDEX.

LATOMUS, JACOBUS, 236.
LYES, a cluster of, selected from the *canons* of the Church of *Rome* relative to marriage, 250—1.
LOCKE, Mr. quoted on association of *ideas*, 306—7.

M

MEAUX, Bishop of, persecutes *Du Pin*, 3
MINUTIUS FELIX, 12.
METHODIUS, Bishop of *Olympus*, 13.
MASCON, Council of, 73.
METZ, ditto, 91, 93, 96.
MENTZ, ditto, 93, 96, 136, 167, 223.
MELPHI, ditto, 120.
MAPES, WALTER, Archdeacon of *Oxford*, 128. His verses on the *Pope*'s forbidding *priests*' marriage, 129.
MICE will not *gnaw* the *consecrated bread*, 113. The contrary allowed, 165.
MATHURINS, divines assembled at, 223.
MARRIAGE, *second*, condemned, and not allowed the priestly benediction, 260. Ceremony *Popish*, 265. *Hottentots*, 266. Preferable to the *Popish*, and why, 268.
MITYLENE, custom at with regard to marriage, 317.
MAGISTRATE, story of one, 326—331. Ought to have jurisdiction over *marriage* as a *civil* contract, 341.
MINORS, their marriages vacated, 345.
MAHOMET, by whom set up, 347. An emblem of the *Christians* setting up the Pope, ib.

N

NEO-CÆSAREA, Council of, 24, 25.
NICE, Council of, 26.
Ditto, 91.
NANTES, ditto, 98.
NICHOLAS, I. Pope, 99.
NISMES, Council of, 122.
NOGAROL, ditto, 179.
NARBONNE, ditto, 180.
NUREMBERG, diet of, 200. The *Pope*'s message to it, ib. The answer, 201. Sends a memorial of an *hundred grievances* to the *Pope*, 203.
NUMA Pompilius pretends to receive his laws from the Goddess *Egeria*, 316.

INDEX.

O

ORIGEN, 12.
ORANGE, Council of, 53.
ORLEANS, ditto, 66, 70, 71.
OXFORD, ditto, 167, 184.
OTAHEITE, inhabitants of, have little notion of marriage-ceremony, 320. Compared with the *Christians*, ib. & 324, 331—333.

P

PELAGIUS II. Pope, 61.
POLYGAMY forbidden, 94, 100, 101, 275.
PARIS, Council of, 78, 166, 184.
PAVIA, ditto, 93, 115.
POLYEUCTA, Patriarch, 103.
————, quarrels with the Emperor, 103.
POICTIERS, Council of, 119.
————, Count of, parts from his wife, 120.
PASCHAL II. Pope, 146.
PETER of BLOIS, Archdeacon of *Bath*, 151.
————, Bishop of *Exeter*, his *canons*, 172.
PRESBURG, Council of, 178.
PALENZA, ditto, 180.
PURGATORY, 165.
PRESS, liberty of, proposed to be taken from the *Lutherans*, 202.
PARR, *Catherine*, 215.
PARIS, divines of, compose *articles* of *faith*, 217.
PHILOSOPHERS, their prejudices against *marriage*, imbibed by the *Christians*, 259. Have holden all manner of absurdities, 319.
POPE, instance of one smartly reproved, 339, n.

Q

QUAKER, observes on our form of matrimony, 265, 268, 300.

R

ROME and MILAN, Councils of against *Jovinian*, 27.
ROME, Council of, under *Innocent* I. 45.
RHEIMS, ditto, 78, 133, 146.
ROME, ditto, under *Gregory* II. 87.
————, under *Zachary*, 88.
————, under *Leo* IV. 94.
ROBERT, King of *France*—dispute about his marriage with *Bertha*, 105.

RATHARIUS,

INDEX.

RATHARIUS, Bishop of *Verona*, 110.
ROME, several Councils of, 116.
ROUEN, ditto, 134, 135.
RAVENNA, ditto, 172, 179.
RAYMOND, Count of *Thoulouse*, persecuted for protecting the *Albigenses*, 177.
RATISBON, Diet of, 215. Assembly at, 206.
RITUAL, *Popish*, relative to marriage, 296—7.

S

SIEGE against the Old Testament begun, 16, and n.
SIRICIUS, *Pope*, makes laws for the *celibacy* of the *clergy*, 20.
SARAGOSA, Council of, 27.
SYMMACHUS, Pope, 55.
SEVIL, Council of, 78.
STEPHEN II. Pope, 86.
SOISSONS, Council of, 89.
SCOTUS, his book burnt, 112.
SELINGENSTADT, Council of, 135.
SAUMUR, ditto, 170.
SALTZBURGH, ditto, 173, 184.
SENLIS, ditto, 180.
SENS, ditto, 185, 219.
SEYMOUR, JANE, 212.
SELDEN, Mr. one of the Assembly of Divines, 225.
SHAKESPEARE—*Much ado about nothing*, quoted, 278, n.

T

TERTULLIAN, condemns *second* marriages, 11.
TIMOTHY of *Alexandria*, 20.
TOLEDO, Council of, 29, 69, 80, 81, 179, 184.
TOURS, ditto, 55, 72, 74, 134, 168.
THEODORUS of *Canterbury*, 76.
TULLIUM, or TOUL, Council of, 94.
TROYES, ditto, 95.
TRIBUR, ditto, 96.
TRANSUBSTANTIATION, disputes about, 111—15. How affirmed by, St. *Chrysostom*, 36.
TRENT, Council of, 238—249.
TURKISH SPY, quoted, 272.

V U

VALENCE, Council of, 26.
VERBERIE, ditto, 89.
VERNEVILLE, ditto, 90.

INDEX.

VIENNA, ditto, 96.
VERSES against *priests'* marriage, 127.
VALLADOLID, Council of, 179.
UXBRIDGE, disputes at, 337, n.
VARMIENSE, Cardinal, absents himself from the council of *Trent*, when the decree was made to vacate clandestine marriages, 344.
VIRGIL's account of the *Cretan* labyrinth, 357.

W

WORMS, Council of, 94.
WALDENSES, or VANDOIS, 173.
WALDENSIS, *Thomas*, 182.
WOLSEY, Cardinal, wants to make a quarrel between the *Emperor* and *Henry* VIII. 209.
WHEATLEY on Common Prayer quoted, 245—46, 249, 250.
WICKLIFFITES endeavour to get their doctrine approved by Parliament, 269, n.
WILLS and *Testaments*, not originally of ecclesiastical jurisdiction, 292, n.
WOMEN, inhumanly treated by the law of *England*, 320. Instances thereof 321—325. By the ecclesiastical courts, 325.

Y

YORK, Synod of, 155, 181.

Z

ZACHARY, Pope, 84.
ZUINGLIUS makes great progress in *Switzerland*, 204. His reply to *John Faber*, 205. Presents a petition to the *Bishop* of *Constance* to allow *priests'* marriage, 205.

www.ingramcontent.com/pod-product-compliance
Lightning Source LLC
Chambersburg PA
CBHW032126010526
44111CB00033B/129